100 Cases

in Clinical Ethics and Law

Second Edition

100 CASES

Series Editor: Janice Rymer

100 Cases

in Clinical Ethics and Law

Second Edition

Carolyn Johnston LLB LLM MA PhD
Adviser in Medical Law and Ethics, School of Medical Education
Faculty of Life Sciences & Medicine, King's College London
Senior Lecturer, Kingston University
Member of the Institute of Medical Ethics Education Steering Group, UK

Penelope Bradbury MBBS MA BSc MRCGP
GP Partner at The Witterings Medical Centre
GP Associate in Accident and Emergency Medicine, UK

100 Cases Series Editor:

Janice Rymer MD FRCOG FRANZCOG FHEA
Dean of Student Affairs and Lead for Twinned Institutions
Professor of Gynaecology
King's College School of Medicine
London, UK

CRC Press

Taylor & Francis Group
Boca Raton London New York

CRC Press is an imprint of the
Taylor & Francis Group, an **informa** business

CRC Press
Taylor & Francis Group
6000 Broken Sound Parkway NW, Suite 300
Boca Raton, FL 33487-2742

© 2016 by Carolyn Johnston and Penelope Bradbury
CRC Press is an imprint of Taylor & Francis Group, an Informa business

No claim to original U.S. Government works

Printed on acid-free paper
Version Date: 20151016
Printed by CPI Group (UK) Ltd, Croydon CR0 4YY

International Standard Book Number-13: 978-1-4987-3933-7 (Paperback)

Visit the Taylor & Francis Web site at
http://www.taylorandfrancis.com

and the CRC Press Web site at
http://www.crcpress.com

CONTENTS

Section 13 Faith, Values and Culture   245

FOREWORD

There are lots of reasons for reading this book. Perhaps you are facing an exam and need to revise. Maybe you did not really understand some of the teaching you had before in your courses and want to make better sense of things. Perhaps you are working or teaching in the area and want practical examples. But it might be that now on the ward or in practice you have come face-to-face with something you don't know how to deal with or you do not think is quite right.

Excellence in medical ethics and law needs to go beyond theory and work properly in practice. Equally, wanting to be a doctor would normally mean wanting to be a good one, but as demanding as it is to be clear about guidelines and frameworks or up to the mark in diagnosis and treatment, achieving this knowledge may still fail to point to what decisions should actually be made and why. Often something more is needed. For instance, deciding between treatments and evaluating side effects will be difficult without finding out about how a patient lives and what she would want to make of her life. There may be a conflict between what the best medical advice suggests and what this patient is prepared to accept. Perhaps what could be done is very expensive, or someone asks if it's really fair to put someone through it all. The patient may be confused, a young child or someone in a new or foreign culture. Perhaps there is pressure on you as medic or adviser to agree to something you do not think is best in the circumstances.

As soon as these sorts of issues crop up, you are in the realm where legal and ethical (or moral – the words for our purpose mean much the same) thinking are vital, the sort of work exemplified by this book. A good clinician or teacher is always prepared to step back and ask 'Is this right?' 'Is this the best thing for this patient?' or 'What does the law require in this sort of situation?' Avoiding facing these questions could mean wasted effort, increased tension and anxiety or worse. Sooner or later someone will make a complaint, or things will go wrong in a bigger way. Even if temperamentally you do not like to think about those possibilities, common sense will tell you that facing them is not going to be an easy experience and is to be avoided in every way possible. We hope you will see that finding good ways of thinking about the ideas raised here will not be just better medicine, but also a happier and healthier way to work.

Medical practice of necessity is often done at speed and in an atmosphere of uncertainty. Try as they might, nobody could be expected to get it all correct all the time. If they were doing their best at the time with the resources and help available, and thought it through, they should not be blamed if things still went wrong. But even if everything worked out well, there still may be a concern as to whether the best was done. How could our care be improved?

One suggestion to a person in practice would be to take anything that has felt uncomfortable in the day's work, and think it through in more detail, alone or with colleagues. As you think and talk, you may see what you should do next time, but you may also be struck by a feeling – a disquiet about something, an annoyance that someone did not help you out, or perhaps an awareness of some strong emotion that the patient expressed that you could not deal with. My claim is that these feelings will nearly always point you to practical moral issues that need addressing.

Once those issues are clarified and if possible named, then the helpful thinking can start, and this book comes into its own. This is partly what the great Scottish philosopher David Hume was talking about 300 years ago when he said, 'Reason is and ought only to be the slave of the passions, and can never pretend to any other office than to serve and obey them'. A doctor who was reasoning properly, on this basis, would still start by listening to what emotions (Hume's 'passions') were indicating in the situation, and then take rational thinking carefully on from there.

Giving an example of my own might make things clearer. As a general practitioner I looked after a proud and private man who in his late sixties became seriously ill with lung cancer. (Rumour had it that he was one of the best diamond 'fences' in Europe, but that was not in the notes!). His wife called me after evening surgery to visit him at home. I found he had become suddenly jaundiced and very weak. A group of us had just opened a community hospital that was designed to provide good terminal care. As it was late at night and not much could be done then, I suggested I admit him to the new hospital. His wife was exhausted and keen on this plan. His pain and other symptoms were well controlled with medication. I came to say goodnight to him in the hospital and told him I was in a bit of a hurry but would see him in the morning. He gave me a look that I did not understand. In the morning I found that he had died quietly in the night.

The relatives, in spite of their grief, were pleased with his care and his peaceful end: but for me that look of his would not leave me, in some way I had let him down. I won't ever know what the look was about, of course, or whether I had interpreted his glance correctly, but when I put myself in his situation, I began to see what might have been happening. I am sure he knew he was in his last hours, was surprised I did not know that (or did not tell him), and he wanted to talk about something important. He was alone, away from his family and the circumstances that he knew. There were no mobiles: perhaps he had no chance to deliver important final messages.

I was left with disquiet. Nobody could fault my clinical care. I had acted entirely within the law. No one was making a complaint. I had used the hospital exactly as it was intended. And yet some part of my care had not been right. Discounting my own sadness – I liked him and we had worked hard together in his last illness – on a human level my care was deficient, because it had not crossed my mind that this might be his last night. Even a company telephonist is trained to ask, 'Is there anything else I can help you with?' It was the moral equivalent of the old surgical joke: the operation was successful but the patient died. The medical care was excellent but there was still something wrong, something that could have been done better, and I had to learn it.

You may at this stage think I am setting the bar too high. How can we all possibly practise under pressure and still offer the best possible care? But that experience helped me to understand what 'a moral problem' really is: something that happens in the transactions between people that *could* and *should* have been done better. Ethicists often say 'ought implies can'. If something is impossible, there is no case to answer. In my situation, however, my values were wrong. I was still on duty, and I *did* have the time and the opportunity to ask my patient that key question: since I knew he was very ill I *should* have thought about what his needs were at that time. It is even possible, on a practical level, that by being so proud of my new hospital I had moved an elderly ill man out of his home unnecessarily and I had precipitated his death. The philosopher Geoffrey Warnock (in his book *The Object of Morality* [1971]) suggested that 'it is the proper business of morality ... to expand our sympathies, or ... to reduce the liability to damage inherent in their natural tendency to be narrowly restricted'. Because we are all only human we sometimes give ourselves excuses for actions or thoughts that really ought to have been better. Giving ourselves a let-out clause may help us get through the day, but may not help us get through the nights that follow.

This marks one difference between ethics and law. The law defines areas of right and wrong as they affect a whole society, and so is talking 'headlines' as it were: big issues or prohibitions that a whole society can sign up to and still be able to live together flexibly and peacefully. But these laws are usually derived from moral ideas. So, for instance, the law's thinking on contract derives partly from our ordinary thinking about promises, and the law of consent from our concern to have control of our own life and not to be harmed by other people. Though law may differ from era to era and country to country, and individuals (or cultures) may be free to make their own decisions about what is right or wrong in their interactions, the impulse to moral thinking is universal. By defining the framework within which medical action is carried out (for instance, who can be thought of as doctors and how their powers and duties differ from people who are not), the law might have something to say about any case. Ethics similarly may want to raise questions about what is right or wrong *in the system* of medical care or about the *relationship* between people.

In most countries now an official group such as the General Medical Council in the UK produces guidelines according to which doctors can be expected to work, but these may not deal adequately with the conflicts we perceive. We need the 'arguments' – the reasoning – of the different ways of thinking that are described in this book. We can structure these in different ways – for instance by appealing to principles – or back up our decisions with reference to the *duties* we see people having, the *consequences* of different actions, or the best sort of characteristics we should like to have (*virtues*) when making that sort of decision; or by using some other cogent and consistent approach.

Certain sorts of processes are required. We should listen to what other people have to say. We need to think if there are other points of view (other 'voices') that are not being expressed but have a bearing on the decision (like the 'voice' of the unborn child). Even if a certain argument does not 'win' in deciding *what* we do, it should still be powerful in determining *how* we do what we do. Unlike philosophers (and sometimes lawyers) we have to do this in a tight time frame, so we have to set *limits* on the process. Others will have to know why in the circumstances we did what we did, so the decisions and their *reasons* have to be succinctly written down. And afterward, we must go back with others to *check* if what we did was the best.

Luckily, in all this we learn more about our chosen profession, about good arguments and bad arguments, about what makes people tick and about ourselves. Our decision making improves, and work moves from just being scary to being very exciting. That is why people admire doctors and envy their work: and why, if professionals in medicine find themselves getting bored and this kind of book does not open things up again, they should probably go off and do something else.

Roger Higgs, MBE
Professor Emeritus in General Practice and Primary Care
King's College London, UK

INTRODUCTION

Welcome to the second edition of *100 Cases in Clinical Ethics and Law*. It has been eight years since we wrote the first edition, and because of our increased experience, we feel that this new edition will offer real insight into some of the more complex ethical issues that are encountered whilst treating patients both in the community and in hospital.

The National Health Service has changed significantly over the past few years, and as an organisation its future in its current form is becoming less certain. Irrespective of this, professional integrity should remain the cornerstone of health and social care provision in the UK. *100 Cases* aims to provide a holistic guide on the skills that medical students and junior doctors need to acquire in order to achieve this. Healthcare courses, and especially medical degrees, are full of factual information, physiological responses, anatomical abnormalities and pharmaceutical interactions. The art of medicine is in using this knowledge and applying it to the individual patient in front of you. It is about exploring the impact and significance that their disease process has on them; whether it be the need for minor surgery, chronic disease management or a terminal diagnosis.

Teaching medical ethics aims to turn students into trustworthy and honest healthcare professionals with advanced communication skills and impressive standards of professionalism. The aim of this book is to demonstrate *why* these skills are essential and how even the simplest of situations can provide real ethical dilemmas. Although a good understanding of ethical theories and law is important, most problems encountered in practice can be solved through simple communication and discussion with the patient and other members of the healthcare team.

In 2010 the Institute of Medical Ethics published an updated core content of learning for medical ethics and law, and all of those topics are covered in this book. However, the cases explored in this edition are by no means exhaustive and are intended to provide a springboard from which to develop your own analysis and understanding of the situation. Consider what your gut instinct is telling you and then try and work out why you feel that.

Of particular interest in this edition is the inclusion of more cases examining how to manage the changes in societal expectations and the impact that social media has had on health concerns. Changes within society have made the GP the first port of call in many situations – medical, social, financial and even due to loneliness – they are accessible to all and as such, the NHS is beginning to crack under the strain of increased demand. We need to examine why this is happening and what can be done to stem the tide of demands and needs. We have also included new cases highlighting the importance of self-care and resilience.

We hope you enjoy the new edition and that it gives you a tantalising taste of the privilege of being a healthcare professional and the positive impact that good ethical decision making can have on patients and their families when they are at their most vulnerable.

Carolyn Johnston
Penelope Bradbury
2015

CONTRIBUTORS

The authors would like to thank those listed below for contributing cases, and for their comments and advice, although the authors remain responsible for any errors.

Victoria Butler-Cole
Chambers of Stephen Tromans QC
and Neil Block QC
London, UK

Rose Crowley
Paediatric registrar
Whittington Hospital
London, UK

Ruth Gailer
Academic GP
London, UK

Kazim Ghafoor
Medical student
GKT School of Medical Education
Faculty of Life Sciences and Medicine
King's College London
London, UK

Rowan Hearn
Consultant in palliative medicine
University College London Hospital
and
Clinical tutor in medical ethics and law
King's College London
London, UK

Bala Karunakaran
Specialist registrar in obstetrics
and gynaecology
Wessex Deanery
Hampshire, UK

Selena Knight
Academic clinical fellow in general
practice
Chelsea and Westminster Hospital and
King's College London
London, UK

Ali Mears
Consultant in genitourinary medicine
and HIV
St Mary's Hospital
London, UK

Vinnie Nambisan
Consultant in palliative medicine
Saint Francis Hospice
Romford, Essex, UK
and
Tutor in medical ethics and law
University College London
London, UK

Laura Nightingale
Specialist registrar in palliative medicine
London, UK

GLOSSARY OF TERMS

Advance decision (directive): Decisions made when a person is competent to refuse specified medical treatment to take effect if mental capacity is lost in the future.

Assisted suicide: A person takes the final act to end his life with the help of another person, e.g., medication obtained from another person in quantities large enough to cause death.

Autonomy: Self-rule, freedom from external constraint and the ability to exercise critical mental capacity.

Basic care: Procedures which provide comfort or alleviate symptoms or distress – includes oral nutrition and hydration.

Battery: Physical touching without consent or legal authority.

Beneficence: Provision of benefit and contribution to welfare.

Best interests: The criterion for determining whether treatment for patients lacking capacity is legally and morally justified. It includes consideration of the benefits and harms of the proposed treatment and the values and views of the patient, where known.

British Medical Association: The trade union and professional body for doctors in the UK.

Capacity: The legal ability to make healthcare decisions.

Casuistry: The morally appropriate course of action determined by considering the particular features of a case and making a comparison with prior experiences from similar situations.

Competence: The ability to understand, retain and weigh up information in order to make a particular healthcare decision. This term tends to be used interchangeably with capacity.

Confidentiality: The obligation to keep safe and not to disclose health information provided in the course of a professional relationship.

Conscientious objection: The right to refuse to participate in certain medical procedures based on religious or ethical grounds.

Consent: The agreement to a treatment or procedure.

Consequentialism: A theory which states that the morality of an action depends on its (good) consequences, rather than the means by which those consequences are achieved.

Declaration: A statement from the court that proposed medical treatment is lawful because it is in the best interests of a patient who lacks capacity.

Deontology: A moral theory based on rights and obligations.

Doctrine of double effect: An action that has an unintended although foreseen harmful effect is permissible as long as the directly intended effect is beneficial. Often used in the context of pain relief for terminally ill patients where a side effect may be that death is hastened.

Euthanasia: A 'good death'. An action to deliberately bring about the death of a person with the aim of relieving suffering.

Foundation Doctor (FY1/FY2): A qualified doctor undertaking formal postgraduate training; usually the first 2 years after completing medical school.

Futile treatment (futility): Medical interventions that will not achieve the identified goal of treatment; those which result in little or no benefit to a patient.

Gametes: The male or female reproductive cell; sperm and ovum.

General Medical Council: An independent organisation which sets educational standards for all UK doctors, manages the UK medical register; investigates and acts on concerns about doctors and checks their knowledge and skills through revalidation. It publishes professional guidance.

Gillick competence: Children under 16 can consent to medical treatment if they have sufficient understanding and intelligence regarding the nature, purpose and likely consequences of the proposed treatment.

Informed consent: The choice of a patient to consent to medical treatment based on the provision of sufficient, understandable information.

Justice: Fair, equitable and appropriate decision making. Distributive justice refers to considerations of fairness in the allocation of scarce resources.

Narrative ethics: Ethical issues explored through the values, experiences and perspectives of those involved.

National Institute for Health and Care Excellence (NICE): NICE provides national guidance on the promotion of good health and the prevention and treatment of ill health and on new and existing medicines and treatments.

Negligence: Conduct that falls below the standard reasonably expected in the circumstances. Damages can be awarded in compensation for harm caused. The purpose of damages is to compensate the claimant for harm caused/loss suffered as a result of negligence.

Non-maleficence: 'Do no harm' – the obligation to avoid or minimise harm.

Parental responsibility: The duties and rights which parents have in respect of their children.

Passive euthanasia: Withholding or withdrawing life-prolonging medical treatment resulting in that person's death, for example, turning off an artificial ventilator.

Paternalism: Overriding a person's known preferences based on the justification that this will benefit them or avoid harm to them.

Percutaneous endoscopic gastrostomy: Provision of nutrition directly into the stomach through a tube.

Pre-implantation genetic diagnosis: A technique performed *in vitro* to identify embryos with specific inherited conditions with a view that such embryos are not selected for implantation.

Quality-adjusted life year (QALY): A measure of calculating the cost-effectiveness of treatment, combining the quality and quantity of life achieved through a medical intervention.

Quality of life: The value of life assessed by reference to certain attributes including mental and physical abilities, rather than its length.

Sanctity of life: All life has intrinsic value irrespective of the features or quality of a particular life.

Substituted judgement: The decision maker makes the decision that the patient would have made in the particular situation. This requires that the patient's preferences, expressed when the patient had capacity, are known.

Suicide: An act performed by an individual with the knowledge and intention that the action taken will result in their death.

Surrogacy: An arrangement through which a woman carries a baby on behalf of another.

Therapeutic privilege: Deliberate withholding of information about risks of treatment in order to prevent harm to the patient.

Utilitarianism: A consequentialist moral theory which provides that the right course of action is that which promotes the greatest happiness for the greatest number.

Viability: The stage of development at which the human foetus is normally capable of surviving outside the mother's womb.

Virtue ethics: A moral theory which provides that an action is morally right if it is what a virtuous agent would do in those circumstances.

SECTION 1

ETHICAL PRINCIPLES

CASE 1: PRINCIPLISM

Ophelia is a 27-year-old woman who has struggled with anorexia nervosa since she was 11 years old. She is extremely intelligent, and having gained a first class degree in history at Oxford University, she is now halfway through her PhD. It is at times when her life is most stressful that she struggles with her anorexia. The first time she was admitted to hospital was when she was 13. She was being badly bullied at school and had stopped eating in order to become thin to prevent being teased about being overweight. Being able to lose so much weight gave her the sense that she had some control over at least one aspect of her life.

Ophelia has spent the past 14 years in and out of hospital. On two occasions she had to be admitted to intensive care as she had lost consciousness. During these admissions she was fed by a nasogastric tube. She also has a history of obsessive-compulsive disorder and has been receiving cognitive behavioural therapy. A year ago she had managed to stabilise her weight at 50 kg – she is 1.7 m tall. With the stress of her PhD and the breakdown of her relationship with her boyfriend, when you initially see Ophelia she weighs less than 35 kg. Although you want to feed her by nasogastric tube to prevent her needing a third admission to intensive care, she adamantly refuses to have this. She tells you that she does not want to die, but neither does she want to be force fed. She is extremely frail and needs constant supervision by a healthcare assistant. Due to a shortage of beds on the psychiatric ward, Ophelia is currently being nursed on a general ward. The older women in her bay are complaining about the amount of personal attention she is receiving, as when they need assistance to change position or to go to the bathroom there is often a long wait due to staff shortages.

Questions
- What is principlism?
- How can the four principles be applied to this case scenario to offer guidance to the doctor about whether Ophelia should be force fed?

ANSWER 1

Beauchamp and Childress are American bioethicists who coined the four principles approach (principlism) for analysing ethical dilemmas in medicine.

! Principlism
The four principles are the *prima facie* moral obligations of • Respect for autonomy • Beneficence (promote overall benefit) • Non-maleficence (avoid causing harm) • Justice

The four principles approach is the most well known ethical theory. Medical students are often taught this theory to demonstrate how to approach (and solve) medical dilemmas.

The first step is to analyse how each principle may be relevant to the situation, i.e., what is the scope of the principle. The principles are non-hierarchical, although respect for autonomy has gained in importance in the era of patient-centred care. Respect for autonomy requires that the decision-making capacities of the individual are acknowledged. A person may not be fully autonomous in all situations, but increasingly the views of those with limited autonomy are being recognised and respected. Just because a patient lacks capacity to make a particular decision does not mean that a doctor should override their wishes. When a patient voices an opinion, every effort should be made to respect that decision.

The moral obligation of beneficence is not owed to everyone in general. However, there is a moral obligation for healthcare professionals to benefit their patients. This is underscored by the legal duty of care, and a doctor must act in a patient's best interests when they lack the autonomy to make decisions about their healthcare. In contrast, the *prima facie* obligation of non-maleficence is a general requirement to avoid causing harm. Most medical treatment incurs an element of potential harm. However, the risk of harm may be justified by balancing it against the anticipated benefits. The principle of justice often takes a backseat to the other principles. It is used in ethical arguments to ensure fair allocation of services and treatment within society. At an individual level, it is used to promote equality among patients from all walks of life, irrespective of nationality, culture or religion.

When there is conflict between the principles, a choice must be made to prioritise one over another. If Ophelia is not sectioned under the Mental Health Act (MHA), the doctor can only impose treatment if there is evidence that she lacks capacity. Anorexia nervosa is a complex illness. Affected individuals feel that they do not have control over their life and so use refusal of food to demonstrate that there is some aspect of their life that they can control. But does this mean that Ophelia lacks autonomy? It may be in her best interests to force feed her if she is at a critically low weight to avoid irreparable harm and restore her autonomy for future decision making. However, restraint and force feeding may destroy any trust she has built with her doctors. The principles of beneficence and non-maleficence should be weighed up to produce the outcome with overall net benefit. It could be claimed that the special nursing that Ophelia is receiving is an unfair allocation of limited health resources.

CASE 2: CONSEQUENTIALISM

Pippa has a 3-year-old son and a 13-month-old daughter. Her son had the triple measles, mumps, rubella (MMR) vaccination just over a year ago after Pippa had been reassured that it was extremely safe and would protect her son against dangerous childhood illnesses. Unfortunately, he had a bad reaction to the injection, with a high temperature, a rash around the injection site and a seizure. Although he seems fine now, Pippa is worried that having a seizure is an indication that he will develop autism or bowel problems. She has read the contradictory evidence about the risks of the triple MMR vaccine in newspapers and recognises that the evidence suggesting a link between MMR and autism has now been disproved. However, she is still concerned about having her daughter immunised against MMR in case the same thing happens to her.

Questions

- What is consequentialism?
- How can this ethical theory be applied to the case scenario to determine whether or not Pippa should have her daughter immunised?

ANSWER 2

Consequentialist theory states that the morally correct course of action is that which results in the best overall outcome, irrespective of the means used to achieve those consequences. The inherent wrongness or rightness of an act is not considered. One example of consequentialist theory is utilitarianism, which was first proposed by Jeremy Bentham in the late eighteenth century and further established by John Stuart Mill in the nineteenth century. Utilitarianism is the most influential consequentialist theory. The principle of utility provides that the morally correct course of action is that which promotes the greatest happiness of the greatest number. So the right thing to do is determined by the action that will result in the greatest overall happiness. The term *benefit* is now used in the context of healthcare. Intuitively, this seems an attractive and simple theory, but it does require impartiality since the theory does not allow room for the promotion of individual interests nor those of family and friends. The consequences of an action must be considered across time. There is no preference for happiness now, and the consequences for both the present and future generations should be taken into account.

The net happiness must be calculated, taking into account any unhappiness that a course of action will cause. The theory not only considers the consequences of actions but also the consequences of failures to act. It is a hugely demanding theory because it requires us to constantly analyse the potential outcomes of everything that we do or do not do and thus allows insufficient moral breathing space.

Consequentialism can be considered to conflict with the demands of justice. Plucking a healthy person off the street and using his body parts to save the lives of six people who need organ transplants may produce the greatest happiness. But does this mean that we can do disagreeable things if the consequences are good enough? The theory is so focused with ends that it overlooks the importance of means, in contrast with deontological theory.

The main problem with consequentialism is that it is difficult to apply to real-life scenarios because accurately predicting the possible consequences of an action is impossible. In this scenario there are several possible outcomes of Pippa having her daughter immunised against MMR. In theory, she may suffer immediate short-term harm (fever) but gain long-term benefits (disease resistance). Although it is not possible to predict whether this child will benefit from immunisation, there is scientific evidence to suggest that childhood immunisation schemes offer overall benefit to society. If sufficient numbers of children are immunised, *herd immunity* is achieved and eventually diseases may be eradicated altogether. This will protect future generations from the side effects of disease and subsequently increase happiness. The future benefit of immunisation outweighs the unhappiness caused by any potential side effects to this child and other children receiving the vaccination.

CASE 3: DEONTOLOGY

Patrick is a 45-year-old mature student nurse in his last year of training. His friend Carlos has had human immunodeficiency virus (HIV) infection for many years. He is now in the terminal stages of the disease and is in constant pain and suffering. Carlos and Patrick have been friends for a long time and Patrick has always said that he would be there to support Carlos. Carlos now asks him to travel with him to Dignitas in Switzerland so that he can be assisted to end his life. Patrick wants to be there for his friend. Personally he does not have any ethical quandaries about whether he should prevent Carlos from making a decision to seek assistance to end his own life. However, he is worried that he now has professional responsibilities and duties, which would be compromised by travelling to Switzerland with Carlos.

Questions

- What does deontological theory say about duties and obligations?
- To what extent must duties be followed irrespective of the consequences?
- According to deontological theory is it morally acceptable for Patrick to take his friend to Dignitas?

ANSWER 3

Deontological (Greek *deon* = duty/obligation) theory focuses on duties and rules rather than consequences. Some acts are intrinsically wrong irrespective of the good consequences that may follow, for example, torture, lying, murder. Immanuel Kant, who propounded the deontological theory Kantianism, considered that duties arise from application of reason by rational human beings and that moral rules must apply universally, i.e., to all people in similar situations. This may seem particularly harsh as it does not take into account either the consequences of an action or the emotions and needs of an individual. The rule 'never kill' may echo intuitive moral understanding, but should this constraint apply in all situations? Would it be ethically justifiable for the police to shoot one terrorist to prevent him from blowing up a train full of people?

In his work on the categorical imperative, Kant stated that an individual should 'act only according to that maxim by which you can at the same time will that it should become a universal law' (Groundwork of the Metaphysics of Morals, 1785). This implies that moral rules should be used only if they can be applied to every situation equally. Deontological theory can be criticised because it does not provide a definitive list of duties, nor does it state what should be done where two duties conflict. On the other hand it provides 'moral space'. People can act freely so long as they do not violate moral constraints. In comparison, consequentialist theory could be said to be far more demanding as it constantly requires an assessment of consequences.

Deontological constraints are usually negatively formulated, e.g., do not kill, do not lie. What is outside these boundaries is not forbidden; it could be argued that withholding the truth is morally acceptable if it does not amount to lying. It is also important to consider the nature of the constraint on action and how narrowly it is framed. For example, Kant considered that it is always wrong to deliberately end the life of an innocent human being. Therefore, it does not preclude killing of animals or murderers. It is more concerned with action rather than inaction. It may be wrong to take life but what about not saving it?

Does the application of deontological theory help in deciding whether it is morally permissible for Patrick to go with his friend to Dignitas? According to the theory it is wrong to deliberately end the life of an innocent human being. If Carlos is injected with a lethal dose of barbiturates, then the person doing this would breach the moral imperative, but what if Carlos is supplied with the drug to self-inject? Patrick is not acting to kill his friend, he is merely enabling such an act to take place. But Kant's categorical imperative requires us to act in a way that we would wish to be treated, which could be applied as a universal law. A universalisable law may forbid assisting a suicide.

CASE 4: VIRTUE ETHICS

Scenario 1

Sara, a 15-year-old girl, has suffered from leukaemia since the age of 6 years. She has had multiple courses of chemotherapy and a bone marrow transplant, all of which have failed. She is constantly in hospital and as such has had a disrupted education and little opportunity to make lasting friendships. She and her parents have accepted that further treatment is unlikely to be beneficial, and she wishes to return home to die in peace. Her doctors are unwilling to accept her decision as she is only 15.

Scenario 2

Tasha, a 15-year-old girl, was born with a congenital heart defect that was repaired at birth. She now needs a heart transplant to enable her to live an active life. She is, however, adamant that she does not want to live 'with someone else's heart beating inside me'. The prognosis of recovery after the heart transplant is good. Her parents are prepared to accept whatever decision she makes as they believe she will have to live with the consequences.

Questions

- What is virtue ethics?
- Which virtues do you think would make a good doctor?
- Can virtue ethics be applied to these two case scenarios to offer guidance to the doctor about whether Gillick competent children should have the right to refuse life-saving treatment?

ANSWER 4

Virtue ethics was first introduced as a concept by Aristotle in his *Nicomachean Ethics* and as such was one of the first true moral theories to shape the history of civilisation. According to virtue theory every action taken by a virtuous individual achieves 'eudaimonia'. Philosophers have attempted to translate this and describe it as 'human flourishing'. Aristotle believed that to be virtuous is to be able to rationally identify relevant characteristics (virtues) and then incorporate them in the decision-making process, which would ultimately result in human flourishing. Virtue theory does not comment on which particular virtues are important.

! Some virtues of a good doctor	
• Honesty	• Empathy
• Compassion	• Trustworthiness
• Respect	• Self-awareness
• Non-judgemental	• Enthusiasm
• Courage	• Professionalism
• Benevolence	• Personable
• Conscientiousness	• Altruism
• Confidence	• Discernment
• Humility	• Integrity

Typically in a doctor–patient relationship the main virtues are honesty, compassion, integrity and justice, although the list is not exhaustive. The choice of which virtues to apply in specific situations is highly subjective. This is both a strength and a weakness of virtue ethics theory. Can virtue theory be used to assess whether Sara and Tasha should be allowed to refuse potentially life-saving treatment?

The virtuous doctor should have a good knowledge of both the *facts* of the cases and the *emotions* of the patient. She should also consider her own emotional response and then reflect on which virtues should be applied in order to attempt to reach a moral conclusion. Benevolence, compassion and discernment are three virtues that could be applied to the two scenarios.

When applied to medicine, *benevolence* means to act in a way that best serves the interests of the patient. Sara is suffering and has little prospect of recovery. It is in her best interests to value the time she has left. Tasha, however, has a good chance of leading a normal life. It would not be in her best interests to die. Compassion means being able to identify with the patient's situation and show empathy. A discerning doctor would weigh complex emotional issues and understand the reasoning behind the patient's decision. She would perhaps understand that Tasha does not want to die but that she has fears surrounding the operation and the consequences of having a transplant. These issues should be discussed with the patient to enable her to cope with her fear.

Thus it would seem that virtue theory would suggest that Sara's wishes should be respected but Tasha's should not. Virtue theory does not give definitive answers to moral dilemmas, but it can help guide decision making after careful analysis. It enables individuals to reflect on the dilemma in question and come up with workable solutions.

CASE 5: CASUISTRY

You are the Foundation Year 1 (FY1) doctor on call when you are called to the ward to see an elderly, confused man. He is wandering around and crying out. The nurses have tried persuading him to stay by his bed or at least in his bay, but he is refusing to listen to them. One female patient has become upset because he keeps going to stand at the end of her bed and stares at her. The nurses are worried that as well as upsetting other patients, he is very unsteady on his feet and they fear he may fall over and injure himself. You read his notes to try to find a cause for his confusion. You learn that Micky, 76 years old, was an elective admission yesterday for a laparoscopic cholecystectomy. Two weeks earlier he had been admitted to Accident and Emergency with shortness of breath and pleuritic chest pain. He was kept in for 3 days and treated with intravenous antibiotics. There are at least two possible causes for his confusion: a recurrence of his pneumonia (or other sepsis) or a reaction to the general anaesthetic. You decide to speak to Micky and try to take some blood. Micky refuses to cooperate and actively pushes you away from him, shouting and swearing. He then tries to leave the ward, claiming he is well enough to go home and it is illegal for you to keep him a prisoner. The nurses suggest he should be physically restrained so that you can take blood and assess him, and that it may be a good idea to give him a sedative so that he does not continue to upset the other patients.

Questions
- What is the ethical principle of casuistry?
- Should you use restraint in this case?

ANSWER 5

Casuistry is a method of applying theories. It is much more practical than other theories and consequently is considered easier to use in clinical practice. Casuistry is broadly defined as a 'case-based' approach to solving an ethical dilemma. A case with a clear-cut course of action is used as a 'paradigm' case. New cases are analysed in detail, paying particular attention to the minutiae, and then compared with the paradigm case. If a new case is similar to the paradigm case, then the same course of action can be taken. If it is significantly different, then a different course of action should be taken. Therefore, choices are made depending on what decisions were previously made in similar cases. It is also a reflection of what happens in common law, where individual cases are examined and judgements are made based on precedent.

In deciding whether to restrain Micky, any of the other ethical theories could be used. Deontology may argue that a patient should never be restrained against their will, but consequentialists may argue that it would be ethical to restrain the patient because it would prevent the other patients from being upset and prevent possible harm occurring to the patient himself. Casuistry would examine similar cases and assess the outcome based on previous decisions. The most striking difficulty with this method of decision making is that in reality junior doctors often do not have the experience to make difficult ethical decisions based on what they have done previously. In the above scenario the FY1 doctor rang her senior to ask for his advice on whether it would be appropriate to restrain the patient to assess and treat him.

In this specific case, the patient was given a little longer to calm down, and when this failed he was safely sedated and assessed. He turned out to have a recurrence of his pneumonia, which responded to intravenous antibiotics, and 24 hours later his confusion resolved and he did not remember anything that had happened. This indicates that biochemical restraint to treat a patient can be argued as ethically justifiable. However, compare it with a slightly different case. A patient with dementia and acute-on-chronic renal failure does not understand what is wrong with him. The doctor knows that his chances of survival without dialysis are poor. However, the patient is unable to comprehend that he needs to stay seated for several hours a day, several days a week. He finds the dialysis sessions extremely traumatic. It is suggested that he is sedated while he is having dialysis. This was considered inappropriate because ongoing restraint was not thought to be in his best interests, and the decision was made to discontinue dialysis.

Casuistry forces the decision maker to examine all the facts of a case carefully before employing appropriate ethical theory to make a decision. A very slight change in case detail can shift the emphasis and can lead to a different decision and, hence, a different outcome.

CASE 6: NARRATIVE ETHICS

You are the FY1 doctor attached to a general medical firm. During a typical on-call you admit a 78-year-old man with shortness of breath. He is acutely unwell. Investigations reveal that he has right lobar pneumonia. He also has dementia and ischaemic heart disease. Despite intravenous antibiotics and fluids, he does not make much improvement over the next few days. He is lethargic, yet occasionally agitated and needs full nursing care. You decide to discuss his medical issues with his wife and son to see how they had been coping at home before the pneumonia. You discover that there had been a gradual decline in his general well-being over the past 6 months. In particular, his son comments how his father seemed to have had increasing difficulty swallowing. He used to hold food in his mouth for long periods of time before swallowing and had choked on several occasions. You decide to get a swallowing assessment. The speech and language therapist grades him as unsafe to swallow and he is made nil by mouth. A nasogastric tube is inserted so that he can continue to be fed but he pulls it out on three occasions. He continues to deteriorate and his albumin drops due to sustained lack of intake. The only way to improve this would be to insert a percutaneous endoscopic gastrostomy (PEG) tube, but you feel that in a patient with so many comorbidities this may not be in his best interests. You discuss the pros and cons of PEG feeding with the patient's relatives. You explain to them that without a PEG you can let him return home and continue to eat normally but that this may result in a fatal aspiration pneumonia at some point. The alternative is a PEG tube and keeping the patient nil by mouth permanently. A PEG tube is associated with a mortality of 3% and serious complications. You inform the relatives that the medical opinion of the team is to allow the patient to return home but that you would be willing to consider a PEG if the family felt that the patient would continue to have a good quality of life with one.

Questions

- What is narrative ethics?
- Which 'voices' should be listened to in this scenario?

ANSWER 6

Medical ethics is not just about hugely controversial issues, such as euthanasia and abortion, but is central to every decision made about the welfare and treatment of a patient. It is unrealistic to assume that every doctor will know the details of ethical theories. However, there is one theory that has been suggested that can help improve the doctor–patient relationship by enabling the doctor to take account of the views of those involved.

Good doctors have been using narrative theory instinctively for centuries. But the theory and its role in medicine have only been fully explored in the past few decades. The theory has two essential elements, which in practice are often intertwined: (1) use of cases as stories for their content, and (2) analysis of these stories to create an analytical and reflective approach to learning. It has a more substantial role than other ethical theories in the education of healthcare professionals and in the solving of everyday medical dilemmas.

Looking at a case as a story gives a holistic approach to medicine. Every individual's role in the story is examined and analysed. Every character's narrative is listened to in order to determine their beliefs and wishes and to act in their best interests. However, the patient's voice should always be listened to first. This is reflected in the way doctors start by taking the patient history. The patient's story is the first clue in discovering how the illness is affecting them – physically, psychologically and socially. A joint narrative is constructed by the doctor listening to the patient without interrupting them and then filling in any gaps with more direct questioning. Non-verbal cues displayed by the patient should also be picked up.

The scenario above is an interesting one in which to examine the application of narrative theory since the primary voice is silent. The patient has severe dementia and cannot voice his wishes. However, body language and actions are often a subtle but significant indication of what a patient wants. In this case, the patient keeps removing his nasogastric tube. We do not know if this is an expression of his wishes not to be fed or because he finds the tube uncomfortable. The doctor should also listen to the patient's relatives and take into account what they think the patient would have wanted. Nursing staff and other healthcare professionals involved in his care should also be listened to. Do they think the patient should have a PEG tube? Do they think the patient would be happier at home in his own environment, irrespective of the risk of aspiration?

Application of narrative ethics is essential when practising medicine. It enables the doctor to focus on the individual rather than the disease. However, it does not give clear-cut guidance about how to solve an ethical dilemma. In this respect it may be argued that the theory is best used in conjunction with other ethical guidance, where, for example, principlism could be used to decide on a course of action with narrative ethics providing a more detailed understanding of the different voices involved.

CASE 7: RIGHTS AND DUTIES

Xavier is a 72-year-old man who is admitted to the intensive care unit where you are an FY1. He was clearing out a gutter when he fell off the ladder and hit his head on the pavement. Passers-by immediately called an ambulance, and he was taken straight to theatre, where a large subdural haematoma was drained. Subsequent tests indicate that he fell from his ladder because he suffered a massive myocardial infarction. He has yet to recover consciousness, and it is thought that he has had irreparable brain damage due to anoxia. He is married and has three sons. His eldest son works as a radiographer in the hospital. His second son is an evangelist with the Pentecostal church, is married and has three young children. His youngest son is travelling around Australia. The intensive care unit has a family room, which has been taken over by Xavier's family. It is also constantly filled with well-wishers from the church who hold prayer and song meetings around the clock. Relatives of other patients are complaining about the lack of access to the family room and the noise levels. However, when the senior staff nurse asks them to keep the noise down, Xavier's son threatens the hospital with legal action for religious discrimination. He also says that the hospital is impeding the chances of his father's recovery because if they cannot hold a prayer meeting, the hospital is preventing the possibility of a miracle from God. Despite full active medical treatment and round-the-clock prayers, Xavier makes no improvement over the next 6 weeks. The medical team decides to discuss the possibility of allowing him to die in peace by withdrawing supportive medical intervention. He has multi-organ failure and has not regained consciousness. Xavier's wife and one son refuse point blank to allow this to happen and insist that everything be done for him, including resuscitation. The staff on the unit are becoming upset that Xavier is not being allowed to die with peace and dignity.

Xavier's eldest son supports the advice of the medical team and attempts to discuss it with his brother and mother. However, they threaten him with becoming a family outcast and divine retribution. They also continue to threaten the hospital with lawsuits as they do not believe that Xavier is being cared for properly. No joint decision is ever made, and after 11 weeks Xavier has a cardiac arrest and dies following a 60-minute cycle of resuscitation.

Questions
- What are 'rights' and 'duties'?
- What is the difference between positive and negative rights?
- Who has 'rights' in the above scenario?

ANSWER 7

There are different types of rights: political, religious and personal rights, such as a right to bodily integrity and a right to life. Rights are also attached to groups within society, for example, students' rights, patients' rights and parental rights. One important distinction is between rights which are legally recognised and moral rights. Some might argue that only rights which are substantiated in law are true rights and that sanctions cannot be imposed on anyone who interferes with a moral right, although if someone has a moral right to something, it could be said that they ought to be given it. But not all moral claims involve a claim of rights that should be legally upheld. There may be a moral obligation of fidelity within marriage, but to involve the law to uphold such a right seems inappropriate.

There is a difference between positive and negative rights. A negative right implies a right to non-interference, for example, a right not to be killed. In contrast, positive rights impose positive duties of support or assistance on others. A positive right to life imposes the duty to provide proper healthcare and ensure that life is saved. Only the person with the right can demand that the duty is performed or can waive that right.

There are very few absolute rights. An absolute right is one that may not be justifiably overridden in any circumstances. What counts as an absolute right – a right to life? In some countries the death penalty is still used as a form of punishment. Healthcare professionals may decide to withdraw life-supporting treatment from a patient whose quality of life is considered extremely poor. It could be argued that there is no right to a life of intolerable suffering. There are also situations where rights conflict, for example, the right to life and the right to self-defence. How and who should determine which right should predominate in such situations?

Consider the rights of all the characters in the above scenario:

- Who has rights?
- Why do they have them?
- What duties does the existence of these rights impose on other people?

Xavier has a prima facie 'right to life'. However, a tragic accident led to deterioration in the quality of his life. The duty of the medical team to provide intensive medical care and support for him has been fulfilled but is proving futile. With the patient incompetent to make a decision about whether the duty to provide medical care should be continued, who should make the decision? The law states that treatment should be provided in a patient's best interests and that no one has a right to insist on the continuation of futile treatment. Xavier's family does not have a legal right to insist on treatment.

Xavier's son also complains about the interference by hospital staff with his right to religious expression. In the UK, there is both a legal and moral right to allow people to express their religious, cultural and political beliefs. However, this is not an absolute right and can be outweighed where the exercise of the right infringes on the rights of others. In this case the constant singing and praying is causing distress to other patients and families on the intensive care unit, which may be an infringement of their rights.

ETHICS AND LAW IN CLINICAL PRACTICE: HOW TO DEAL WITH AN ETHICAL DILEMMA IN CLINICAL PRACTICE

Identify the ethical issue

- Determine why you feel that there is an ethical dilemma.
- How would you frame the ethical dilemma?
- Is this a clinical issue that you need more information about?

Clinical information

- Is the diagnosis clear?
- What other information do you need and how will you get it?
- How are you going to clinically manage this case: what options are possible, what prognoses are possible?

Do you know what the patient wants?

If the patient is *competent*

- Have they expressed a preference (informed/after dialogue)?
- Can the patient's expectations/choices be met – legally/clinically?
- Is the patient making an 'unusual' choice indicating that further dialogue is necessary and/or capacity is formally assessed?

If the patient is *not competent*

- Is there an advance decision – is it valid and applicable?
- Has the patient appointed a proxy to make decisions?
- What treatment option is in the patient's best interests?
- Can the patient's relatives/carers provide insight into what the patient would have wanted?

If the patient is *a child*

- Have the parents been informed and consulted about the treatment options and likely outcomes?

Resolving the ethical dilemma

Identify the main ethical principles that are relevant, including:

- Patient autonomy
- Confidentiality
- Provision of information
- Duties – to the patient, to colleagues, to oneself, to others
- Best interests
- Avoid/limit harms
- Competence

Is there a tension between any of these ethical principles – which ones?

Which ethical principle do you think carries the most weight? Justify why.

Seek advice or a sounding board

- Always speak to your consultant, your educational supervisor or another consultant.
- Does professional guidance clarify the issue?
- Can you refer the matter to a clinical ethics committee?

Make a decision

- Who should be involved in the decision-making process?
- When does the decision need to be made?
- What are the foreseeable consequences of your decision?
- What would be the implications of your decision if it applied in all similar cases?
- Can you justify this decision to: the patient or the patient's family; to your consultant; and to your peers?

Review your decision with the benefit of experience and learn from it!

ETHICS AND LAW IN CLINICAL PRACTICE: BEGINNING OF LIFE

CASE 8: *IN VITRO* FERTILISATION

As a member of your local clinical commissioning group (CCG), you are involved in setting up a specialist clinic for GPs to refer patients for consideration for fertility treatment funding. You have been asked to draw up some guidelines so that GPs know which patients would be eligible for fertility treatment on the National Health Service (NHS). Part of the discussion within the group has been to consider the interpretation of the National Institute for Health and Care Excellence (NICE) guidance and its application for funding decisions in practice. Points raised in a rather heated debate considered whether

- Fertility treatment should be offered to only those with a medical reason for infertility
- There should be a time frame as to how long a couple has been trying to conceive
- There should be any consideration of the financial implications of raising a child or the existence of other children
- It would be appropriate to fund the use of donor gametes, for example, using donor sperm for single women wishing to raise a child alone

You quickly realise that this is quite an emotive subject and individuals within the group have very strong views on when fertility treatment should be available. You decide more information is needed before guidance can be drafted and delegate fact finding tasks to the other members of the team.

Questions
- How does the law regulate assisted conception both privately and on the NHS?
- Are there limits to provision of NHS fertility treatment?
- Is there a 'right' to have a child?

ANSWER 8

Infertility is a common problem. It is estimated that approximately 7% of heterosexual couples having regular intercourse will not be able to conceive within two years. Fertility treatment is defined as a medical intervention to help conceive a child, and includes ovarian stimulation, intrauterine insemination (IUI), *in vitro* fertilisation (IVF) as well as the use of donor gametes and surrogacy. All fertility treatment is regulated by the Human Fertilisation and Embryology Act 1990 (as amended in 2008). The Human Fertilisation and Embryology Authority (HFEA) was set up in order to license, monitor and collect data on any clinic carrying out the above procedures. A licence is needed for any clinic involved in the use, storage and disposal of gametes and embryos. In 2012 there were 77 licensed clinics in the UK that performed 66,607 procedures (IVF or Donor Insemination) on 49,687 women.

The HFEA regulatory principles* reflect much of the content of the Human Fertilisation and Embryology Act and incorporate key ethical concepts including equality, confidentiality and consent. They also include guidance on assessing the welfare of the child to be born, clinical safety and data transparency and research.

The latest NICE guidance recommends that infertility treatment should be offered to individuals or couples who have a medical cause of infertility or those who have unexplained infertility after trying to conceive for 2 years.

Current NICE criteria for treatment include

- Women under 40 who have been trying for more than 2 years should be offered three full cycles of IVF
- Women aged 40 to 42 should be offered one cycle of IVF provided they have had no previous IVF cycles, they have no evidence of low ovarian reserve and they are made aware of the increased risks arising from pregnancy at this age
- Treatment is only recommended if the woman has a BMI of between 19 and 30

Despite this guidance data demonstrates that only 40% of IVF cycles performed in 2012 were funded by the NHS.

CCGs are responsible for developing specific area criteria for funding and in reality they impose far more restrictions on funding fertility treatment in line with limitations on their budgets. Some CCGs refuse to offer any funding in any circumstances (Case 57) and this 'postcode lottery' funding has come under heavy scrutiny. Restrictions commonly imposed by CCGs include funding provided for explained infertility problems only, longer waiting times before treatment is offered, much more stringent age and BMI restrictions, smoking history and that no partner must have another living child.

Welfare of the child

Section 3 of the Human Fertilisation and Embryology Act states that prior to any fertility treatment the clinic must take account of 'the welfare of any child who may be born as a result of the licensed treatment provided by them and any other child who may be affected by that birth'. In 2005 the HFEA published *Tomorrow's Children*, setting out a more focused interpretation of the welfare requirement under the Act. It states that there is a presumption in favour of providing treatment for those who seek it unless there is any evidence that any child born to an individual or couple, or any existing child of the family, would face a serious risk of medical, physical or psychological harm. Consideration may be taken of previous

---

* http://www.hfea.gov.uk/184.html

convictions relating to harming children, chronic physical illness, mental health problems, drug or alcohol addiction and any family history of inheritable genetic diseases.

In 1990, when the Act was originally passed, the 'need for a father' was included when considering the welfare of the child. This clearly discriminated against single women and same-sex couples. The 2008 Act replaces that with the need for 'supportive parenting'. This is defined as 'a commitment to the health, well-being and development of the child'.

Older women who may need donor eggs and would not meet criteria for NHS funding are still able to ask for self-funded IVF treatment irrespective of age, although there may be concerns for the health of older women undergoing treatment and pregnancy.

Donor anonymity

The Human Fertilisation and Embryology Authority (Disclosure of Donor Information) Regulations 2004 provide that any child resulting from gamete donation after April 2005 has the legal right to receive information about the donor when they reach the age of 18. This includes identifying information such as name, date of birth, physical characteristics and last known address. Of course, not all children will be told that they are conceived as a result of conception with donor gametes. Since regulations came into effect there has been a decrease in the number of sperm donors. Donor identification does not apply in some European countries or America, and because of this, more self-funding couples are making the decision to have fertility treatment abroad.

Is there a right to have a child?

Article 12, European Convention on Human Rights (ECHR) provides a 'right to found a family'. However, this is not an absolute right. A refusal to fund infertility treatment for women over an age where it is clinically less effective may be justifiable in the light of limited resources.

For the vast majority of people the decision to seek fertility treatment demonstrates that they are committed to becoming parents and raising a child. Putting up a barrier to fertility treatment based on social reasons could be perceived as medical professionals making judgements on who would make a fit parent. By comparison people with a history of unfit parenting are not prevented from conceiving naturally. It could, therefore, be considered ethically unjust for the State to judge the suitability of people with fertility problems to become parents. Conversely, it could be argued that because assistance is being provided by a third party, an ethical duty is owed to ensure that the child being created will be adequately cared for.

 Key Points

- There is marked disparity between NICE guidelines and local guidelines about eligibility for NHS funded fertility treatment.
- The welfare of the child must be considered in the provision of fertility treatment.
- The 'need for a father' has been replaced by the 'need for supportive parenting'.
- Any child born as a result of donor gametes will have a right to identifiable information about their donor.

CASE 9: SAME-SEX PARENTING

As part of your clinical duties as a gynaecology trainee, you have been asked to see some of the patients in the fertility treatment clinic. These patients have usually been referred by their GP for specialist advice and information provision when struggling to conceive naturally. You are therefore surprised to discover that one couple is in a same-sex relationship. They tell you they had their civil partnership 6 months ago and would now like to start a family. Neither of them have had children previously and they are interested in finding out more about the different options of fertility treatment available to them.

Questions

- Are same-sex couples entitled to fertility treatment?
- Who can legally be named as a parent on a birth certificate?
- What are the ethical arguments against same-sex parenting?

ANSWER 9

Civil partnerships and marriage for same-sex couples are recognised in law. The fertility options available to same-sex couples are numerous. The GP or obstetric specialist will usually be the first professional approached for information, and it is important they are able to have an open and honest discussion about potential different methods. Fertility options vary from DIY insemination at home – where many lesbians without fertility problems choose to use donor sperm from either a male friend or an online sperm provider – to formal surrogacy arrangements for gay men. However, it is rare for fertility treatment to be funded on the NHS as most CCGs do not cover the costs of using donor gametes, irrespective of sexuality.

In 2008, changes to the Human Fertilisation and Embryology Act enabled same-sex parents to be recognised as legal parents. For any child conceived after 6 April 2009, *both* parents could be named on the birth certificate and so be entitled to parental responsibility so long as the couple were in a civil partnership at the time of conception or the child was conceived via fertility treatment at a licensed clinic. For a lesbian couple both women are documented as legal parents on the birth certificate. The non-biological mother is listed as 'parent' which has replaced 'father'. This gives both women joint and equal parental responsibility. In 2005, it also became legal for same-sex couples to foster and adopt children as a couple rather than as individuals.

Many of the moral arguments against same-sex parenting used to be based on the possibility of a same-sex couple not being able to meet the welfare of a child. There were concerns that societal stigma would significantly impact upon the child. Multiple research studies in many different countries have disproved this theory and it is now recognised that the style of parenting is more important than the nature of the family the child is raised in. Golombok has argued that 'the quality of family relationships and the wider social environment are more influential in children's psychological development than are the number, gender, sexual orientation or biological relatedness of their parents or the method of their conception'. (S. Golombok. *Modern Families: Parents and Children in New Family Forms*. Cambridge: Cambridge University Press 2015.)

 Key Points

- Same-sex couples are lawfully able to access fertility treatment; however, this is rarely funded by the NHS.
- Both lesbian partners can be named on a birth certificate as long as either they are in a civil partnership at the time of conception or fertility treatment has taken place in a licensed clinic.

CASE 10: SURROGACY

You are a lawyer specialising in family law. To celebrate your new job, your best friend, Tessa, and her husband have come round to dinner. They have been having trouble conceiving and have had several failed IVF attempts. After dinner Tessa takes you to one side and confides that the fertility clinic they have been using mentioned the option of surrogacy. Tessa has been thinking it over but is unsure about the legalities of surrogacy in the UK and so asks for your advice. She has seen several documentaries on the television about high-profile couples using a surrogate but had always assumed it would be extremely expensive.

Questions

- What is surrogacy?
- Is surrogacy lawful?
- What ethical concerns may arise from surrogacy?
- Who in law are the parents of a child born as a result of surrogacy?

ANSWER 10

The original meaning of the word surrogate is 'a substitute'. Historically, a surrogate was used only in circumstances where a woman was unable to carry a child of their own. However, it is also now being used by homosexual couples who wish to raise a family.

There are two main types of surrogacy:

- Traditional surrogacy – the surrogate uses her own eggs and is the biological mother but conceives with sperm from the intended father.
- Host surrogacy – an embryo is created by IVF using the sperm and eggs of the commissioning couple. The embryo is implanted in the surrogate. She therefore has no biological link to the child.

The Surrogacy Arrangements Act 1985 was passed following the first high-profile surrogacy case in the UK – 'Baby Cotton'. The Act makes 'commercial surrogacy' illegal and no enforceable contract can be made between the surrogate and the commissioning couple. Although a surrogate cannot be paid, the Act states that reasonable expenses can be covered. This is very open to interpretation but there have been several cases which have reviewed payments made to a surrogate which state that the sums paid to the surrogate were not disproportionate to reasonable expenses. There are currently two not-for-profit organisations that assist childless couples in finding a surrogate: Surrogacy UK and Childlessness overcome through Surrogacy (COTs.)

As contracts are not enforceable, either party can change their mind until a parental order is issued. The surrogate is the legal mother irrespective of the genetic makeup of the child. A parental order must be granted (usually between 6 weeks and 6 months of age) in order to transfer parental responsibility from the surrogate to the commissioning couple. Up until this occurs, the surrogate has the right to change her mind.

It is also not risk-free for the surrogate. There are inherent medical risks associated with any pregnancy as well as the risk that the commissioning parents will not accept the baby either due to a change in their circumstances or due to unexpected complications that may result in medical problems with the baby. Although not legally recognised, a surrogacy agreement is usually drawn up between the commissioning couple and the surrogate.

There have been two significant reports published in 1984 and 1988[*] which raised concerns about the ethics of surrogacy. However, surrogacy is now more widely accepted and public opinion has changed. Surrogate parents now have equal rights as other couples with regard to maternity leave (Children and Families Act 2014).

For many, surrogacy is seen as a virtuous, altruistic act. However, opponents to it argue that there is potential to take advantage of the vulnerability of both the surrogate and the parents-to-be. The arguments against surrogacy include the commodification of babies and the potential health risks of pregnancy and childbirth, which outweigh the virtue of carrying a baby for another woman. Relatives may also feel coerced into surrogacy by being unable to say no to a request from someone they love. Some people feel that surrogacy can never be truly altruistic.

	Key Points

- Surrogacy is lawful but contracts cannot be enforced.
- Some argue that surrogacy enables the commodification of a child.

---

[*] The Warnock Report (1984), www.hfea.gov.uk/2068, and the Brazier Report (1998), http://webarchive. nationalarchives.gov.uk/20130107105354/http://www.dh.gov.uk/prod_consum_dh/groups/dh_digitalassets/@ dh/@en/documents/digitalasset/dh_4014373.pdf.

CASE 11: PRE-IMPLANTATION GENETIC DIAGNOSIS

Mike and Lauren, both in their late 20s, have been happily married for 4 years. Lauren has congenital deafness due to a known gene mutation, and Mike is an unaffected carrier. They have a one-in-two chance of having a deaf child, and they wish to avoid that risk. They are referred to the Pre-implantation Genetic Diagnosis (PGD) clinic as they are seeking *in vitro* fertilisation with PGD so that an embryo without the mutation causing deafness can be selected for implantation.

Questions
- What is pre-implantation genetic diagnosis?
- Does the law allow pre-implantation genetic diagnosis for a condition which does not require medical treatment?

ANSWER 11

This couple is seeking IVF not because they are infertile but in order that embryos can be created *in vitro* and tested for a genetic mutation. An unaffected embryo would be implanted and others frozen for future use. Embryos which do have the genetic mutation would be discarded. The HFEA issues licences for conditions for which PGD can be used. It must consider that the genetic condition is sufficiently serious before it grants a licence to test for it. Advances in knowledge of genetic mutations have resulted in an increasing number of conditions for which PGD is considered appropriate.

The 2008 amendments to the Human Fertilisation and Embryology Act 1990 provide that embryo testing is acceptable where there is a significant risk that the child to be born will have or develop a serious illness or disability. The HFEA Code of Practice provides that in deciding whether to offer PGD the clinic should consider factors such as the likely degree of suffering associated with the condition, the availability of effective treatment, the degree of any intellectual impairment and the social support available.

The genetic mutation here results in deafness, but this is not a life-shortening condition and there are no other clinical manifestations of the condition. The World Health Organisation states that a disability is not just a health problem but reflects the interaction between features of a person's body and features of the society in which he or she lives. Some members of the deaf community consider that deafness is not a disability.

Lauren and Mike feel strongly about the issue, and their views are an important factor for the clinic to consider. They view the state of deafness to be a harm which they want to avoid for a future child, and Lauren's experience of deafness informs this stance. They may feel that they do not have the support and resources to try to give a deaf child the same opportunities in life as a hearing child.

The clinical team should discuss with Lauren and Mike the seriousness of the condition and their perception of the level of risk. The HFEA has granted a licence for PGD to be offered for this condition. Respecting Lauren and Mike's autonomy entails providing them with relevant information and allowing them to make a choice about which embryos are implanted, according to their perception of harm.

PGD is an alternative to prenatal diagnosis. A couple with a genetic mutation could conceive naturally and the woman could choose to have a termination if antenatal tests detect the foetus has the condition. This may not be an acceptable choice to some couples. PGD is preferable for those who consider that a foetus has greater moral value than an embryo *in vitro*.

 Key Points

- PGD can be used for adult-onset conditions such as Huntington's disease and lower penetrance late-onset genetic conditions such as BRCA 1 and 2.
- It cannot be used to prefer selection of embryos which would develop serious disability or illness.
- Implantation of non-affected embryos eradicates the genetic mutation for future generations.
- Destruction of embryos is morally contentious for those who consider life begins at fertilisation.

CASE 12: MORAL STATUS OF THE FOETUS

Adele is a 39-year-old solicitor. She has been married to her husband for 8 years. Although they have both always wanted a family, Adele initially wanted to focus on her career and then struggled to conceive. When she finally fell pregnant, both Adele and her husband were thrilled. Unfortunately, following her first trimester scan, a nuchal screening test indicated that the foetus had a high risk of suffering from Down's syndrome. She decided to undergo further diagnostic testing, and amniocentesis confirmed Down's syndrome. The couple is distraught. They had waited a long time to conceive and wanted the 'perfect' baby to fit into their busy lifestyles. Adele does not feel she would ever be able to return to work if she had to care for a disabled child and thinks having to give up her career would be detrimental to her mental health. After much deliberation she visits her doctor to discuss termination of pregnancy.

Questions

- What is the extent of a woman's reproductive autonomy?
- At what stage of gestation, if at all, does the moral status of the foetus limit a woman's right to choose?

ANSWER 12

When a woman wishes to terminate a pregnancy, her reproductive autonomy is in direct conflict with the interests of the foetus. Although a foetus has no legal rights, it could be argued that it has a moral claim to a right to life, which trumps the woman's right to procreative autonomy. However, there are various ways in which abortion can be defended morally.

The personhood argument states that only 'persons' can claim rights. The definition of *person* is therefore crucial. If *person* is defined as someone who can make choices, is self-aware, has a conception of their future, and can evaluate from past experience, then a foetus is clearly not a person and has no claim to a right to life. However, according to this definition, patients in a permanent vegetative state and neonates will not count as persons and therefore will lack a right to life, but surely it is precisely those who lack autonomy who need protection.

Many religions believe that all human life is sacred and that because life begins at conception, the moral status of the foetus limits a woman's right to reproductive autonomy. In comparison, the potentiality argument recognises the foetus as a potential person. As pregnancy progresses there is a gradual increase in the probability that the foetus will become a person capable of independent life. So, an abortion at 6 weeks gestation may, on these grounds, carry less objection to one at 36 weeks. Of course, the concept of potentiality also applies to egg and sperm as they are capable of generating future life, and this could be used as an ethical argument against contraception.

An alternative view is that a foetus develops a moral right at viability because this is the point at which it has the capacity to survive outside the womb. However, so-called 'social' termination of pregnancy up to 24 weeks gestation (Case 13) seems at odds with advancements in neonatal care since babies born at 22 weeks gestation have survived, even if that might be with significant comorbidities. So at what point of development would a foetus gain a right to life – conception, the appearance of a nervous system, viability? If such a right is acquired from conception onward, then all abortion would be wrong; but if such rights are acquired from viability, early abortions would be permitted but not late ones.

It can be argued that as it is the mother who is the patient and has a 'contract' with the doctor, it is the doctor's duty to respect the mother's autonomy and enhance her ability to participate in the informed decision-making process. Those taking this stance will state that the clinician's moral perspective on abortion is irrelevant.

Key Points
• Abortion highlights the conflict between maternal reproductive autonomy and the moral status of a foetus.
• There are differing views on when a foetus acquires a moral claim to a right to life.

CASE 13: TERMINATION OF PREGNANCY

Sophie has had her 20-week anomaly scan and has discovered she is expecting another boy. This is her fourth pregnancy. She already has three sons and she and her husband decided to have another child in the hope of having a daughter. Sophie and her own mother had a very close bond growing up, and she had dreamt of recreating the mother–daughter bond with her own child. This desire had been made stronger due to the recent death of her own mother.

You are her GP and when she comes to see you she is visibly distressed. She confides that she has already booked an appointment with a counsellor at the British Pregnancy Advisory Service. She does not want to continue with the current pregnancy as she does not feel she could give enough love to another son. She also tells you that her husband is supportive of any decision she chooses to make as he too has a preference to have a daughter.

Questions
- What are the grounds for a lawful termination of pregnancy?
- Is it lawful to terminate a pregnancy on the grounds of foetal sex?
- Does the potential father have any legal rights?

ANSWER 13

The Offences Against the Person Act 1861 creates an offence of procuring a miscarriage. The Abortion Act 1967 provides that no offence is committed if the criteria in the Abortion Act are met: two registered medical practitioners are of the opinion, formed in good faith, that one of the four statutory grounds exists, that it is carried out by a registered medical practitioner on approved premises and that the abortion is notified to the chief medical officer.

The Abortion Act provides that a doctor can agree to a termination of pregnancy in the following circumstances:

- That the pregnancy has not exceeded its 24th week and that the continuance of the pregnancy would involve risk, greater than if the pregnancy were terminated, of injury to the physical or mental health of the pregnant woman or any existing children of her family; or
- That the termination of the pregnancy is necessary to prevent grave permanent injury to the physical or mental health of the woman; or
- That the continuance of the pregnancy would involve risk to the life of the pregnant woman greater than if the pregnancy was terminated; or
- That there is a substantial risk that if the child were born it would suffer from such physical or mental abnormalities as to be seriously handicapped.

The vast majority of terminations are performed under the first ground, colloquially termed 'social' abortions. In fact, the risks of pregnancy will always outweigh the risk of a termination at this stage. Anti-abortion groups argue that this ground is too liberal and that anyone can have an abortion for 'social' reasons. When the Abortion Act was amended in 1990, the time limit under this ground was lowered from 28 to 24 weeks. There have been many unsuccessful attempts by pro-life groups to lower this even further, particularly since there are now children who have survived despite being born at 22 weeks. In 2006 Nadine Dorries, MP, wanted the gestation limit dropped to 20 weeks. Her argument focused on the belief that it is at 21 weeks that sentience develops and a foetus may feel pain. The British Medical Association (BMA) stated that there is no scientific justification to reduce the limit for this reason, and the Termination of Pregnancy Bill was heavily defeated.

However, despite the ability to undergo termination up to 24 weeks under this criteria, statistics demonstrate that most social abortions are performed before 12 weeks gestation. In 2013 there were a total of 185,331 abortions performed in England and Wales and 97% of these came under the first ground; 91% of all abortions were performed before 13 weeks gestation, suggesting that although abortion can be lawfully performed up to 24 weeks it is rarely performed during the second trimester.[*]

With advances in neonatal care there is very little need for termination to occur due to risks to foetal or maternal health. Generally the child is wanted in these circumstances and so the woman is more likely to undergo early delivery of the foetus with appropriate medical intervention to save its life.

The most ethically contentious ground is termination for serious disability. Approximately 1% of all abortions in England and Wales are carried out under this ground. There are two issues here – the likelihood of risk and the nature of the risk. There will be some situations

---

[*] Abortion Statistics, England and Wales: 2013, Department of Health.

where antenatal tests show that the baby will undoubtedly be born with disabilities. In some cases, however, a definitive diagnosis cannot be made. There is no definition of serious disability, and the Royal College of Obstetricians and Gynaecologists (RCOG) has stated that this would be impracticable. There are insufficient advanced diagnostic techniques to detect malformations accurately and it is not always possible to predict the 'seriousness' of the outcome in terms of the long-term physical, intellectual or social disability on the child and the effects on the family. The RCOG believes that the interpretation of 'serious disability' should be based upon individual discussion between the parents and the mother's doctor.*

In the scenario Sophie wishes to terminate on the grounds that having another boy will have a detrimental effect on her mental health. The law does not expressly prohibit gender-specific abortions. This gives a wide discretion to doctors when assessing the mental health risks to a pregnant woman. In 2012 the BMA stated that

> It is normally unethical to terminate a pregnancy on the grounds of f(o)etal sex alone, except in cases of severe sex linked disorders. The pregnant woman's views about the effect of the sex of the foetus on her situation should nevertheless be carefully considered. In some circumstances doctors may come to the conclusion that the effects are so severe as to provide legal and ethical justification for a termination.
>
> Medical Ethics Today: The BMA's Handbook of Ethics and Law, 3rd Edition 2012

Rights of the father

The father-to-be has no right to insist that a woman continue with the pregnancy. This was clarified in the case of *Paton v British Pregnancy Advisory Service Trustees* (1979). Mr Paton tried to prevent his wife from having an abortion using both his right as a potential father and the right to life of the unborn child as justification. He failed on both accounts.

 Key Points

- The Abortion Act provides clinicians with a defence for performing terminations, providing specific criteria are met.
- There is no right to termination, and two doctors in good faith must agree that a ground exists.
- The father of an unborn foetus has no legal right to either insist on or prevent an abortion.

---

* Abortions for fetal abnormality and syndromatic conditions indicated by cleft lip and/or palate, RCOG, July 2008.

CASE 14: CONSCIENTIOUS OBJECTION

Adele is a 39-year-old solicitor. She is 16 weeks pregnant with her first child. Following her first trimester scan at 13 weeks she was informed that she was high risk for having a child with Down's syndrome. She underwent further diagnostic testing in the form of amniocenteses which confirmed the diagnosis. The couple is distraught as they had tried for a long time to conceive, but Adele does not think she can cope with a baby with Down's syndrome. Despite counselling, Adele is now sure that she wants to terminate the pregnancy. She visits her GP to request a termination. However, the GP is a practising Roman Catholic with a strong faith, and he does not wish to participate in abortion services.

Questions

- In what circumstances can a healthcare professional refuse to be involved in a termination of pregnancy?
- Are there any other medical situations when conscientious objection can be used by a healthcare professional?

ANSWER 14

Doctors, nurses and midwives are permitted to refuse to 'participate in treatment' by virtue of a conscientious objection clause in the Abortion Act 1967. Section 4 provides that 'no person shall be under any duty … to participate in any treatment authorised by this Act to which he has a conscientious objection, except where treatment is necessary to save the life of or prevent grave permanent injury to the pregnant woman'. The onus is on the person claiming to rely on conscientious objection to prove it on religious or ethical grounds. As there is no statutory definition of *conscientious objection*, there may be practical difficulties in interpreting these grounds.

Conscientious objection applies only to participation in treatment. The Supreme Court in *Doogan v Greater Glasgow and Clyde Health Board* (2014) held that 'participate' means taking part in a hands-on capacity and so, for example, making a telephone call to arrange terminations of pregnancy and paging anaesthetists are not covered. Doctors relying on the conscientious objection clause still have a duty to signpost the patient to appropriate services.

Professional guidance also gives recognition to conscientious objection in a wider context. The General Medical Council (GMC) guidance provides that 'you may choose to opt out of providing a particular procedure because of your personal beliefs and values, as long as this does not result in direct or indirect discrimination against, or harassment of, individual patients or groups of patients' (GMC, Personal Beliefs and Medical Practice, 2013). A doctor must not refuse to provide treatment because of the individual attributes of a patient. The person wishing to exercise conscientious objection must do his/her best to make sure patients are aware of this.

The view of the BMA is that doctors should have a right to conscientiously object to participation in abortion, fertility treatment and withdrawal of life-sustaining treatment.

However, there is an argument that healthcare professionals have a duty to their patients which transcends their personal beliefs. Julian Savulescu considers that 'if people are not prepared to offer legally permitted, efficient, and beneficial care to a patient because it conflicts with their values, they should not be doctors. Doctors should not offer partial medical services or partially discharge their obligations to care for their patients' (Savulescu 2006).

The GMC Education Committee recognises that medical students have a range of ethical and religious beliefs, but these cannot compromise their medical training, and core educational outcomes must be demonstrated for graduation.*

 Key Points

- Healthcare professionals are not required to participate in termination of pregnancy if they conscientiously object for ethical, moral or religious reasons.
- The healthcare professional must still provide information about appropriate services.
- The burden of proof lies with the person seeking to rely on conscientious objection.

---

* GMC Core Education Outcomes: GMC Education Committee Position Statement para 10, (2006).

CASE 15: PRE-NATAL INJURY

Angela is 19 years old and during her pregnancy with her first child drank heavily. All those who provided antenatal care gave her information about the risks that this posed to her unborn child and urged her to stop drinking or significantly reduce her intake. Angela did not do so, and her baby was born with foetal alcohol syndrome, which is characterised by intellectual disability and physical defects.

Josephine was 8 weeks pregnant when her 3-year-old daughter was covered with red spots and diagnosed as having German measles. Josephine told her GP that she would want a termination rather than risk giving birth to a disabled child. She had two blood tests but the results were contradictory. The GP did not check with the laboratory nor did he run new tests. Instead he reassured her that all was well. In fact, Josephine gave birth to a boy who was blind, deaf and severely brain damaged, which could be attributed to German measles exposure in utero.

Questions

- Is a woman morally or legally responsible for the harms she causes her child in utero?
- Can a claim be made against a healthcare professional whose negligent acts prenatally give rise to a child born disabled?

ANSWER 15

If we see a pregnant woman smoke or drink we may instinctively feel that it is wrong because of the potential harm that may be caused to her unborn baby. A pregnant woman could be said to owe a moral duty to the unborn child due to the impact that her actions may have on its future well-being. However, legal status is only acquired when a child is born (*Paton v BPAS* 1979), and an unborn child therefore has no rights until birth.

A mother cannot be sued in negligence for harm caused in utero (unless the harm occurred as a result of a road traffic accident where insurance would fund a claim for compensation). In the case of *CP (A Child) v First-tier Tribunal (Criminal Injuries Compensation)* (2014) a claim was made that a woman who drank heavily during pregnancy, despite warnings of the consequences, resulting in the child being born with foetal alcohol syndrome had committed a crime against her unborn child. Section 23 Offences Against the Person Act 1861 provides that it is unlawful to administer to any other person any noxious agent to inflict grievous bodily harm. The alcohol was a noxious agent but the claim failed because the court held the foetus was not a person at the time it was taken. There would be profound implications if a mother could be held liable, in negligence or through a criminal act, for harms to her unborn child, and this could change the relationship she has with healthcare professionals during her pregnancy.

A healthcare professional owes a duty of care to the pregnant woman as his patient. During pregnancy the foetus is not a legal person, so how can it be owed a duty of care? The Congenital Disabilities (Civil Liability) Act 1976 enables the child once born to make a claim for compensation for disabilities which occurred before birth as a result of a breach of duty owed to one of his parents. Once born any claim crystallies and relates to harm sustained in utero. Josephine's baby was born disabled as a result of exposure to the rubella virus. As the two blood tests were contradictory, the doctor's failure to check with the laboratory or run a new test could be negligent (Case 41), and if so, the child born could sue in respect of the disabilities incurred.

A 'wrongful life' claim is one made by a child alleging that but for the negligence of the doctor he would not be born because the mother was deprived of the choice not to continue with the pregnancy, i.e., Josephine's lack of option to have an abortion because she was not properly informed of the risk of giving birth to a child with such disabilities. English law does not recognise a claim for wrongful life because it is impossible to compare a life of poor quality with no existence at all.

Key Points
• A healthcare professional whose pre-natal negligence results in harm to the child when born could be subject to a legal claim.
• A pregnant woman could be said to owe moral duties to her unborn child but has no legal duty in respect of injury caused in utero.

CASE 16: NEONATAL CARE: LEGAL AND ETHICAL ISSUES

You are working as an ST2 in a neonatal intensive care unit. You and your consultant are called to the delivery of baby Ayesha, who has just been born at 25 weeks following a normal pregnancy. When you arrive, she is not breathing spontaneously and has a slow heart rate. She is intubated and ventilated and requires a brief period of cardiopulmonary resuscitation. Following this, she is able to be stabilised on the ventilator and is transferred to the neonatal unit. Although she appears reasonably stable over the next 48 hours, a cranial ultrasound scan shows large bleeds into her brain (bilateral grade IV intra-ventricular haemorrhages).

Your consultant has a meeting with the family and explains that the likely impact of the bleeding is that Ayesha will be very severely disabled, with severe four-limb cerebral palsy, cognitive impairment and potentially visual and hearing impairment. He explains that she is unlikely to be able to breathe on her own at the moment, and that it may well be in her best interests to remove her from the ventilator and withdraw intensive support rather than prolonging her suffering. Her parents are horrified by the idea that medical treatment could be withdrawn from their child and are adamant that she continues to be ventilated. They have strong religious beliefs, maintain that only God can decide when someone should die and are praying for a miracle to make her recover. Ayesha is their only child, her mother is 42 years old and this baby was much longed for after years of trying to conceive. They understand that she is likely to be disabled but could not countenance ending her life and think that her life will still be worthwhile if she is very severely impaired. The treating team feel it is wrong to prolong Ayesha's suffering by continuing to ventilate her and to perform invasive and painful procedures when her brain is known to be so severely damaged. Even if she might manage to breathe on her own when she is a few days or weeks older, some think it would be kinder to withdraw intensive care now, given how severely brain damaged she is likely to be.

Questions

- Was it the correct decision to resuscitate Ayesha at birth?
- Does Ayesha have a right to life?
- When parents' views conflict with doctors', who decides what treatment is given to a neonate?
- What impact do parents' religious beliefs have?
- Does the financial cost of continuing intensive care make any difference to what should be done?

ANSWER 16

Professional guidance

The Nuffield Council on Bioethics 2006 document *Critical Care Decisions in Fetal and Neonatal Medicine: Ethical Issues* offers guidance on the resuscitation of extremely premature babies. This would support the decision to offer full cardiopulmonary resuscitation at birth at 25 weeks' gestation. At earlier gestations, the low probability of a successful outcome means that a decision to offer limited resuscitation or not to resuscitate may be reasonable. The Nuffield guidance states that at 24 weeks a baby should be offered full invasive intensive care and support *unless* the parents and the clinicians are agreed that in the light of the baby's condition (or likely condition) it is not in his or her best interests to start intensive care.

The Nuffield guidance also outlines the circumstances in which withholding or withdrawing life-sustaining treatment in neonates should be considered, and given the severity of Ayesha's intracerebral haemorrhages and likely brain damage, it is understandable that the treating team now feel it is not in her best interests to continue treatment.

The Nuffield guidance should be read in conjunction with the Royal College of Paediatrics and Child Health (RCPCH) 2015 guidance *Making decisions to limit treatment in life-limiting and life-threatening conditions in children: a framework for practice*. This outlines three situations in which continued treatment may not be in a child's best interests: when their life is limited in quantity (when death is imminent or inevitable or brainstem death has been confirmed); when life is limited in quality (the burden of treatment or suffering from treatments or the child's underlying condition outweighs any benefit in sustaining life); and competent refusal by an older child or adolescent, supported by parents and clinicians. If clinicians and parents disagree over whether life-sustaining treatment should be continued, every effort should be made to reach consensus through clear and sensitive discussion of the issues. If this is unsuccessful, the RCPCH recommend obtaining a second opinion from an independent clinical team, the involvement of a Clinical Ethics Committee, chaplain or religious leader and mediation as possible strategies for resolving disputes.

Ethical issues

The conflict between the parents and doctors in this case is a conflict over whether sanctity of life or quality of life should be the primary concern when deciding on further medical treatment. The parents strongly believe that Ayesha's life should be preserved at all costs, and as in many cases of dispute between parents and clinicians, this is partly founded in religious belief.

Although there is a strong presumption in favour of prolonging life, the quality of life approach also takes into account other factors: is this individual's dignity being compromised? Is the burden of treatment and suffering so great that harm (maleficence) is being done? Clearly, gauging the quality of life of a neonate, or the severely disabled child Ayesha is predicted to become, is extremely subjective. The situation is further complicated because the neonatal brain is constantly developing, making it difficult to predict the consequences of damage. There is also some evidence that preterm babies who survive into adulthood report a quality of life much higher than doctors would predict.

A further ethical issue is that of justice, with the allocation of resources for prolonged and potentially futile treatment in neonatal intensive care depriving other patients of timely treatment. This is used in allocating resources at a national level (e.g., recommendations for treatment by the National Institute for Health and Care Excellence) but should not be used to guide treatment decisions about withdrawal of care for individual patients. The Nuffield guidance recommends that clinicians 'continue to do the best possible for the "patient in front of them"' but debate continues over whether using scarce resources to offer intensive care for extremely preterm babies is just.

Legal issues

The overriding principle is clearly that further management be determined in Ayesha's best interests. 'Independent of gestational age, children of 6 days, months or years are each worthy of equal consideration' (Nuffield Council on Bioethics 2006). Neonates have the same status as older children and adults in respect of their Article 2 ECHR right to life, although Article 2 does not impose a positive obligation for continuation of medical treatment where it is no longer in the patient's best interests. John Harris has argued that a neonate should have the same moral status as a foetus as neither have the attributes of 'personhood' i.e. entities which value existence, take an interest in their own futures, and take a view about how important it is for them to experience whatever future existence may be available.[*] A person in PVS may not have these attributes; nevertheless we still accord value to their existence.

There is no legal distinction between withholding and withdrawing treatment. UK law does not, however, permit active neonatal euthanasia (clinicians taking deliberate action to end life). By contrast, the Netherlands' Groningen Protocol offers a defence for doctors who administer medication to end the life of a neonate suffering unbearably if stringent criteria are fulfilled and parents agree.

There is a substantial body of case law relating to parents' requests that intensive care be continued against medical advice. Judgments have taken into account a 'balancing exercise' of the benefits and burdens of continued treatment on a case-by-case basis, without regard to parental religious belief. Factors considered may include pain, suffering, mental distress and capacity for independent survival, pleasure and relationships with others. The inherent subjectivity of quality of life becomes particularly problematic when weighing potentially incommensurable factors against each other, such as the pleasure a severely disabled child derives from their relationship with their parents versus the pain of invasive medical procedures (see, for example, *An NHS Trust v. MB* 2006 and *Kings College Hospital NHS Foundation Trust v Y*, 2015). This is even more difficult in a neonate who has not had any opportunity to indicate preferences. Although parental views are considered, the judiciary have stopped short of forcing doctors to provide continued treatment they believe is futile.

 Key Points

- Decisions about withholding and withdrawing neonatal intensive care are extremely complex and sensitive: everything possible should be done to achieve consensus between parents and the treating team.
- If conflict arises between clinicians and parents, the best interests standard is considered to determine further treatment for neonates, as it is with older children.
- Very severe impairments or extremely low probability of survival need to be present before quality of life is deemed so poor that life-sustaining treatment should be withheld or withdrawn.

---

[*] Harris, J. The concept of the person and the value of life. *Kennedy Institute of Ethics Journal*, 1999; 9 (4): 293–308.

SECTION 4

ETHICS AND LAW IN CLINICAL PRACTICE: CHILDREN AND ADOLESCENTS

Seven-year-old Megan is on a school trip to the Isle of Wight when she slips on the edge of the swimming pool and lands awkwardly on her wrist. She is taken to the local Accident and Emergency department by her teacher. X-rays reveal she has a nasty comminuted fracture of her radius, and the orthopaedic team believes that it is going to need manipulation under anaesthesia in order to achieve satisfactory realignment. Your surgical ST6 has asked you to complete the necessary pre-theatre checklists and to complete the consent form. You try to explain to him that the parents are not present, but he reassures you that the teacher can sign instead since she is the accompanying adult.

Questions
- Who can consent to medical treatment for young children?
- What happens in an emergency?

ANSWER 17

A person with 'parental responsibility' has decision-making authority regarding the child, including the right to make healthcare decisions. The biological mother automatically has parental responsibility. Both parents have parental responsibility if they are married, or for children born after 1 December 2003 (in England and Wales), if they are named on the birth certificate. It is also possible for another person to acquire parental responsibility through a court order, or it may be given to a legal guardian or a local authority if they have care of the child.

Legally, consent is required only from one person with parental responsibility. However, it is clearly good practice to involve both parents where possible, particularly if treatment is invasive or the benefits of treatment do not overwhelmingly outweigh the burdens. In situations where there is disagreement between parents, a clinician may still proceed with treatment if it is in the child's best interests. However, there are a small group of decisions which should not be taken by one person with parental responsibility against the wishes of another, e.g., non-therapeutic male circumcision and immunisations.

Where there is disagreement between parents and clinical team, a court order should be obtained before any treatment is given where there is time to do so. The European Court of Human Rights in *Glass v UK* (2004) stated that a failure to refer such cases to the court is a breach of the child's Article 8 rights.

When a child presents for treatment, it is good medical practice for staff to inquire about the relationship the accompanying adult has with the child. Rarely would this need to be verified through other means. Adults other than parents, such as a child-minder or a teacher, cannot give consent to treatment. Nevertheless the Children Act 1989 authorises a person with care of a child to do 'what is reasonable in all the circumstances of the case for the purpose of safeguarding or promoting the child's welfare'. This would mean that another adult could bring a child for a routine assessment and facilitate examination for simple treatment, for example, tonsillitis.

In an emergency where no parent is present or contactable, urgent treatment which is in the child's best interests may be given. This is the case in the above scenario where delay to examination under anaesthesia could result in long-term problems.

 Key Points

- Only one person with parental responsibility needs to consent except in contentious or serious situations.
- Any treatment can be given in an emergency if it is in the child's best interests and the person with parental responsibility is not contactable.

CASE 18: PARENTAL REFUSAL OF TREATMENT

A 7-year-old boy is being treated for medulloblastoma, a type of brain tumour. He has had surgery and is due to start a treatment protocol that involves radiotherapy and chemotherapy. His parents (who were married at the time of his birth) are now separated, and although his father agrees to the treatment protocol, his mother is strongly opposed to radiotherapy. She is very worried about the impact it may have on surrounding brain tissue, citing evidence that it may reduce his IQ and make him infertile. The treating team is worried that his chances of survival will be much decreased if he does not have radiotherapy, which has been shown to increase the chance of disease-free survival from 35% to 80%.

His mother wants to explore other treatment options, including an alternative form of radiotherapy called proton beam irradiation (which is not recommended for this type of tumour in this country) or using hyperbaric oxygen rather than any form of radiotherapy. The clinicians are very worried that any delay in treatment will reduce the chances of the radiotherapy being successful. They have sought a second opinion from a paediatric oncology team in a separate hospital, who are wholly in agreement with their treatment plan.

Questions

- If parents refuse treatment for their child against doctors' advice, how should we decide whether or not to proceed with treatment?
- Does it matter whether it is one parent or both who are opposed to treatment?
- Does it make any difference if they are divorced or separated?

ANSWER 18

This case is based on the situation affecting a 7-year-old boy in *An NHS Trust v SR* (2012), which highlights the tension between parents' rights to decide on their child's treatment and the need to act in the child's best interests.

Consent for treatment can be sought from either parent if both have parental responsibility (Case 17). In this case, the father and mother share parental responsibility as they were married at the time of birth, and subsequent separation or divorce does not change this. Although consent need only be obtained from one parent, it would be unreasonable and impracticable to proceed with a course of treatment as serious and prolonged as radiotherapy against the wishes of one parent without a declaration from the court.

The guiding principle for deciding whether to proceed with treatment must be the child's best interests. In this case, Bodey J was clear in concluding that it was in the boy's best interests to proceed with radiotherapy, given the evidence that his chances of survival would be drastically improved even at the risk of long term side effects, commenting that 'one cannot enjoy even a diminished quality of life if one is not alive'. An interesting comparison can be made with a more recent case in which a 5-year-old boy with medulloblastoma was removed from a hospital by his parents and taken abroad because they wished him to have proton beam rather than conventional radiotherapy (*Re Ashya King (A Child)* 2014). In this case, greater importance was accorded to the rights of parents to decide their child's treatment, given that a unit in Prague was willing to commence the alternative treatment immediately, even though it is not recommended in this country. As Baker J commented:

> It is a fundamental principle of family law in this jurisdiction that responsibility for making decisions about a child rests with his parents. In most cases, the parents are the best people to make decisions about a child and the State [...] has no business interfering with the exercise of parental responsibility unless the child is suffering or is likely to suffer significant harm.
>
> *Re Ashya King (A Child)* 2014

When parents oppose a strategy of treatment clinicians feel is necessary, the first question to answer is how urgent the situation is. In all non-emergency situations, an application should be made to the court if the situation cannot be resolved through further discussion. The degree and likelihood of harm must be significant for parents' decisions to be overruled: for example, parental refusal of immunisation is respected (Case 60), while medically necessary blood transfusions have been given by court order, against parental wishes.

 Key Points

- Many disagreements between parents and clinicians can be overcome through a process of discussion and negotiation, but if this fails an application should be made to the court.
- Parents have the right to take decisions about their child's healthcare, but this is not absolute: the presumption in favour of respecting their decision can be overruled if the child is at risk of significant harm.

CASE 19: REQUEST FOR NON-THERAPEUTIC TREATMENT

Michael is 8 years old. His parents have brought him to see the GP as they are concerned that his ears are very prominent and stick out. They tell the GP that Michael seems very withdrawn when he comes home from school, and a discussion with his teacher alerted them to the fact that he is being teased about his ears – he is called Dumbo and Mr Spock. Michael is wearing a hat throughout the consultation. His parents ask whether a referral could be made so Michael could have his ears pinned back. The GP explains that this is a cosmetic procedure and that it may be better to see how Michael feels about his ears when he is older. The GP also informs them that as it is considered cosmetic surgery it would not be funded on the NHS. Nevertheless they insist that something is done to stop Michael's suffering.

Questions

- Is it in Michael's best interests to have a non-therapeutic procedure?
- Should cosmetic surgery be performed on children?

ANSWER 19

Michael's parents have 'parental responsibility', which means they have the authority and responsibility to make decisions about his medical treatment. It is assumed that parents will make decisions in their child's best interests because they know the emotional and welfare needs of their child and more often than not will want their child to be happy and flourish.

Doctors must safeguard and protect the health and well-being of children and young people. 'Well-being includes treating children and young people as individuals and respecting their views, as well as considering their physical and emotional welfare' (GMC 0-18 years: guidance for all doctors, 2007).

The medical and non-medical benefits and disadvantages of the proposed treatment should be considered in deciding whether it is in the child's best interests. Michael's parents consider that pinnaplasty will enable him to have a more 'normal' look so he will not be bullied, and this will benefit his emotional needs. But any benefits should be balanced against the harms and burdens. There is no medical need for this surgical procedure. It will be performed under anaesthesia, which carries risks. The effectiveness, risks and side effects of this particular procedure are relevant considerations.

Michael's parents are requesting a referral for a surgical procedure for him. Although Michael does not have capacity to make the decision, he should be involved in discussions so he can express his views about what he would want to happen and why. Although he is not able to give valid consent, he may assent to the procedure.

Michael's parents are expressing their concerns for the well-being of their son and his future welfare. Their views about his emotional and welfare needs are important. It would be sensible for their GP to refer to an ear, nose and throat specialist to evaluate Michael's needs and to have an informed discussion about surgery and other possible alternatives. As with any cosmetic surgery, this would have to be self-funded.

 Key Points

- Parents can give or refuse consent for medical treatment or procedures, but this must be in the best interests of the child, without regard to their own interests.
- The medical and non-medical benefits, such as emotional benefit, should be considered.
- Doctors cannot be compelled to perform a procedure that they do not consider to be in the best interests of a child.

CASE 20: ASSESSING COMPETENCE IN CHILDREN

The asthma nurse at your surgery has asked you to come and review a 15-year-old girl, Shania, who has booked in to discuss her medication. She was diagnosed with asthma at the age of 6 and has had several admissions to hospital with severe asthma attacks. She is now at boarding school and feels that over the past few months her asthma has not been as well controlled as before, despite taking her inhalers regularly. On closer questioning you discover that she is only really symptomatic during extreme exertion, but Shania feels that she would like to try stronger treatment as her breathing is affecting her during running and she wants to compete at county level at the upcoming cross-country sports events.

Questions

- When is a young person considered competent to make healthcare decisions?
- Are there any limitations on what treatments a young person can consent to?
- What is the role of parents of a competent child in healthcare decision making?

ANSWER 20

At 18 years a person is an adult and capacity is presumed rather than proven. Young people aged 16–17 years are presumed to be competent to give effective consent to surgical, medical and dental treatment, and associated procedures such as investigations and anaesthesia. However, there is no presumption of competence to consent to organ donation, non-therapeutic procedures or research. For these more unusual situations capacity has to be assessed before consent is valid.

Young people under 16 years of age can also consent to medical treatment but only if they can demonstrate that they are competent to do so. This is called 'Gillick competence' because the legal principle was clarified in the case of *Gillick v West Norfolk and Wisbech Area Health Authority* (1985). If a young person has sufficient intelligence and understanding to understand fully what is proposed, the advantages and disadvantages, then they can consent to the procedure or treatment without either the knowledge of or the consent of their parents.

The Age of Legal Capacity (Scotland) Act 1991 provides that minors younger than 16 may consent to medical treatment if, in the opinion of the health professional, they are capable of understanding the nature and possible health consequences of the procedure or treatment.

The ability to consent, therefore, is much more dependent on intelligence and psychological maturity than on age. Experience of life, and perhaps particularly of illness itself, will point toward a better ability to weigh the issues in the decision-making process and to predict outcomes. As in adults, capacity is functional, i.e., it depends on the nature of the decision to be taken. A high level of understanding would be expected for an invasive procedure, in contrast to something more minor such as consent to phlebotomy.

The assessment of competence is a matter for the healthcare professional conducting the examination, providing the treatment or performing the intervention. If there are doubts about the young person's capacity, a second opinion should be sought.

Where a minor is not competent to give or withhold informed consent, a person with parental responsibility may give consent for investigations or treatment which are in the minor's best interests. This is the case whether the minor is 17, 16 or younger than 16 years.

In the scenario Shania has demonstrated a good understanding of her asthma and has been able to explain the impact it has on her life. She has lived with her condition for many years and has made the sensible decision to talk to a specialist about her ongoing problems. This would be enough to demonstrate that she has capacity to make simple decisions about further treatment options.

 Key Points

- A 'Gillick-competent' child refers to someone under the age of 16 who is deemed to have capacity to make relevant healthcare decisions.
- Competence is often related to psychological maturity and experience of illness rather than age.
- The nature and amount of information provided can influence capacity.

CASE 21: UNDERAGE CONTRACEPTION

Lilianna has booked in to see you at a walk-in family planning clinic. She has come to discuss contraceptive options as she is thinking about starting a sexual relationship with her boyfriend. She tells you that she has not had sex yet but they have talked about it and she would like to be sure she cannot fall pregnant. Although Lilianna looks and acts much older, she is not quite 15.

Questions

- What questions ought you to ask?
- Can you lawfully prescribe contraception?
- As Lilianna is under the legal age for sexual intercourse should this be reported?

ANSWER 21

Legal issues

In the case of *Gillick v West Norfolk and Wisbech Area Health Authority* (1985), Mrs Gillick, a mother to five daughters, challenged a policy that a doctor could provide teenagers with contraception without informing a parent. The House of Lords held that a doctor can provide contraceptive services to under-16s in the following circumstances:

- The young person understands the health professional's advice
- The health professional cannot persuade the young person to inform his or her parents or allow the doctor to inform the parents that he or she is seeking contraceptive advice
- The young person is very likely to begin or continue having intercourse with or without contraceptive treatment
- Unless he or she receives contraceptive advice or treatment, the young person's physical or mental health or both are likely to suffer
- The young person's best interests require the health professional to give contraceptive advice, treatment or both without parental consent

These are known as Fraser Guidelines and apply specifically to contraceptive and sexual health guidance.

In 2004, the Department of Health issued *Revised Guidance for Health Professionals on the Provision of Contraceptive Services for the Under-16s*. This recommends that when a person under 16 requests contraception, doctors and other health professionals should discuss the risks of pregnancy, sexually transmitted diseases and the pros and cons of the various contraceptive options. A doctor or health professional can provide contraception (and sexual and reproductive health advice and treatment) without parental knowledge or consent, to a person under 16, provided that:

- She understands the advice provided and its implications
- Her physical or mental health would otherwise be likely to suffer and so provision of advice or treatment is in her best interests.

The courts have also recognised the importance of maintaining confidentiality of young people who access contraception and abortion services because without this reassurance they may fail to seek sexual health advice. Although the clinician in the case scenario should encourage Lilianna to confide in her mother or another responsible adult, she should not break confidentiality unless she felt Lilianna was at risk.

In order to establish risk the doctor should try to gain as much information about Lilianna's future sexual partner as he/she can, for example, how they know each other, where they meet up and what their joint interests are. It is an offence for a man to have sex with a girl under 16, although it would not normally be in the girl's best interests to involve the authorities if the ages of the patient and her partner were similar and they were engaging in a normal teenage relationship. However, Lilianna would be considered potentially vulnerable because of her age and it should be ascertained that there is no power imbalance in the relationship, either because of age difference or the nature of the relationship. If there are concerns about this, a referral should be made to the appropriate authorities.

Young people over 16 and under 18 are not deemed able to give consent if the sexual activity is with an adult in a position of trust or a family member as defined by the Sexual Offences Act 2003. Children under 13 are not deemed competent to consent to sex (Sexual Offences

Act 2003), and consideration would have to be given as to whether it would be in the young person's best interests to report to a statutory agency. This would usually be the case, and although there is no requirement for mandatory reporting, the issue should always be discussed with the child safeguarding lead.

Ethical issues

An individual's choice about her sexual activities and preferences is an aspect of private life which deserves respect. Respecting the autonomy of a competent young person provides a benefit in itself – an increased sense of worth and dignity. However, this must be balanced against the potential for harm. As Lilianna is already planning on having sex with her boyfriend, there is potentially more harm in denying her safe access to contraception as the chances are she would proceed with intercourse anyway. By forging a trusting relationship with her it is possible that Lilianna can be protected long-term by educating her about the importance of using barrier methods of contraception to prevent infection, regular sexually transmitted infection (STI) screening and in the future, engagement with the cervical screening programme.

 Key Points

- A child under the age of 13 cannot legally consent to a sexual relationship.
- When providing sexual health advice to adolescents between the ages of 13 and 16 it is good medical practice to ensure that they are Fraser competent and to establish the nature of the sexual relationship they are in.
- If there are any doubts about the person being vulnerable, confidentiality may be broken by discussing the case with the child safeguarding lead.

CASE 22: ADOLESCENT REFUSAL OF LIFE-SUSTAINING TREATMENT

Patricia is 17 and has taken an overdose of paracetamol. She has been rushed to the Accident and Emergency department and doctors tell her that she needs urgent treatment; otherwise she is at risk of permanent liver damage or death. Patricia refuses, she says her life is awful and she does not want to live anyway. She has been diagnosed with emotional intensity disorder and has had a recent brief admission under the Mental Health Act, although she was discharged last week.

John is 16 and has been involved in a road traffic accident. He needs urgent treatment, which would include blood products. He tells the doctors that he is a practising Jehovah's Witness and in all circumstances he refuses blood products in any form.

Joshua is 15. Over the past 3 years he has been in and out of hospital for treatment of leukaemia. Unfortunately, following a check-up, the doctors tell him that he now needs further aggressive chemotherapy. Without treatment his prognosis is poor, and he is likely to die within 6 months. Joshua has had enough. He does not want to go into hospital again nor receive any more treatment, which he knows through experience makes him feel very sick. He wants to be at home with his family and have a peaceful end to his life. The doctors consider that with this treatment he will have a 30% chance of remission in 5 years.

Questions
- Can a minor refuse medical treatment?
- Does it make a difference if they are 15 or 17 years old?

ANSWER 22

Respect for patient autonomy

The refusal by a young person of clinically indicated treatment questions the extent to which patient autonomy should be respected when it is at odds with our perception of what is 'best' for them. As a society should we allow young people to make healthcare decisions that we think will harm them, and if not, is it appropriate for healthcare professionals to force treatment on a competent young person who is adamantly refusing?

Firstly we should consider whether the patient is sufficiently autonomous to make the decision. Different factors may enhance or compromise autonomy. If a young person has prior experience of illness and medical treatment(s), then their decision is likely to be more informed and the implications of treatment and non-treatment better understood. Generally, age and greater life experience can enhance decision-making abilities. Adolescents tend to engage in risky behaviour due to their neurocognitive development and may be under pressure from their peers to do so. Nevertheless some authors consider that adolescents are just as able to make rational decisions as adults (Doig & Burgess 2000). Provision of understandable information within a supportive and therapeutic relationship will enhance decision-making capabilities.

Capacity

A person is considered to be autonomous if they have capacities for understanding, reasoning, deliberating and making an independent choice, and a competent person is considered to possess these features. Young people 16 and over are presumed to have capacity to make healthcare decisions (although the presumption does not apply for organ donation and research) and those under 16 may be able to demonstrate that they are Gillick competent to make a particular decision (Case 20).

Consent

If a young person has capacity to consent to treatment, that consent is valid, and parental consent is not also required. The Family Law Reform Act 1969 provides that consent of a person aged 16 and 17 shall be as valid as if he was an adult. Patricia and John could, unless there was medical evidence which rebutted the presumption of capacity, consent to treatment including blood transfusions. A discussion with Joshua would enable his doctor to decide whether he understands the procedure, why it is necessary and the short- and long-term implications with and without the treatment. If Joshua is considered Gillick competent, he could provide valid consent to chemotherapy.

Refusal

Just because a young person can consent to treatment, should they be able to refuse it, or should the State act paternalistically to save the young person from harm, and if so what might be the level of harm to justify overriding their autonomy?

Although it is recognised that it will normally be in the best interests of a competent young person to make an informed choice about treatment, especially if it is invasive, in a series of cases in the 1990s the court adopted a protective stance. 'An individual who has reached the age of 18 is free to do with his life what he wishes, but it is the duty of the court to ensure so far as it can that children survive to attain that age' (*Re W (A Minor) (Medical Treatment: Court's Jurisdiction)* 1993).

Since then the Human Rights Act 1998 has been implemented, which incorporates into domestic law the rights enshrined in the European Convention on Human Rights. Article 8 ECHR encompasses considerations of a patient's personal autonomy and quality of life. The wishes of a young person should be taken into account as part of their Article 8 rights. Nevertheless there is a positive obligation arising from Article 2, 'right to life', to take preventive measures to protect an individual whose life is at risk. So, although the wishes of a competent young person are important, they are not decisive and his welfare is the paramount consideration. An Article 8 right of self-determination can be outweighed by a young person's right to life under Article 2.

This is not to say that any refusal can be overridden. Interference with competent decision making of a young person is limited to circumstances where a refusal of treatment would probably lead to death or to severe permanent injury. However, it would be impracticable and unduly burdensome to carry out ineffective treatment, and a court would not authorise treatment of a distressing nature which offered only a small hope of preserving life.

Consent is required from only one authorised source. If the young person is refusing, a parent could give consent, but this would be a rather divisive course of action and it may be appropriate to ask the court for a declaration that it would be lawful to perform the procedure against the wishes of the young person in his best interests.

Patricia is refusing treatment which would be effective in saving her life. Even if she was competent to make the decision, her refusal would be overridden because it would be considered to be in her best interests to preserve her life.

In similar circumstances to John, it was reported in the press in 2010 that the refusal by a 15-year-old Jehovah's Witness was respected by the clinicians treating him. They considered him competent to make the decision and they respected his views, although the matter did not go to court. John is also refusing life-sustaining treatment. Should a refusal for religious reasons be accorded greater respect than refusals for other reasons? Perhaps the benefit of a life saved is not accorded as much weight when the life to be lived would conflict with the patient's values, principles and beliefs.

Joshua has provided consent to previous treatments. Although the chemotherapy may save his life, there are significant burdens of treatment, not least the burden of imposing it in the face of his refusal. The therapeutic relationship would be damaged by enforcing treatment, and this is exacerbated as the treatment is ongoing. However, if society should protect young people until they reach adulthood, then overriding their views and wishes in refusing life-sustaining treatment is considered justified.

 Key Points

- A young person may have capacity to consent to treatment but their refusal of life-sustaining treatment may not be respected.
- If they refuse, then treatment could be authorised in their best interests to preserve life or to prevent severe permanent injury.
- It would be harmful to the therapeutic relationship to treat in the face of an abject refusal, especially if this necessitates ongoing force.

CASE 23: NON-ENGAGEMENT WITH THERAPEUTIC MEDICATION

During your final year at medical school you decide to attend the hospital's clinical ethics committee meeting as you have an interest in medical ethics and would like to see what type of cases are brought for discussion. Tonight a diabetes specialist nurse has presented a case of a 16-year-old girl, Stephanie, who has suffered from diabetes since a young age. Stephanie has previously had well-controlled blood sugar levels with a four times daily insulin regime and carbohydrate counting. Over the last year, however, the nurse has become very concerned about a decline in her physical health. She does not think that Stephanie is taking her insulin regularly as she is losing weight, has had recurrent infections and her blood sugars have risen. She has also missed several important appointments including one with the paediatric consultant. Whenever the nurse tries to discuss her diabetic control, Stephanie closes up and insists her medication control is fine. The nurse is at a loss as to how to help Stephanie further.

Questions
- How can Stephanie's non-engagement with treatment be managed?
- How can the medical profession encourage teenagers to engage with healthcare?

ANSWER 23

Respecting an adolescents' individual autonomy and bodily integrity may conflict with a duty of care to ensure that no unnecessary harm occurs on their journey toward adulthood. In rare cases this can create an almost insoluble dichotomy. How can we ethically argue that we are respecting the wishes of a competent, mature adolescent if we remove their right to take responsibility for their own healthcare? What a 15-year-old may consider in their best interests is very much related to the here and now and can lack the maturity to conceive of what may be in their future best interests. An intellectual understanding may be very different to an emotive understanding about the impact that non-engagement with treatment can have on their health in the long term.

The reality of imposing treatment on an unwilling patient is considerably problematic. Gaining consent for a one-off treatment such as an operation or blood transfusion may be easier than ensuring that a teenager is taking regular medication or that they attend for monitoring of their condition.

In these situations advanced communication skills are needed to assess *why* a teenager may not be complying with medical treatment. It may be due to a genuine misunderstanding of why treatment is important or be rooted in much more socially complex problems. As frustrating as non-engagement may be in terms of recurrent missed appointments and waste of NHS resources, it is imperative to remain non-judgemental and attempt to develop a more in-depth rapport with the patient so that their healthcare beliefs and concerns can be explored and discussed openly and honestly.

In the above scenario the diabetes nurse is advised by the clinical ethics committee to invite Stephanie to an appointment which fits in with her schedule rather than issuing an appointment which she may not be able to make. Rather than discussing her diabetes the nurse could ask Stephanie more about how the recent changes in her life are affecting her. Over the next few consultations Stephanie begins to open up more about the fact that she is feeling very isolated at her new school, which she has moved to following her parent's separation. Her need to inject insulin has made her embarrassed about eating with others and she often eats alone during breaks and lunch. She also felt that by decreasing her insulin she would lose weight and be more popular. This knowledge enables the diabetic nurse to suggest ways in which Stephanie could control her diabetes without injecting so frequently and she also can signpost her to a specialist adolescent counsellor to help her come to terms with the effects of living with a chronic illness and her recent parental separation.

Developing a good rapport can open up channels of communication to allow an adolescent to feel much more involved in the decision-making process. Coming to an agreed management plan with patient and clinician input has been widely demonstrated to improve patient concordance and long-term outcomes.

 Key Points

- Establishing trust and respect between the patient and the healthcare professional is essential to ensure concordance with medical treatment.
- Discussing complex patients with colleagues can be a useful way of identifying a better approach to encourage engagement with healthcare services.

CASE 24: WITHHOLDING INFORMATION FROM A CHILD

Adam is a 12-year-old boy being treated for osteosarcoma of the arm in the paediatric oncology unit where you are working as a first year specialist trainee (ST1). Although he initially responded well to treatment, he has suffered a relapse and now has widespread metastatic disease. His parents have been told about his relapse and a further cycle of chemotherapy, with the hope of prolonging his life by a few months, has been suggested. The chances of cure are negligible and the side effects likely to be very significant.

His parents have considered the options and decided they would like him to have further chemotherapy. However, they are adamant that they do not want Adam to be informed that his cancer has spread or that he is likely to die even with the additional chemotherapy. They wish to protect him and are very worried that telling him will cause him great distress. Your consultant has encouraged them to involve him in decision-making and explained that families are encouraged to discuss things honestly with their children, even when the prognosis is terminal. However, his parents continue making plans with him for the following year and telling him he needs further chemotherapy to 'get better'.

Questions

- Should Adam be involved in the decision about whether he has further chemotherapy?
- What ethical principles should be considered when deciding whether to withhold information from a patient?

ANSWER 24

Ethical issues

The question of whether information should be given to or withheld from Adam can be addressed from a consequentialist perspective by weighing up potential benefits and harms to identify the strategy that maximises beneficence and non-maleficence. Adam's parents are understandably worried that psychological harm will result if he is told how unwell he is. This argument has historically been used to justify withholding distressing information even from competent adult patients, but such an attitude would now be viewed as overly paternalistic and not respectful of an adult patient's autonomy. Moreover, withholding information is not without risk of harm. There is considerable evidence that children who are terminally ill are usually aware of this fact and can become anxious and upset if they feel this is being hidden from them. There is also the risk that Adam will find out accidentally, causing him to lose trust in his parents and the treating team.

The question of whether doctors should always tell patients the truth can also be addressed from a deontological perspective. Many people would argue that veracity (truth-telling) is one of the fundamental duties of a doctor upon which trust in the doctor-patient relationship is founded. The GMC guidance document 0–18 years: guidance for all doctors, 2007 requires that doctors are 'honest and open' with children, as with adults. However, it also states that young people 'should not be given access to information that would cause them serious harm'. This is exactly what Adam's parents (arguably the people who know him best) believe would result from disclosure.

Legal issues

At the age of 12, Adam could potentially have sufficient understanding to be competent to consent to treatment (Case 20). Even if he is not, he is being asked to assent to treatment without even the most basic understanding of its purpose. His doctors and parents are in agreement that further treatment is in his best interests, but Adam has not been able to express his own opinion and his autonomy is being ignored. The question must be asked, however, whether this will make any material difference to the outcome: given his age, if Adam refused treatment sanctioned by his doctors and parents, would the courts uphold his right to refuse or be more likely to deem him incompetent (Case 22)?

There is no legal precedent in which the right of a 12-year-old to access their health information or the right of parents to keep information from them has been tested. How would parents' ECHR Article 8 right to 'private and family life' be balanced against the child's Article 8 rights? The UN Convention on the Rights of the Child (1989) gives children the right to express their views, 'the views of the child being given due weight'.

 Key Points

- Young people should be given sufficient information to assent to treatment and the opportunity to exercise autonomy.
- Veracity can be seen as a fundamental duty of a doctor.
- Consequentialist reasoning can occasionally favour withholding information in situations where disclosure is likely to cause significant harm.

ETHICS AND LAW IN CLINICAL PRACTICE: CONSENT, CAPACITY AND REFUSAL OF TREATMENT

CASE 25: VALID CONSENT TO TREATMENT

You are the surgical FY1 on call. A patient comes in acutely unwell with severe abdominal pain. He is reviewed by your seniors, who tell him he needs an operation to investigate the cause of his symptoms. They ask you to obtain consent for laparoscopy and a laparotomy and proceed. When you see the patient he is still in pain and he tells you that he is aware he needs an operation but just wants them to get on with it. He says he does not want to know what risks there might be, 'You do whatever is best, doctor'.

Questions

- Why is consent legally necessary?
- What are the essentials of valid consent?
- Is consent valid if the patient is not informed of risks because he does not want to know?

ANSWER 25

Legal issues

> Every human being of adult years and sound mind has a right to determine what shall be done with his own body, and a surgeon who performs an operation without his patient's consent commits an assault for which he is liable in damages.
>
> *Schloendorff v Society of New York Hospital* (1914)

Consent is the agreement of a patient to being examined or having a procedure performed. Touching a patient without consent or lawful justification amounts to battery (although prosecutions are uncommon). Article 8 ECHR protects bodily integrity from unwarranted interference. Requiring consent for all procedures protects a patient's dignity and bodily integrity and respects the patient's values.

Consent does not have to be given in writing; it can be given verbally or even implied from the circumstances, e.g., holding an arm out for an injection, nodding the head, although care must be taken to ensure the patient has understood what is going to be done and why. Where the investigation or treatment is complex, if it involves significant risks or where there may be significant consequences for the patient's employment, social or personal life, written consent should be obtained (GMC Consent: patients and doctors making decisions together, 2008). Written consent is also needed for any surgical procedure even if there is minimal risk associated with it. GMC guidance also states that 'if, after discussion, a patient still does not want to know in detail about their condition or the treatment, you should respect their wishes, as far as possible. But you must still give them the information they need in order to give their consent to a proposed investigation or treatment' (including information about level of pain and discomfort and serious risks).

In the present scenario it might be tempting to 'just get the form signed' and it is important to document when consent has been given. However, although a signed consent form is *prima facie* evidence of consent, the form itself does not mean valid consent has been given, for example, the patient may later claim that his consent was not voluntary.

There is also the question of who should obtain consent. Most agree that it is good practice for the healthcare professional performing the procedure to obtain consent as it is their responsibility, but in practice this does not always happen. The process of taking consent can be delegated, but the person seeking consent must be suitably trained and qualified, have sufficient knowledge of the proposed investigation or treatment and understand and be able to explain the risks involved.

> **! Essential elements of consent**
>
> - The patient must be competent to give consent.
> - It must be voluntary and not coerced.
> - The patient must be provided with information about the procedure.

Competence is presumed in patients aged 16 and over unless there is evidence to the contrary. If an adult patient lacks capacity to consent, treatment can be given in their best interests.

Relatives do not have the authority to make that decision on a patient's behalf unless there is a Lasting Power of Attorney in place. Arguably a certain amount of coercion occurs in almost all cases, but consent is only considered not voluntary where there is undue, excessive or unwarranted exercise of power or trust (Case 28).

To make a valid choice a person must be given information of the broad nature and purpose of the proposed treatment at the very least – what the procedure involves and why it is needed as well as the likely outcomes. Failure to provide this basic information could give rise to a claim of battery. But this may not be enough to prevent an action for negligence if harm occurs which could have been avoided if the patient had been provided with sufficient information about risks and alternative treatments (Case 42). How much information the patient needs is difficult to judge because particular risks may have significance to certain patients. Doctors have a powerful role as dispensers of information as well as medicines and treatment.

Consent is limited to the procedures which the patient has been informed of and agreed to. Except in an emergency it cannot be exceeded to include other procedures. A surgical consent form will include a term that additional procedures, not included in the scope of the original consent, may be performed if it would be unreasonable to delay the procedure and it is in the patient's best interests. However, it must be immediately necessary and not merely convenient to proceed without explicit consent.

Ethical issues

A patient's right to decide whether to accept or reject treatment, the right of self-determination, is the cornerstone of patient-centred care. Respect for autonomy entails that patient choice is respected even if the decision is not one that most patients in that position would make. Can patients be truly autonomous? There is an imbalance of power between the informed and experienced doctor and the vulnerable patient, whose autonomy may be compromised by illness. Although full autonomy may be difficult to achieve, a patient can be sufficiently autonomous. The nature of information given to a patient and the way in which it is presented can affect the patient's choice, and ultimately whether or not they consent to the procedure proposed. In this scenario the patient is exercising his autonomy in saying that he 'does not want to know'. From a legal perspective this is problematic because consent must be based on an informed decision.

Medical students

Patients should be informed that medical students would like to sit in on a consultation and this should be done prior to the arrival of student observers. Patients should feel able to refuse consent to the presence of students during their consultation and/or examination and they should be reassured that their decision will not affect their treatment (BMA Consent Tool Kit, 5th edition).

 Key Points

- The patient must be competent to give consent.
- Consent must be voluntary and not coerced.
- The patient must be provided with information about the procedure.

CASE 26: ADULT CAPACITY TO CONSENT TO TREATMENT

Cordelia, a 29-year-old woman, presents to the Accident and Emergency department in extreme pain. She fell over on AstroTurf in the afternoon the day before while playing hockey and grazed her knees. Her left knee is now extremely painful, swollen and erythematous, and she cannot bend her leg or weight bear. You suspect that she has a septic arthritis secondary to her knee injury. This is a medical emergency, and without immediate drainage and antibiotic treatment there is a risk of destructive joint damage and permanent disability. You explain to Cordelia that she needs to have the joint aspirated and the risks associated with aspiration. You are not sure that she is taking in what you are telling her because she is in pain and very scared.

Questions
- Is the patient competent to make such a decision?
- How is this assessment made?
- Who makes this assessment?

ANSWER 26

Legal issues

The Mental Capacity Act 2005 (MCA) provides that people in England and Wales aged 16 and over are presumed to have capacity to make decisions although this can be rebutted on medical evidence. Mental capacity is a legal concept informed by clinical advice. The MCA sets out a statutory test for capacity (the terms *capacity* and *competence* tend to be used interchangeably, and *capacity* will be used here).

All steps should be taken to enhance capacity through appropriate communication and support. Where capacity is lacking because of temporary factors such as shock, use of alcohol or drugs, treatment should be delayed, if appropriate, until the person regains capacity and can make an informed decision themselves. In emergency situations or when immediate medical treatment is required if the patient lacks capacity, treatment can be given in the patient's best interests.

A person lacks capacity if he is unable to make the particular decision at the time because of an impairment of, or a disturbance in the functioning of, the mind or brain. Examples include dementia, significant learning disabilities, physical or medical conditions that cause confusion, drowsiness or loss of consciousness and conditions associated with some forms of mental illness (Case 47).

The MCA states that a person is unable to make a decision if he cannot:

- Understand relevant information – the nature of the decision, why it is needed and the likely effects of making a decision one way or another
- Retain that information long enough to make the decision
- Use or weigh that information in making the decision or
- Communicate their decision by any means

Assessment of capacity is decision specific. Is the patient able to understand, retain, use and weigh up the information relevant to *this* decision? Capacity is commensurate with the gravity of the decision – the more serious the decision, the greater the capacity required. There is a cognitive bias in the assessment of capacity; values and emotions are not mentioned in the legal test. Respecting the healthcare choices of competent individuals is clearly beneficial to enable a trusting, therapeutic relationship, but of course some may make decisions which seem counterintuitive to their medical needs. It may be too easy to assume that a patient who makes a decision which is inconsistent with conventional values or with which a healthcare professional disagrees lacks capacity to make it. An 'outcome' approach, which focuses on the final content of the decision, 'penalises individuality and demands conformity at the expense of personal autonomy' (Law Commission 231, Mental Incapacity 1995).

If there are difficulties in deciding whether the patient has sufficient mental capacity, particularly if the refusal may have grave consequences for the patient, it is most important that those considering the issue should not confuse the question of mental capacity with the nature of the decision made by the patient, however grave the consequences. The view of the patient may reflect a difference in values rather than an absence of competence, and the assessment of capacity should be approached with this firmly in mind. The doctors must not allow their emotional reaction to or strong disagreement with the decision of the patient to cloud their judgment in answering the primary question whether the patient has the mental capacity to make the decision.

Ms B v An NHS Hospital Trust (2002)

A patient has a right to make an unwise decision, but if a person repeatedly makes decisions that are out of character or puts them at risk, their capacity should be assessed. Reference to age, appearance or an aspect of the person's behaviour is not sufficient to establish lack of capacity.

If the patient has communication problems, then all practical and appropriate efforts should be made to help them, and this might involve speech and language therapists and specialists in non-verbal communication.

The courts have said that they will be guided by the view of the medical profession regarding capacity. Where there is doubt about a patient's capacity, a medical assessment should be carried out, usually by a consultant psychiatrist.

Decisions made by competent adult patients must be respected. Those who lack capacity to make a particular decision at the time it needs to be made can be treated in their best interests (Case 32).

Ethical issues

The ethical principle of respect for autonomy acknowledges a person's right to make choices based on personal values and beliefs (BMA Ethics Tool Kit for Students). The exercise of autonomy depends on the provision of sufficient, understandable information on which to base that decision. Thus, provision of information about treatment options can directly impact on the patient having capacity to make the decision and being able to exercise an autonomous choice.

In the above scenario Cordelia should be given extra support since she is undoubtedly frightened and in pain. Analgesia should be prescribed and time spent exploring any specific concerns she may have about the proposed management plan.

 Key Points

- Adults are presumed to have capacity to make healthcare decisions.
- Capacity relates to the ability to make a specific decision at the time it needs to be made.
- A person lacks capacity if he is unable to make a decision *because of* an impairment in functioning of the mind or brain.
- A person who lacks capacity should be involved in the decision as much as possible.

CASE 27: CONSENT AND HIV

Scenario 1

A newly qualified nurse is cannulating a very intoxicated patient in the Accident and Emergency department (A&E). She misses the vein on the first attempt and whilst trying again the patient moves his arm away and she stabs the end of the cannula in her finger. The nurse washes her wound out for 10 minutes under running water and then goes to speak to the sister in charge about the needlestick injury policy.

Scenario 2

A homosexual man presents to his GP over a period of months with multiple different infections. The first few occasions he is treated with antibiotics or antifungals. On his fourth appointment he expresses concern that he keeps getting ill and has lost a bit of weight. He would like to know whether there is anything else causing these infections other than being busy and having a stressful job with a poor work–life balance. The GP agrees to do some blood tests but does not elaborate on what she is testing for.

Scenario 3

A 24-year-old male has attended his local A&E department following a minor injury on a night out. He thinks he may have broken his ankle and is requesting an X-ray. The triage nurse also mentions that they are doing routine HIV screening for every A&E attendee and would like to know whether he would like a test.

Questions

- What should be done in the above scenarios?
- Should specific consent be needed for HIV testing?

ANSWER 27

Whether specific consent should be obtained in order to test for transmissible bloodborne viruses is a contentious issue and one that often causes a lot of debate between bioethicists and physicians. Professional attitudes toward HIV have changed considerably over the past decade due to advances in treatment. However, there is still a lot of public stigma attached to a diagnosis, and this should be taken into consideration when thinking about the pros and cons of HIV testing.

Needlestick injury

All hospitals and healthcare settings should have a needle-stick injury policy to provide advice and support to doctors and members of the public on what to do in the event that they are injured by a contaminated needle. It is important to remember that it is not just health-care workers that are at risk of injury – tattooists, refuse collectors and members of the public who may come across discarded drug paraphernalia are all considered at risk.

When assessing a needlestick injury the first thing to do is to consider the risk of contamination by identifying (if possible) the source of the blood and the subsequent likelihood of that individual having HIV. If the source is identified and that individual has capacity, they should be asked sensitively about the risk of them being HIV-positive. Consent must always be gained for testing and it should be obtained from a healthcare worker other than the person who sustained the injury. A pre-test discussion, to establish informed consent for HIV testing, should cover the benefits of testing for the individual and details of how the results will be given. Lengthy pre-test HIV counselling is not a requirement, unless a patient requests or needs it. Healthcare professionals should be able to obtain informed consent for an HIV test in the same way that they do for any other medical investigation. In the scenario above consent can be sought from the intoxicated patient once he has sobered up. If he refuses to undergo testing, that must be respected.

In nearly all cases a blood sample should be taken from the recipient of the injury to test for bloodborne viruses. The risk of bloodborne virus transmission determines what action should be taken. Despite the fear of needlestick injuries the actual risk of contracting a bloodborne infection from a sharps injury is very low. A recent Health Protection Agency report documented that between 2002 and 2011 there were 4381 needlestick injuries in healthcare workers but only 20 cases of hepatitis C infection. There have been no documented cases of HIV seroconversion from a needlestick injury since 1999 (Health Protection Agency, Eye of the Needle 2012).

The law is very clear that tests performed on patients who lack capacity can only be done in their best interests. Unless the individual was known to be at high risk of having HIV and may benefit from treatment, testing without consent would not be in their best interests. Ethically it could be argued that the individual who had sustained the needlestick injury also has a right to be protected from infection. It is questionable, therefore, whether there should be a limit to the rights of a patient, where there is a risk of harm to another individual. Consequentialists would argue that it is justifiable to test an incompetent patient's blood as a blood test is of minimal harm to the patient but can provide information that will prevent harm to a healthcare worker. Usually someone who has sustained a needlestick injury would take post-exposure prophylactic medication as soon as possible to reduce the chance of transmission. This medication may have unpleasant side effects and would not need to be continued if the patient was tested and the test is negative for bloodborne viruses.

HIV testing

In the UK HIV testing is voluntary and confidential. However, there has been a large drive to take away the stigma of testing. Although HIV is not curable it is now treatable, and if diagnosed early, patients can expect to have a normal life expectancy. Studies have demonstrated increased morbidity and mortality with late diagnosis and increased cost to healthcare services. Knowledge of HIV status is associated with a reduction in risky behaviour, and therefore early diagnosis will result in reduced onward transmission.

The British HIV Association UK National Guidelines for HIV Testing (2008) provides that HIV testing should be offered routinely to patients who present for healthcare where HIV, including primary HIV infection, enters the differential diagnosis and where a male patient has disclosed sexual contact with other men. Consent must be obtained for testing. It is recommend that an individual testing HIV-positive should be seen by a specialist at the earliest possible opportunity, preferably within 48 hours and certainly within 2 weeks of receiving the result.

Screening

There are circumstances where HIV testing should be routinely offered and patients need to opt out rather than opt in. This could be considered screening rather than testing as the individual may have no other markers of illness. Areas where this is offered include Genitourinary medicine clinics, antenatal screening and even in areas of the country where HIV has a prevalence of more than 2/1000 population.

Interestingly, a recent study has reported that non-targeted, routine offering of HIV screening in a variety of different healthcare settings not only demonstrated a high uptake but also a positive public perception that this is appropriate (Rayment et al. 2012). Stigma attached to HIV infection is still widespread, yet the at-risk population has changed considerably in the last decade. The availability of effective treatment means that HIV testing should be as socially acceptable as diabetes screening.

 Key Points

- Consent must be obtained to test for HIV no matter what the clinical circumstance or setting.
- HIV testing in patients who lack capacity can only be performed if it is in their best interests.
- Every healthcare professional should feel able to discuss HIV testing in the same way that they would gain consent to test for any other medical condition.

CASE 28: CONSENT AND COERCION

Anne is 68 and has had multiple sclerosis (MS) for more than 20 years. As a result she is completely bed bound and requires full-time care in a nursing home. She saw her GP with a complaint of a change in bowel habits and rectal bleeding and was referred for a colonoscopy. Cancer was diagnosed and originally she consented to have surgical removal of the tumour. Anne has been listed for surgery. Anne's adult daughter, Wendy, was her mother's sole carer prior to her going into the nursing home and she visits Anne every day. Wendy has expressed to the consultant her concern that the operation is not in her mother's best interests. She says that her mother lives a miserable life, in the past she expressed a wish to die and, as the cancer presents an opportunity for her mother to die naturally, intervention would be inappropriate. After Wendy's visit the doctor speaks to Anne, who tells him that she has changed her mind and she no longer wishes to have the operation.

Questions
- Should a change of mind about treatment be respected?
- In what circumstances can discussion with family amount to coercion such that the patient's decision is no longer valid?

ANSWER 28

Autonomy refers to the right of an individual to make informed decisions about their treatment, and respect for patient autonomy entails that such decisions are respected regardless of whether the decision made seems 'wise'. Since Anne has changed her mind about treatment, the surgeon is concerned that Anne's ability to make an autonomous decision might be affected by Wendy's involvement. Anne is entirely dependent on carers for her basic needs, and with the recent diagnosis of cancer she is vulnerable to the influences of others. She seemed to respond firstly to the recommendations of the surgical team to have treatment, and then to that of her daughter. Wendy's influence could be seen as a way of promoting Anne's autonomy by helping and supporting her to come to a decision regarding treatment which correlates with and represents her beliefs and values. As her previous primary carer, her opinion may be useful to her mother in coming to a decision, as long as it is supportive and not coercive. Perhaps Anne only consented in the first place to please the healthcare professionals. She may have felt that she had no choice or that she may be abandoned by services if she disagreed. Conversely, Anne may feel guilty for the burden of care Wendy previously undertook and so may wish to appease her. The influence of others in decision making may be increased if the patient is particularly vulnerable. A patient is entitled to receive and indeed invite advice and assistance from others in reaching a decision, particularly from family members, and it is acceptable that a patient is 'persuaded' by others of the merits of a decision. However, if a decision is 'coerced' it lacks the quality necessary for the consent or refusal to be valid. In *Re T (Adult: refusal of treatment)* (1992) the court said the real question in each such case is 'does the patient really mean what he says or is he merely saying it for a quiet life, to satisfy someone else or because the advice and persuasion to which he has been subjected is such that he can no longer think and decide for himself?'

Taking Anne's experiences into consideration it is clear why she may refuse surgery which may result in the prolongation of a life that she might not necessarily want to live. Although a patient's refusal may appear unwise in light of the inevitable medical ramifications, it may in fact be a rational decision based on weighing the risks of surgery against its benefits. Patients have a right to change their minds, and Anne may be exercising this right. However, the surgeon should endeavor to ensure that this is truly her decision, given the implications, and should reassure Anne that she will still receive optimal care and further treatment should she change her mind again.

 Key Points

- If a decision to refuse treatment is sufficiently autonomous – free from coercion and informed – it must be respected.
- A patient can change their mind about treatment options.

CASE 29: EXAMINATION UNDER ANAESTHESIA

Pamela, a 34-year-old woman with fibroids, was clerked in yesterday by a fourth-year medical student on an obstetrics and gynaecology rotation. Pamela is scheduled to have surgery today for removal of the fibroids, and the consultant asks the student if she would like to scrub in to assist during the operation. The student has assisted the anaesthetist before the operation and has reassured Pamela about the planned operation. Once Pamela is anaesthetised, the consultant asks the student to demonstrate how she would perform an internal examination on a female patient. The student realises that Pamela was not asked for permission to do this and feels that it would be wrong to carry out the examination. However, she also thinks that it would be a good learning opportunity and she is slightly in awe of the consultant and she knows that he has shouted at other students. The student decides to point out that she does not have Pamela's consent, but the consultant reassures her that as Pamela is anaesthetised she will not know anything about it.

Questions
- Should the student perform an internal examination on Pamela?
- What should she say to her consultant if she refuses?

ANSWER 29

Professional guidance underscores the requirement of consent for intimate examinations performed under anaesthetic. GMC, Good Medical Practice, 2013 states:

> Before you carry out an intimate examination on an anaesthetised patient, or supervise a student who intends to carry one out, you must make sure that the patient has given consent in advance, usually in writing.

There is no justification that the procedure is performed in a teaching hospital, and the patient must, therefore, be aware that students will perform examinations as part of their training.

There is a conflict between respecting the patient's dignity and autonomy, the desire of the student to gain experience and the need to train competent doctors. Should the interests of individual members of society be outweighed by the need to promote the training of competent doctors? A consequentialist justification for examination without express consent is that the overall benefit to society in having well-trained doctors outweighs the harm to individual patients. Intimate examinations carry no real risk, may add to patient anxiety and meet with a refusal if asked, thus reducing the opportunity for training. The experience will increase the student's practical skills, which she may then benefit from when caring for future patients.

However, the patient will suffer loss of privacy and dignity, perhaps some psychological harm, and loss of trust in the medical profession if they become aware that this had happened. Do the consequences of informing the patient and requesting consent impede medical education and training? There is no evidence that a significant number of patients would withhold consent as to impact on training. In comparison, Kantian ethics state that people should always be treated as ends in themselves, and never simply as a means to another's ends. Medical procedures performed for training purposes only without any benefit to a particular patient use the patient as a training aid and merely as a means to enhance the student's training and her goals of becoming a better doctor.

It can be hard to stand up to consultants and students may often fear the repercussions on their clinical involvement and assessment if they do not do as a consultant asks them to do. Many medical schools now have a pro forma which must be completed by the student and the patient before performing any examination under anaesthesia. It is the responsibility of the student to ensure that written consent has been given by the patient. In the present case the student should decline to examine this patient but seek consent from the next patient on the list.

Where medical students perform procedures to further their own education, provided it will further the care of the patient (and for which they are suitably trained), for example, cannulation, it is good practice to inform the patient that they are a student (Department of Health 2009). However, consent must be obtained for a physical examination which is performed for training but is not part of a patient's care.

 Key Points

- The requirement to practise ethically and lawfully supersedes the need to practise examination techniques without the consent of the patient.
- Students and trainee doctors must take responsibility for their conduct.

CASE 30: REFUSAL OF TREATMENT

You are a GP doing an evening shift for the local out-of-hours provider. A call comes through from a paramedic requesting an urgent home visit for a 76-year-old man whose wife has called 999 as he was complaining of chest pain. The paramedic is concerned that the patient is having a heart attack but is refusing to be taken to hospital.

On arrival at the patient's house you find that Harry Barker, the patient, is looking very unwell. He is pale and slightly clammy. However, his chest pain has eased a little bit with the aspirin and GTN spray that the paramedics have administered. An electrocardiogram (ECG) taken by the paramedics demonstrates T wave inversion in leads II, III and aVF, suggesting an element of inferior ischaemia. You agree with the paramedics that Harry's chest pain is most likely cardiac in origin and feel he needs an urgent admission to hospital. Although Harry had been completely concordant with investigations and treatment up until this time, he now completely refuses to be transferred to hospital.

You ask him more questions about his past medical history and discover that other than being on medication for hypertension and high cholesterol he has been very well. His father died of a heart attack in his 60s but all his siblings are alive and well. There is no history of dementia or mental health problems.

Questions
- Can a competent patient refuse life-sustaining treatment?
- Can Harry refuse to be taken to hospital?
- What else should be done in the above scenario?

ANSWER 30

There is clear legal guidance on how to assess capacity and how to obtain valid consent to treatment (Cases 25 and 26). This case explores what can be done if a patient is refusing treatment – particularly if it is felt that treatment is medically necessary in order to prevent death or serious harm. The first thing the doctor needs to ascertain is whether or not Harry has capacity. The GP has already established that Harry has no other medical problems that would impair his ability to make an informed decision, and after further discussion he is happy that Harry understands the concerns.

The law is very clear about refusal of treatment. A competent adult has the right to refuse all treatment even if this is likely to result in significant harm or death. Incapacity cannot be assumed merely because decisions appear unwise or irrational.

The GMC supports this in their guidance, Consent: patients and doctors making decisions together, 2008, which states, 'You must respect a competent patient's decision to refuse an investigation or treatment, even if you think their decision is wrong or irrational. You may advise the patient of your clinical opinion, but you must not put pressure on them to accept your advice. You must be careful that your words and actions do not imply judgement of the patient or their beliefs and values.'

In ethical terms this can be seen as principle of sanctity of life yielding to the principle of self-determination. An autonomous individual can make decisions that they deem to be in their best interests in accordance with their religious and cultural beliefs or individual preferences.

Although it is much quicker to simply assess capacity and let Harry make his decision to stay at home and move on to the next home visit, this would not be deemed good medical care from a professional point of view. Although there is no doubt that Harry can make the decision to remain at home, it is still clinically appropriate to explore why he is refusing hospital admission. Is there something he is afraid of? Does he feel that there is a reason he should not leave home, a sick relative or no one to look after a pet, for example? Sometimes concerns can be easily resolved to help the patient feel more comfortable about leaving his home. Even if Harry continues to refuse to go to hospital it would still be clinically appropriate to ensure he had good medical follow-up – a letter to his own GP to visit the following day to perform further tests and review medication would demonstrate ongoing patient care and support. The conversation and explorations of his concerns should be clearly documented.

 Key Points

- Every competent adult has the right to refuse treatment, even if that treatment is life sustaining.
- A patient does not lack capacity merely because their decision may appear irrational.
- Ongoing medical care and attention should be given even if the patient has chosen not to act on the advice of the clinician.

CASE 31: CONSENT AND EMERGENCIES

You are a Year 5 specialist trainee (ST5) in obstetrics. You have been asked to review a patient by her midwife. The woman is a 30-year-old Polish lady in labour named Greta. This is her first pregnancy and she is full term. The midwife has established that her husband is on his way in. Her grasp of English is limited. She is in a lot of pain and not engaging with her midwife. The trace of her baby's heart is classified as pathological. Her liquor is stained with meconium. The clinical picture indicates that the baby is in distress and needs delivering immediately by a caesarean section to prevent intrauterine death.

Questions
- What clinical problems can impact on gaining adequate consent to treatment?
- What could you do if Greta refuses to consent to an emergency caesarean section?

ANSWER 31

The initial approach would be to assess the patient's capacity to provide consent in this situation. GMC, Good Medical Practice, 2013 makes it explicitly clear that doctors should respect patients' rights to make choices over their treatment. But what does this patient want? It is not clear that she is refusing a caesarean; rather, she is not engaging with the midwife and doctor.

If this is because of a language issue and she cannot understand the questions posed, then provision of an interpreter as well as information leaflets in her own language could enable her to understand the situation better. As this is of some urgency, rather than delay waiting for an interpreter the woman's husband may be able to assist in communicating with his wife.

It might be that the woman is not communicating with the team because she is in so much pain. Severe pain, confusion, shock, fatigue and/or the effect of medication may render her temporarily lacking capacity. Reasonable practical steps could include offering the patient adequate pain relief to reduce her pain and enable her to engage in the decision-making process. It may not be possible to wait for an epidural to take effect.

The obstetrician should make a decision about how long it will be before the clinical situation deteriorates, thus putting the health of the patient and her unborn child at risk.

If the patient lacks capacity, and treatment cannot be delayed, you should act in her best interests. The unborn child does not have any legal rights and the focus is the patient's best interests. Best interests encompass the medical interests of the patient and also her social, emotional and welfare interests. It can be reasonably assumed that the woman wants a healthy baby. The obstetric notes would have records of the patient's encounters with healthcare professionals in the past and one would expect records of the patient's key beliefs to be included in her birth plan. Whilst the patient's partner or relatives cannot consent for her, they can inform you about the patient's views and wishes. It would be in the best interests of a woman carrying a full-term child whom she wants to be born alive and healthy that such a result should be achieved if possible, in this case by carrying out the caesarean section.

 Key Points

- Capacity can be fluctuating and every effort should be made to enhance the patient's capacity.
- Previous statements made by the patient will inform a decision about her best interests.
- A competent woman can refuse obstetric intervention even if that results in the death or serious disability of the child to be born.
- In an emergency situation, and where it is not possible to find out a patient's wishes, treatment can be given without consent provided that it is immediately necessary to save her life or to prevent a serious deterioration in her condition.

CASE 32: ASSESSMENT OF BEST INTERESTS

The family and friends of Alice are very unhappy with her care in a NHS neuro-disability unit. Alice is 45 years old, and following viral encephalitis she has been left with severe neurological impairment with no prospect of improvement. She cannot move or speak and is entirely dependent on others for care. She is receiving clinically assisted nutrition and hydration. Alice was close to her father and sister and long-term partner. She does not have children. Her family considers that she would not wish to carry on living in this condition and that feeding should be withheld so she can die peacefully and with dignity.

Paul is 42. He has a severe learning disability and end-stage renal failure secondary to diabetes. Unless he receives an organ transplant, his life expectancy is significantly reduced. He requires dialysis three times a week. He has a needle phobia and due to his learning disabilities becomes physically aggressive and resists attempts by doctors to examine or treat him. In order to carry out dialysis, he would require sedation by general anesthetic, which carries inherent risks. His understanding of the situation is very limited.

Felicity is 55 years old and has a severe learning disability. She has localised cancer of the uterus and her gynaecologist considers that without a hysterectomy the tumour will likely metastasise and lead ultimately to her death.

Questions
- What factors should be considered in assessing the 'best interests' of an incompetent adult patient?
- Who makes the decision about the patient's best interests?
- What if the clinical team and the patient's relatives disagree about what treatment is in the patient's best interests?
- Is it always in the patient's best interests to do what the patient would most probably have wanted if he had capacity?

ANSWER 32

If a patient lacks capacity to make a particular healthcare decision (Case 26), the justification for treatment is that it is in his best interests. The Mental Capacity Act 2005 (MCA) sets out a legal framework for the care and treatment of persons lacking capacity. Although it does not define the term 'best interests', it sets out a checklist of factors that must be considered when determining best interests. The person making the decision must consider, as far as is reasonably ascertainable, the patient's past and present wishes, and the beliefs and values and other factors that could have influenced their decision if they had capacity. This assessment of best interests looks to what the person lacking capacity would have wanted, and therefore takes non-medical issues into account. In addition to the checklist, 'all relevant circumstances' should be considered. For example, a doctor would need to consider the 'clinical needs of the patient, the potential benefits and burdens of the treatment on the person's health and life expectancy and any other factors relevant to making a professional judgement' (MCA Code of Practice). The doctor performing the particular medical treatment or procedure is responsible for ensuring that the best interests of the patient have been considered by discussion with those interested in the welfare of the patient. Wherever possible, the patient should be involved in the decision-making process.

The best interests test is not the same as 'substituted judgement'. Judges have stated that although the past and present wishes of the patient are very important in assessing best interests, they are not determinative. Despite her learning disabilities, Felicity has a good quality of life and enjoys regular outings and visits from family. She has indicated that she does not want surgery as she is frightened. However, without treatment she is likely to die. The stress and anxiety that she may experience in having treatment is balanced against the fact that the surgery is likely to be curative and therefore life preserving. There is a strong presumption that it is in a person's best interests to stay alive. The MCA requires that the treatment must be no more than is necessary in order to treat them effectively (the least restrictive intervention principle).

The MCA requires that, where practical and appropriate, others who are close to the patient should be consulted about what might be in the patient's best interests. Alice's family may be able to give examples of conversations indicating her previous views which might be relevant to her situation now, although even if that is possible they may have changed in light of her current situation. When there is a conflict of opinion about whether a particular treatment is in the patient's best interests, which cannot be otherwise resolved, the Court of Protection may be asked to adjudicate.

If the treatment proposed is overly burdensome in relation to the prospect of recovery or quality of life which may be prolonged after treatment, then it may not be in the patient's best interests to initiate or continue it. Section 5 MCA enables the use of reasonable force to carry out treatment. For Paul, although dialysis is life-preserving, the burdens of treatment are relevant in determining whether it is in his best interests. Ongoing treatment requiring general anaesthetic, force and restraint and consequent apprehension and loss of dignity may be too harmful to continue on a long-term basis.

Lasting power of attorney

A personal welfare lasting power of attorney (LPA) is a legal document which allows a person to appoint someone (the attorney) to make healthcare decisions for them in the event of loss of capacity. There may be restrictions about the types of decisions that can be taken, and decisions about life-sustaining treatment can only be made if authority to do so is stated in the LPA. Healthcare staff must discuss their proposed care plan with the person appointed and obtain their agreement to it. Where the healthcare team disagrees with the attorney's assessment of the best interests of the patient, the case should be discussed with other medical experts. Ultimately, the issue may have to be resolved by the Court of Protection.

Independent mental capacity advocate

Independent mental capacity advocates (IMCAs) represent the views of vulnerable people lacking capacity to make important decisions about serious medical treatment when there are no family members or friends who can be consulted. They act as a check to ensure that the proposed treatment is in the person's best interests and therefore have the right to see relevant healthcare records. They can challenge decisions that they do not think are in the patient's best interests, and they must be instructed and consulted in certain circumstances, e.g., providing, withholding or stopping serious medical treatment and where the person will stay in hospital longer than 28 days.

Ethical issues

The assessment of a person's best interests uses consequentialist criteria. A 'balance sheet' should be drawn of the benefits and harms of treatment. A procedure that is invasive and has harmful side effects would be in a patient's best interests only if the benefits to be gained outweigh the harms of treatment. The assessment of best interests could take into account overall *future* benefit despite the immediate harm of carrying out treatment which the patient does not want.

 Key Points

- Alice, Paul and Felicity lack capacity, and therefore treatment decisions must be taken in their best interests.
- The patient's views and those of the carers and relatives should be taken into account.
- A 'best interests' assessment is not relevant where a person has made a valid and applicable advance decision.
- Staff should ask whether the patient has a LPA.
- Where an incompetent patient has no one to represent his best interests, an IMCA must be consulted in connection with decisions about major medical treatment.

CASE 33: DEPRIVATION OF LIBERTY

Mr Alan Moore is a 46-year-old man who lives in a nursing home. He has a severe learning disability, and the nursing home provides one-to-one nursing and care support for him. Although he does wander around the home on occasion, he has never tried to leave the nursing home, and the nursing home staff report that he seems happy and free of pain and other distress. If he ever did try to leave, staff would prevent him from doing so, to avoid him coming to harm. He seems to enjoy some activities, such as watching television and being read to. He requires assistance with feeding and toileting and is given regular medication by staff at the home. Although he does vocalise, no coherent conversation is possible. He has no family and does not receive any visitors.

Questions

- How do the Deprivation of Liberty Safeguards relate to both the Mental Health Act (1983) and Mental Capacity Act (2005)?
- What is the difference between a restriction of liberty and deprivation of liberty?
- Should the nursing home staff apply for an authorisation under the Deprivation of Liberty Safeguards?

ANSWER 33

Deprivation of Liberty Safeguards and the Mental Health Act 1983 and Mental Capacity Act 2005

The Deprivation of Liberty Safeguards (DoLS) were created as part of the Mental Health Act (MHA) when it was revised in 2007, as an addition to the Mental Capacity Act (MCA). They contain elements of legislation from the MHA and apply to those people who are deprived of their liberty, who lack capacity to consent to that deprivation, and whose deprivation is not covered by the MHA.

What is the difference between a restriction of liberty and deprivation of liberty?

There is no clear criterion; the difference is one of degree, i.e., whether the curtailment is extensive enough to amount to a deprivation of a person's liberty rather than just a restriction of it.

In 2014, the case of *P v Cheshire West and P & Q v Surrey County Council* (known as the Cheshire West case) had a significant impact on the way in which the DoLS were interpreted and applied. The case was heard in the UK Supreme Court and referred to the care of three people with learning disabilities. As a result, liberty is now considered to be deprived if all aspects of the following 'Acid Test' are met:

THE ACID TEST

- The person is subject to the *continuous supervision* and *control* of those caring for him or her (both aspects must apply).
- The person is *not* free to leave, were they to try to do so.

The following factors are no longer relevant in determining whether or not a deprivation of liberty is taking place:

- The person's compliance or lack of objection (i.e., it does not matter if the person is going along with the deprivation, or if they are not actually trying to leave)
- The relative normality of the placement (i.e., it does not matter if the deprivation is normal for someone with that condition or diagnosis and of similar age)
- The reason(s) or purpose behind a particular placement (i.e., it does not matter if it is being done for the benefit of the person – although for a deprivation to be successfully authorised, it must be in the person's best interests)

If a person's liberty is being deprived, this must be approved under the DoLS legislation. This applies to patients in all hospitals (including hospices) and registered care homes in England and Wales, aged 18 and over, who:

- Suffer from a 'mental disorder' within the meaning of Section 1(2) of the MHA, excluding drug/alcohol dependency, but including learning disability
- Lack the capacity to give consent to the arrangements made for their care or treatment
- Can only be given such care and treatment in circumstances that amount to not just a restriction on, but a deprivation of, their liberty
- Require such a regime as a necessary and proportionate response in their best interests to protect them from harm

If a hospital or care home is depriving such a person of their liberty, they must first consider whether they can still provide safe and effective care with a lesser level of restriction. If they cannot, they must immediately self-authorise that deprivation (called an 'urgent authorisation'; 7-day maximum duration), whilst also applying to the Local Authority (LA) for a 'standard authorisation' (1-year maximum duration). The LA must complete six relevant assessments within a statutory timescale of 7 days (if an urgent authorisation is in place) or 28 days (if the application is being made in advance, before the person's liberty will be deprived, e.g., whilst still at home). These assessments ensure that the person meets the conditions for an authorised deprivation of liberty under DoLS; that the deprivation is in his/her best interests; and that safeguards are put in place for review of the deprivation. Under DoLS terminology, the care home or hospital is known as the 'managing authority', and the LA as the 'supervising body'.

In this case, Mr Moore meets the criteria listed above. He lacks relevant capacity as a result of a mental disorder, is under continuous supervision and control, and is not free to leave; therefore, the Acid Test is met. An urgent authorisation must be undertaken by the nursing home immediately, and an application for standard authorisation must also be made at the same time.

 Key Points

- After the Cheshire West case (2014), liberty is now considered to be deprived if the Acid Test is met.
- If deprivation is necessary for the care of an individual who lacks capacity to consent to it, it must be authorised, and safeguards, called Deprivation of Liberty Safeguards (DoLS), put in place.

SECTION 6

ETHICS AND LAW IN CLINICAL PRACTICE: CONFIDENTIALITY

CASE 34: CONFIDENTIALITY

Daisy is a nurse working on an orthopaedic ward. She has established a rapport with a patient, Janine, who has been admitted under the orthopaedic team for surgical repair of a fractured wrist. Janine told the consultant that her injuries were sustained falling down the stairs. However, during a chat with Daisy, Janine asks 'is everything I tell you confidential?'. She then confides to Daisy that her husband has become increasingly violent and pushed her down the stairs.

Daisy does not know if she should tell anyone.

Questions
- Who is owed a duty of confidentiality?
- In what circumstances can information be disclosed without consent of the patient?
- Should Daisy disclose the fact that Janine has suffered domestic abuse?

ANSWER 34

Medical problems can often be embarrassing and frightening and can be associated with stigma. Keeping patient information confidential helps to ensure that the patient will trust their doctor sufficiently to divulge personal information to enable optimum healthcare. Although few healthcare professionals purposely break confidentiality, it is important to be aware how easily information can be shared between people who do not have a right to that information.

All information which can identify a patient is confidential, including images of the patient. A constellation of clinical information combined with the patient's NHS number or full postcode could identify the patient. There are legal, ethical and professional obligations to maintain confidentiality. The duty of care owed by a healthcare professional to a patient includes the duty to maintain confidentiality and the General Medical Council (GMC) issues guidance to doctors about maintaining confidentiality and grounds for disclosure (GMC, Confidentiality, 2009). The Data Protection Act 1998 provides safeguards in relation to processing sensitive personal data, and Article 8 ECHR gives a right to respect for private and family life and correspondence.

Sharing information within the healthcare team

Patient information needs to be shared with other members of the team in order to facilitate care, and patients are taken to implicitly agree to share their personal information within the healthcare team (GMC, Confidentiality, 2009). The British Medical Association (BMA) states that information sharing in this context 'is acceptable to the extent that health professionals share what is necessary and relevant for patient care on a "need to know" basis' (BMA, Confidentiality and disclosure of health information toolkit, 1st edition). In contrast, disclosure of information to social services usually requires explicit consent from competent patients, although for patients lacking capacity, information can be shared on a need-to-know basis if it is clearly necessary in the patient's interests and not against his known wishes.

Patients who lack capacity

A duty of confidentiality is owed to all patients; however, when a patient lacks capacity their healthcare information may need to be shared with others to facilitate a decision in the patient's best interests. Parent(s) make healthcare decisions for their child who is unable to do so and so they need clinical information of the child's diagnosis, prognosis and treatment options to make decisions. For adult patients who lack capacity, information may need to be shared with relatives, friends and carers in order to assess the patient's best interests; but a judgement may need to be made about sharing sensitive information, and if there is evidence that the patient did not want information shared, this must be respected (BMA, Confidentiality and disclosure of health information tool kit, Card 7, Adults who lack capacity).

Disclosure of information

The duty of confidentiality is not absolute, and so the common expression that *'everything you tell me will be confidential'* is not accurate. Confidential information may be disclosed if

- The patient consents to the disclosure
- The disclosure is required by law, e.g., to regulatory bodies which have statutory powers to access patients' records
- It is justified in the public interest

Disclosure in the public interest can be justified when it is 'essential to prevent a serious and imminent threat to public health, national security, the life of the individual or a third party or to prevent or detect serious crime' such as murder, manslaughter, rape and child abuse (British Medical Association, Confidentiality and disclosure of health information toolkit). This might be where the patient has a medical condition which puts others at serious risk of harm or poses a risk to public safety, for example, the patient has a condition where he is a risk to others if he continues to drive.

There are clear harms in breaking confidentiality including a patient's loss of trust with the healthcare service and potential disengagement with treatment. However, a consequentialist approach recognises that the harms of disclosure may be outweighed by the harms of non-disclosure. The harms and benefits of disclosure should be weighed in deciding whether to breach patient confidentiality. In any event the disclosure of confidential information should be to an appropriate person or authority who can use the information to eliminate or reduce the risk of harm. The patient should be informed that disclosure will be made in the public interest, unless this would create a risk of serious harm or would prejudice the purpose of the disclosure.

Particular difficulties may arise where two or more patients who have a relationship to each other are registered in the same GP practice. The doctors will owe a duty of care and confidentiality to all of them, and this can result in a potential conflict of interest.

Janine is a competent adult patient. If she refuses to allow a healthcare professional to disclose information to help her, then this decision should be respected. The GMC states, 'It may be appropriate to encourage patients to consent to disclosures you consider necessary for their protection, and to warn them of the risks of refusing to consent; but you should usually abide by a competent adult patient's refusal to consent to disclosure, even if their decision leaves them, but nobody else, at risk of serious harm' (GMC, Confidentiality 2009). Disclosure would be necessary if children may be at risk.

Of course, Janine should be provided with information and support to contact appropriate agencies if she wishes. In the highest-risk cases of domestic abuse, a local Multi-Agency Risk Assessment Conference (MARAC) may share information in order to create a safety plan for the individual. The Caldicott Guardian (Case 36) makes the judgement about whether to share information and should authorise MARAC information sharing.* The justification for information sharing without consent is prevention and detection of crime or prevention of serious harm.

If a patient who lacks capacity may be a victim of neglect or physical, sexual or emotional abuse, information *must* be disclosed to the appropriate authority if it is in the patient's best interests or to protect others from risk of serious harm.

 Key Points

- Maintaining patient confidentiality is necessary to ensure that patients trust doctors with personal and sensitive information.
- Information can be disclosed to avoid or reduce the risk of serious harm to others.
- Information should be disclosed to the appropriate person or authority.

---

* Department of Health, 'Striking the Balance' Practical Guidance on the Application of Caldicott Guardian Principles to Domestic Violence and MARACs (Multi-Agency Risk Assessment Conferences), 2012.

CASE 35: CONFIDENTIALITY AND CHILDREN

Paula is 17 and has an inherited metabolic disease. She has been attending a specialist clinic on a yearly basis for monitoring. Sometimes Paula attends with her parents, although patients are encouraged to increasingly take an independent approach. At the latest appointment Paula specifically asked to speak to the consultant without her dad being present. She asked the consultant of the risks of developing a metabolic crisis associated with illicit drug use. She admitted that she occasionally uses recreational drugs. She insisted that her parents should not be informed of this and from previous conversations with her parents it is clear that they do not know of the drug use.

The team has advised Paula about the implications and risks of her behaviour in terms of her health and the fact that it is illegal, but the consultant wonders whether he should inform Paula's parents of her drug use.

Questions
- Is a duty of confidentiality owed to Paula?
- What circumstances justify breaching confidentiality?

ANSWER 35

At 17 years old Paula is not yet an adult. Young people, however, are owed a duty of confidentiality and General Medical Council (GMC) guidance states that 'you have the same duty of confidentiality to children and young people as you have to adults' (GMC, 0–18 years: guidance for all doctors, 2007). Paula has been involved in decisions about her treatment and is competent to do so. Therefore, although her parents are aware of her diagnosis and treatment, there is no need for disclosure of her healthcare issues to her parents in order to obtain their consent to treatment. She seems able to articulate the reasons for taking drugs, and her request is to understand the risks to her health rather than as a cry for help.

Paula has specifically requested that the information about her drug use is not shared with her parents. Is there a justification for disclosure to her parents in the face of her refusal? GMC guidance states that information should be disclosed if it is necessary to protect the child or young person, or someone else, from risk of death or serious harm (GMC, 0–18 years: guidance for all doctors, 2007). Such cases may arise, for example, if 'a child or young person is involved in behaviour that might put them or others at risk of serious harm, such as serious addiction, self-harm or joy-riding'.

Even if informed of her drug use, Paula's parents are perhaps unlikely to be able to stop it. If they were informed they could be alert to signs of worsening health or a sudden deterioration, but as they are aware of the metabolic condition they will be monitoring her health anyway. If Paula did come to harm and her parents found out that healthcare professionals had known about drug use and not told them, they may feel they were deprived of their chance to intervene and let down by the team caring for their child.

However, Paula is engaging well with the team and wants to make a reasoned and informed choice about taking drugs. It could be argued that the degree of criminality and potential harm is not sufficiently severe to justify disclosure to her parents in the face of a refusal to do so. Informing her parents against her express refusal would be very damaging to the relationship she has established with the team and may impact on future engagement with treatment.

 | **Key Points**

- A duty of confidentiality is owed to all children and young people.
- Disclosing information to parents without the consent of the young person may have a negative impact on the long-term relationship between the healthcare team and the patient, and also the patient and their parents.
- Even where a young person is competent and refuses to allow disclosure to parents, a reasonable effort must be made to persuade the child to involve parents for important or life-changing decisions.

CASE 36: ACCESS TO HEALTHCARE INFORMATION

One of your patients has recently died from ovarian cancer. She had presented to the surgery twice with vague symptoms prior to being referred for an ultrasound scan which demonstrated advanced cancer. Despite aggressive treatment with chemotherapy and surgery, she died less than 6 months after diagnosis. Her family is understandably distraught, and her daughter has written to the practice manager requesting a full copy of her medical records as they are wondering whether the cancer could have been diagnosed earlier. As the complaints lead for the practice, you have been asked to respond to the letter.

Questions
- Does confidentiality continue after death?
- Can a relative request access to a patient's medical records?
- What processes are in place to protect confidentiality and medical records?

ANSWER 36

Data protection

Medical records often contain sensitive information – both about the individual and in some cases third parties. Anyone who has access to medical records should be aware of how easy it can be to inadvertently break confidentiality. They should also be aware of who can legally request access to patient data. The Data Protection Act 1998 (DPA) deals with the use and handling of confidential information. Data protection principles state that personal data shall be processed fairly and lawfully, obtained only for one or more specified lawful purposes, be adequate, relevant and not excessive, be accurate and up-to-date, and not be kept for longer than necessary. The DPA entitles patients to view their own medical records. Individuals can request to see their medical records, but a doctor has the responsibility to remove any information in the records that pertains to a third person.

The Caldicott Report (1997) gives guidance on how the DPA should be employed within the framework of the NHS and states that each NHS trust and GP practice must appoint a 'Caldicott guardian'. A Caldicott guardian acts as an adviser in situations in which confidentiality is at risk of being breached. This role has a wide remit including ensuring that waste paper containing patient information is disposed of in a secure way, dealing with drug companies that may want anonymous prescribing data and general practitioners who want to make email referrals without having in place encryption protection on their personal computers. The Caldicott Principles recommend that a healthcare professional must always justify the need for information, use the minimum amount of information possible, ensure that patient information is shared on a strict need-to-know basis only, and ensure that the people with access to information are aware of the importance of keeping the information confidential.

Confidentiality

The duty of confidentiality to a patient also remains after death. The GMC Confidentiality guidance (2009) gives guidance on what to do when information is requested by others about the nature of a patient's death. It highlights circumstances in which confidentiality should be maintained but also looks at the emotional needs of any relatives that have questions about the nature of a person's death. Relevant information about the patient's death should be disclosed in some circumstances, including the following:

- To help a coroner, procurator fiscal or other similar officer with an inquest or fatal accident inquiry
- On death certificates, which must be completed honestly and fully
- When a parent asks for information about the circumstances and causes of a child's death
- When a partner, close relative or friend asks for information about the circumstances of an adult's death, and there is no reason to believe that the patient would have objected to such a disclosure
- When a person has a right of access to records under the Access to Health Records Act 1990

In the above scenario perhaps the best course of action would be to invite the relatives in to have a conversation about the nature of the patient's presentation, investigations and ongoing treatment. It would allow the relatives a chance to ask questions and for the GP to give open and honest answers. If the relatives still had concerns or felt that negligence had occurred, then the next step would be to ask them to make a more formal complaint. In most cases, being able to have a conversation about the circumstances of an individual's death is enough to support the relatives in coming to terms with the death of a loved one.

There has been a lot of public interest in medical record keeping in recent years due to government plans to increase access to medical records both in terms of ease of access by other healthcare workers and by outside organisations in the form of anonymised data. The National Programme for IT aims to provide online electronic access to medical records by healthcare professionals so that patient information can be accessed from anywhere in the country.

The care.data programme allows information from GP records to be passed to the Health and Social Care Information Centre (HSCIC), which will collate information to promote health and social care. In theory this data should be anonymised as the patient's name will not be shared. However, other identifiable information will be shared including NHS number, date of birth and postcode, which leads to a risk of medical records being identified. The information passed to the HSCIC would also include BMI, smoking habits and early indicators of disease. Although in theory this information will only be used in healthcare promotion and research, there is no guarantee that is could not be accessed or sold to non-medical organisations such as insurance companies, which could then increase premiums based on non-individual data. The most controversial aspect of care.data is that inclusion in the programme is 'opt-out', which means vulnerable and elderly patients may have their medical data disseminated due to a lack of understanding that it is happening. Due to public concerns, care.data is currently under review.

 Key Points

- Maintaining patient confidentiality is necessary to ensure that patients trust doctors with personal and sensitive information.
- Personal data should be kept safe, used for a proper purpose and only be shared with relevant healthcare professionals.

CASE 37: CONFIDENTIALITY AND HIV

James, a 25-year-old white man with no symptoms, attends the genitourinary medicine clinic. He reports that Tom, his boyfriend of 2 years, has advised him to attend. He says Tom was diagnosed and treated for syphilis the week before at the same clinic. James has had no other partners since his last negative tests 2 years ago and says Tom had a negative HIV test last year. James consents to all tests including an HIV test.

While the patient is waiting for his tests, the doctor pulls out Tom's file. She confirms that Tom was diagnosed with syphilis last week but also notices that Tom is HIV-positive and has attended this centre for the past 4 years for HIV care. Tom's next appointment is in 2 days.

Questions
- How should the doctor proceed with this consultation? What should she say to James?
- Does the fact that both patients are under the care of the same clinic affect the doctor's decision?
- What should be said to Tom at his next appointment?
- Would the doctor be liable if she breached Tom's confidentiality *or* if she did not inform James of his ongoing risk?

ANSWER 37

Following James's consultation, the doctor is now aware that Tom has concealed his HIV-positive status, which may have put James at risk of HIV transmission. She should proceed with the consultation, ensuring appropriate sexual health advice is provided, and address any of James's concerns. At this stage, the doctor would not be justified to disclose to James any of the information she has found out about Tom as it would result in a breach of confidentiality. The doctor has not yet had the opportunity to discuss issues of disclosure with Tom, and unless Tom himself consents to the disclosure of his HIV status, or disclosure is necessary in the public interest, she has both a moral and legal duty to maintain confidentiality.

Taking a full sexual history from James is important to assess his risk (and it is important not to make assumptions). Other information which may be useful in consultation includes their sexual practices, e.g., whether they have anal sex and if they use condoms regularly. An uninfected individual is thought to be most at risk of acquiring HIV by unprotected receptive anal sex. The results from James's tests will also crucially determine how he will be managed. If he is found to be HIV-positive he will need to be counselled sensitively. James will also need to be seen by an HIV specialist within 2 weeks (the standard for HIV clinical care). Even if James is now HIV-negative, failure of disclosure from Tom may result in HIV transmission to James in the future. As both James and Tom are patients under the care of the same clinical team, they are both owed a duty of care. The important but difficult issue is identifying in which circumstances the duty of confidentiality is outweighed by the interests of others.

During Tom's next consultation it would be important to ascertain his feelings regarding disclosure of his status to his partner. It is the doctor's duty to properly advise him of the nature of the disease and ways of protecting others from infection. Tom should be encouraged to disclose his HIV-positive status to James, regardless of condom usage. It would be important to inform Tom that lack of disclosure and choosing not to use condoms could amount to 'reckless' transmission of HIV, which has been seen in UK courts as a criminal offence resulting in prosecution (this was clarified by the Court of Appeal in *R v Dica* 2004). Acting recklessly means that the individual must have been aware that he was placing others at an unreasonable risk. Tom should be advised that sharing information about his HIV diagnosis with his partner allows for informed decision making about their sexual behaviour. Also, disclosure would enable James to seek post-exposure prophylaxis following accidental unprotected sex and therefore reduce the risk of transmission. The case would be discussed by a multidisciplinary team and a deadline agreed with Tom by which he needs to have disclosed. It would be made clear to Tom that if this deadline was breached the clinic would step in and inform James that he has been at risk and needs HIV testing (but not telling him outright that Tom has HIV). It is rare for a person to refuse to disclose when supported. Any disclosure to Tom – about James attending the clinic – needs to be authorised by James first.

If James was to become HIV-positive as a result of Tom failing to disclose, it is questionable whether the doctor could be held accountable for failing to prevent onward transmission of HIV. Some court decisions have suggested that the doctor could be held civilly liable (that is, liable in damages) if the third party was also a patient of the doctor and independently owed a duty of care. Therefore, in the event that the doctor has sufficient reason to believe Tom is not following the advice given and cannot be persuaded to do so, and is putting James at ongoing risk, it may become necessary to disclose information. In these circumstances the doctor should inform Tom before the disclosure is made, and must be prepared to justify the decision to disclose.

In the UK, it is unlikely that doctors would be held civilly or criminally liable for failure to prevent onward transmission of HIV. The General Medical Council's guidance on confidentiality and disclosure should be followed. The guidance does not suggest that there is a 'duty' to disclose ongoing risk to a third party, but indicates the ability to disclose if the doctor, in discussion with the patient and with other colleagues, feels that ongoing risk to a known individual outweighs the risk to the existing patient relationship and trust in confidentiality.

Ethical issues

Individuals have a moral obligation to avoid harming others where possible. But they also have a responsibility to protect themselves from known harm. A person consents to assume and accept a risk which they were aware of (where there is a choice to avoid that risk). But can James be said to have assumed the risk of acquiring HIV when he has been deceived by Tom about the reality of the risks? Society places strong emphasis on an individual's autonomy. James's decision to have sex with Tom can only be said to be truly autonomous if he is made aware of all the facts (as condoms do not protect against HIV 100%). This does not negate the public health message that everyone should take responsibility for their own health (and not put themselves at risk), which is particularly prudent given that one-third of all cases of HIV in the UK remain undiagnosed.

Key Points
• The duty of confidentiality is an important cornerstone of the provision of medical care but it is not absolute.
• Disclosure can be justified to protect a person from risk of death or serious harm, e.g., sexual contact of patient with HIV who has not been informed.
• Inform the patient before disclosure.
• Do not disclose to others who are not at risk of infection.

CASE 38: USE OF INTERPRETERS

Carol, a 40-year-old woman, has come to see you to discuss treatment for menorrhagia. Carol was born with congenital deafness and has brought her 16-year-old son with her to act as an interpreter. She lip reads a little but feels more comfortable using sign language.

Carol tells you that she has had enough of her heavy bleeding and she is keen to undergo a hysterectomy. However, you are slightly concerned that she also reports some inter-menstrual bleeding and you need to discuss your concerns that this may be something more sinister and that you need to refer her urgently for more investigations.

You are aware both that Carol is relying on a non-medical person to translate your concerns into sign language and that the person doing the translation is her teenage son. He may feel uncomfortable discussing his mum's intimate problems and worried when you start talking about possible tests for cancer.

Questions
- What could the GP do in this situation?
- What other scenarios can you think of where communication may be problematic?
- What services are available to provide support in consultations where the patient cannot communicate in English?

ANSWER 38

There are many scenarios where consultations are impeded due to communication barriers. Hearing impairment is just one example. More commonly encountered difficulties include language barriers and other verbal communication difficulties such as learning disability or dysphasia. When encountering a patient with communication difficulties it is up to the clinician to decide how best to address the problem. In non-urgent scenarios it is often best to organise a consultation with a professional interpreter present so that a face-to-face consultation can occur. In emergency situations telephone interpretation services should be accessible in every healthcare setting.

Professional interpreters should be expected to

- Act in an impartial and professional manner
- Be fluent in the language specified
- Not pretend to understand something when they have not
- Interpret accurately without anything being omitted or added from the interaction (Croydon Translation and Interpreting Service: Best Practice Guide. www.croydon.gov.uk.)

Occasionally it may be appropriate to ask other medical professionals to act as interpreters. However, using friends and relatives or other workers within a hospital should be discouraged.

One of the most important reasons for using a professional interpreting service is that medical information being obtained or given needs to be accurate. Misinterpretation, whether accidental or intended, could lead to misdiagnosis or suboptimal treatment. Where consent needs to be obtained to undergo a procedure, the consent would be invalid if the person interpreting fails to ensure that the patient fully understands what they are consenting to.

Ethical concerns may arise when using non-professionals to interpret. Professional interpreting services are bound by the same professional code of conduct as healthcare professionals, whereas using a friend or relative means that confidentiality could be broken by the other person present as they are not bound by any professional duty. Patients themselves may also be reluctant to fully disclose potentially embarrassing or sensitive information in front of their relatives. This can be easier when using an impartial third person.

Increasingly, patients are presenting with their children and asking them to act as interpreters. Although this may seem useful in straightforward situations, it should not be encouraged, as often children themselves may not understand the medical information they are being asked to translate and it may cause them unnecessary distress and anxiety to discuss their parents' symptoms, particularly if they are in pain or very unwell.

In the above scenario the GP should ask the son to explain to his mother that the GP does not feel comfortable using him as an interpreter due to the sensitive nature of the questions they need to ask. An interpreter should be booked for a face-to-face consultation within the next few days if at all possible or the consultation could potentially be carried out by written communication.

 Key Points

- Hospitals and general practices have a legal obligation to provide interpreter services.
- Using non-professional interpreters can inhibit the doctor–patient relationship and raises issues of translation mistakes and confidentiality.
- Family members should be used as interpreters only in an emergency where there is no other option.

CASE 39: DISCLOSING GENETIC INFORMATION

Doug is 51 and married with three adult children. He has been treated by his GP for depression for the last 7 years. More recently he has developed abnormal facial movements and spasms in his legs which are occurring at rest. The GP suspected that his low mood and lethargy over the past 7 years may be due to Huntington's disease, which is now only becoming apparent with the onset of new clinical features. Doug was referred to a specialist for genetic testing, and sadly the result has come back positive and he has now been given a definite diagnosis of Huntington's disease. Doug was adopted at birth and has no knowledge of his biological parents. He feels relieved that he was unaware that one of his parents would also have had the condition as he would not have wanted to find out his diagnosis before becoming symptomatic. Doug has told his wife, and together they have decided that they do not want any of their children to know about his diagnosis. They have been informed by the counsellor at the genetics clinic that their children might want to know because they each have a 50% chance of having the gene mutation. Although Doug and his wife have been offered support to share the difficult news with their children, they strongly resist telling them as they feel the knowledge would be a burden to them – 'and what can they do about it anyway?'

Questions

- Should genetic information belong to individuals or families?
- Do Doug and his wife have an ethical obligation to tell their children they are at risk of a genetic condition?
- Are there any circumstances in which genetic information can be disclosed without their consent?

ANSWER 39

Genetic testing provides information about whether the person tested has a genetic mutation for a specific disease such as Huntington's or a predisposition to develop a disease; for example, BRCA 1 and 2 gene mutations increase the likelihood of breast cancer. Genetic screening, by comparison, is carried out to identify individuals who are carriers of specific genetic disorders and may not develop the disease themselves but could pass the genes on to their children, which in combination with DNA from the other parent may result in disease, for example cystic fibrosis. Genetic information differs from other medical information because it reveals information about other family members. Huntington's is autosomal dominant, and as Doug has the gene, his children have a 50% chance of also having the gene.

The Joint Committee on Medical Genetics (Consent and confidentiality in clinical genetic practice 2011) states that during the consent process for genetic testing a discussion should cover the fact that genetic test results may have a significant impact for other family members and therefore communication of certain aspects of information is recommended. Doug and his wife are refusing to inform their children of his genetic condition. This is highly sensitive personal information and the medical specialists owe him a duty of confidentiality. However, this duty is not absolute and in certain circumstances breaching confidentiality may be justified to avoid serious harm (Case 34). The GMC guidance on Confidentiality (2009) states that 'if a patient refuses consent to disclosure, you will need to balance your duty to make the care of your patient your first concern against your duty to help protect the other person from serious harm'. The harms of breaching confidentiality should be weighed against the potential benefits to the relatives of doing so. There is a public interest in maintaining a confidential health service. Disclosing information without consent may lead to loss of trust in the therapeutic relationship. If information about Doug's test results is disclosed to his children, would this knowledge be effective to reduce or prevent 'serious' harm?

Of course, his children either will or will not have the genetic mutation for Huntington's. GMC guidance states that sharing genetic information with relatives may enable them to get prophylaxis or other preventive treatments or interventions, make use of increased surveillance or other investigations or prepare for potential health problems (GMC Confidentiality 2009). Huntington's disease affects the brain and nervous system. It is a progressive condition which affects body movements and can lead to a change in behaviour. Treatment aims to control symptoms but the condition is incurable. If Doug's children were informed that he has the gene they could choose to seek testing themselves, and an affirmative test result means they could make plans for their futures, including perhaps an informed choice not to have children or to seek pre-implantation genetic diagnosis (Case 11). However, knowledge of genetic inheritance can be a burden and may lead to 'morbidification' – falling victim to an inescapable fate through knowledge of an existing disease (Danish Council of Ethics, Ethics and mapping of the human genome, 1993). More discussion and support should be offered to Doug and his wife. They may wish that their children be contacted by the genetics unit on their behalf. If they continue to refuse to disclose, the genetics unit should maintain confidentiality as Huntington's has no medical cure and nothing can be done to prevent the condition from developing.

 Key Points

- Genetic information may not be considered to be private where it is observable.
- The harms of breaching confidentiality by informing a relative 'at risk' without consent must be weighed against the benefits of disclosure: is there a cure or lifestyle measures that can be taken to prevent or ameliorate harms?

CASE 40: GENETIC TESTING OF CHILDREN FOR ADULT-ONSET CONDITIONS

Pearl and Dean have been married for 12 years and have a 6-year-old son. Dean's father and grandfather died from cancer when they were in their early 40s. Because of the strong family history of cancer, Dean wanted to have a genetic test to find out his level of risk. Although no clear diagnosis was possible, tests indicated that he was at risk of hereditary non-polyposis colorectal cancer. Now Dean is feeling tired and unwell, and has a colonoscopy. The test reveals that he has inoperable bowel cancer. Pearl is concerned that their son might also be at risk of colon cancer when he is older, and she wants him to be tested to see if he is at risk.

Questions

- Should parents be allowed to have their children tested for adult-onset genetic conditions?
- Do children have a right to know about their genetic risks?

ANSWER 40

Legal issues

Pearl is requesting genetic testing for her son. As he is so young he clearly lacks capacity to understand and give consent for tests himself. Pearl could give consent for testing if it is in his best interests, but information provided by the test would not benefit the child now because he will remain asymptomatic for decades to come. At his age there is no therapeutic intervention and there are no steps that can be taken to reduce any future risk.

How far are Pearl's interests intertwined with her son's? Does the fact that she may be an overly concerned mother if she does not know whether he is at future risk affect his best interests? It is hard to conceive a situation where the mother's distress caused by the uncertainty would so affect her parenting to impact on his best interests. The only benefit for testing the child now is to give Pearl possible peace of mind if the test is negative.

The assessment of best interests should also include consideration of the burden of knowledge if the test proves positive. The child is too young to be told now and there is no control over when and how Pearl will tell him in the future and whether counselling would be sought. If the test is positive, when he is told he is likely to find the information burdensome and upsetting. A positive test does not necessarily indicate certainty of developing this cancer, nor does it provide information about the time of onset and severity of the condition. A positive test result far from clarifying the position may actually harm the child. The potential for genetic discrimination and the possibility that insurance will be denied also need to be considered for some genetic conditions.

The British Society for Human Genetics recommends that where genetic testing will not be of medical benefit to the child for some time there is a presumption of delay until a child is old enough to choose for him- or herself, unless there are compelling reasons to test earlier.

Ethical issues

Pearl's interest in knowing could be set against her son's right not to know of his genetic inheritance. Usually availability of information is considered a good thing because it allows informed choices about healthcare options. Patient autonomy is based on the ability to understand relevant information, but Pearl's son cannot make autonomous choices yet. Parents *are* allowed to make decisions which limit the future choices for their child but only where it is in the child's best interests, i.e., the benefits outweigh the burdens of the intervention.

 Key Points

- In the future Pearl's son may choose to be tested himself when he can make an autonomous choice.
- Genetic testing now would limit this child's open future without any commensurate benefit.

Section 7

ETHICS AND LAW IN CLINICAL PRACTICE: NEGLIGENCE

CASE 41: STANDARD OF CARE AND NEGLIGENCE

Joe is on a busy ward round with his consultant. The round is post-take and he has seen 23 patients so far. One of his patients is septic and needs a prescription for intravenous antibiotics. The consultant tells Joe to put him on ciprofloxacin. However, Joe is aware that the hospital protocol has changed and that ciprofloxacin is no longer the first-line antibiotic due to the increasing incidence of *Clostridium difficile* infection after its use. He suggests giving intravenous co-amoxiclav instead. The consultant agrees and appears impressed that Joe is up-to-date with the antibiotic guidelines. Joe prescribes the antibiotic. A few hours later he is called to the ward urgently as the septic patient is having difficulty breathing and has developed urticaria. He has had an anaphylactic reaction to co-amoxiclav. Joe realises that the allergies box on the drug chart states that the patient is allergic to penicillin. He puts out a medical emergency call and after further assessment the patient is transferred to ITU. After 24 hours on ITU the patient returns to the ward. No permanent damage has occurred.

Questions
- What is clinical negligence?
- Has Joe been negligent?
- What can he do to protect himself against a claim in negligence?

ANSWER 41

A healthcare professional owes a duty of care toward his patients. This duty is to exercise reasonable skill and care in diagnosis, treatment and provision of healthcare information (Case 42). The healthcare professional breaches his duty of care if he falls below the standard of care. For a doctor, this is the standard of care practised by a responsible body of doctors professing that skill. A patient who has been harmed as a result of medical care may bring a claim in negligence seeking compensation.

A patient has to prove that a doctor is negligent by demonstrating that

- The doctor owed the patient a duty of care
- The doctor failed to give an appropriate standard of care
- But for the failure of care, the harm would not have occurred and the harm is reasonably foreseeable

The claim must be brought within 3 years of the date when the harm occurred or the date when the patient knew or should have realised that he may have a claim. Experts provide evidence about the appropriate standard of care and will consider professional guidance issued by the relevant speciality. If the claim is successful, compensation will be awarded and damages can be very high. In 2012 compensation worth £10.8 million was awarded to enable full-time care and equipment for a girl who suffered injuries after doctors failed to notice that her heart had stopped shortly after birth.

The NHS hospital trust is vicariously liable for negligence of its employees. A claim is brought against the NHS trust employing the doctor who is alleged to have caused the harm. The National Health Service Litigation Authority handles claims against the NHS in England. It reported that there was a 10.8% increase in clinical claims (from 9,143 claims in 2011/12 to 10,129 in 2012/13) but less than 1% go to a court hearing. Nearly one-fifth (£22.7 billion in 2012) of the NHS annual budget is set aside for compensation payments.

Litigation is a stressful and costly experience for claimants and has a negative effect on NHS staff. The Francis Report published in 2013 following the inquiry into care at the Mid Staffordshire Hospital recommended an open and transparent culture within the NHS. There is now a 'duty of candour' on all NHS trusts in England which requires them to be open and honest with patients and their families, admit their mistakes and apologise when things go wrong.

In this scenario it was Joe's responsibility to check before prescribing medication that the patient did not have any allergies. However, the nurse who gave the drug also has a responsibility to check allergies. Although Joe failed in his care to the patient, because there was no long-term harm, it is unlikely that a claim for negligence would be pursued.

 Key Points

- Clinical negligence claims are increasing and a large part of the NHS budget is set aside for compensation awards.
- A duty of candour requires healthcare professionals to be open and honest with patients when something goes wrong.

CASE 42: PROVISION OF INFORMATION

Rachel was very excited to be pregnant with her first child but was not having an easy pregnancy. She is naturally petite and had developed gestational diabetes, which was not detected until 30 weeks into her pregnancy. She was then referred to a specialist obstetrician as her pregnancy was considered high risk.

As Rachel had been diagnosed with gestational diabetes she was more likely to have a larger baby. In her case this was particularly worrisome due to her small frame. She was considered at significant risk of the baby developing shoulder dystocia (the shoulder getting stuck) during delivery. This is a major obstetric emergency associated with short- and long-term neonatal and maternal morbidity and associated neonatal mortality.

Although Rachel was told that she was having a larger-than-usual baby, she was not told about the risks of her experiencing mechanical problems during labour and she was not told about the risk of shoulder dystocia. Rachel had repeatedly expressed concerns about the size of the foetus and about the risk that the baby might be too big to be delivered vaginally but she had not asked her consultant specifically about this risk.

During the birth the baby did develop shoulder dystocia. There was a 15-minute delay between the baby's head appearing and the delivery, and during this time the baby was deprived of oxygen. At a few months old, her son was diagnosed as suffering from severe cerebral palsy, caused by deprivation of oxygen. If Rachel had been given the option of having an elective caesarean section her son would have been born uninjured.

Questions
- What information should be discussed with patients prior to consent for a procedure?
- What if a patient does not ask questions about risks?
- Can a doctor not disclose information about risks if he thinks that information will be harmful to the patient?

ANSWER 42

The law on disclosure of information is generally considered to be founded on the patient's 'right to choose' whether or not to have a particular treatment. To make an autonomous choice, the patient must be able to understand and reason and therefore needs sufficient information to be able to do so. The healthcare professional's legal duty of care includes the duty to disclose information of inherent risks, alternative treatment(s) and comparative risks of different treatment options and the implications of non-treatment.

A failure to disclose such information deprives the patient of the opportunity to decide whether they are willing to undertake the risks of treatment. A patient who has consented to a procedure, having been informed in broad terms of the nature and purpose of the procedure, has given valid consent (Case 25); but the patient has a claim in negligence if they can show that the doctor breached his duty by failing to provide enough information and that if the patient had been properly informed they would not have agreed to the treatment or procedure, thus avoiding the risk that in fact did materialise.

What information must be disclosed?

GMC guidance (Consent: patients and doctors making decisions together, 2008) advises that the doctor must tell patients if treatment might result in a serious adverse outcome, even if the risk is very small, and should also tell patients about less serious complications if they occur frequently. The BMA states that 'the amount of information doctors provide to each patient will vary according to factors such as the nature and severity of the condition, the complexity of the treatment, the risks associated with the treatment or procedure and the patient's own wishes' (BMA Consent tool kit). A healthcare professional will breach his duty if he has fallen below the requisite standard of disclosure. Numerous cases have considered the standard of disclosure of information. The Supreme Court decision of *Montgomery v Lanarkshire Health Board* (2015) reviews the prior case law and gives a judgment strongly focusing on provision of information which is sufficient to protect the patient's right of autonomy and her freedom to decide what shall and shall not be done with her body.

> A doctor is under a duty to take reasonable care to ensure that the patient is aware of any material risks involved in any recommended treatment and of any reasonable alternative or variant treatments. The test of materiality is whether, in the circumstances of the particular case, a reasonable person in the patient's position would be likely to attach significance to the risk, or the doctor is or should reasonably be aware that the particular patient would be likely to attach significance to it.
>
> *Montgomery v Lanarkshire Health Board* (2015)

Whether a risk is material does not depend solely on the statistical magnitude of risk. In the past a 10% risk of stroke was considered material and should therefore be disclosed. *Montgomery v Lanarkshire Health Board* identifies that whether a risk is material depends on the magnitude of risk to the patient and so is sensitive to the needs, concerns and circumstances of the individual patient, to the extent that they are or ought to be known to the doctor.

To understand the importance of potential harms of treatment for the patient requires a dialogue and 'the exchange of information between doctor and patient is central to good decision-making' (GMC, Consent: patients and doctors making decisions together, 2008). Information should be given in a manner that is readily understandable by the patient, and consideration should be given to issues of language, cognitive ability and stress of the patient. The duty to disclose will not be fulfilled if the doctor merely bombards the patient with technical information which the patient does not understand.

Asking questions

If the patient asks questions, they must be answered fully and truthfully. Rachel had raised general concerns but had not asked specific questions about the baby getting stuck during delivery. In *Montgomery* it was noted that 'the more a patient knows about the risks she faces, the easier it is for her to ask specific questions about those risks, so as to impose on her doctor a duty to provide information; but it is those who lack such knowledge, and who are in consequence unable to pose such questions and instead express their anxiety in more general terms, who are in the greatest need of information'.

Therapeutic privilege

It could be argued that a patient may be unduly alarmed by disclosure of serious risks of treatment even if they are statistically unlikely to occur, thus perhaps resulting in the patient forgoing treatment which is considered beneficial. 'Therapeutic privilege' refers to the withholding of information by the clinician during the consent process in the belief that disclosure of this information would lead to the harm or suffering of the patient. The GMC says that information necessary to make a decision should not be withheld 'unless you believe that giving it would cause the patient serious harm. In this context "serious harm" means more than that the patient might become upset or decide to refuse treatment' (GMC, Consent: patients and doctors making decisions together, 2008). There is no justification for a doctor to fail to disclose material information because he believes the patient may choose an alternative treatment which he thinks is contrary to their best interests.

The virtue of trust in the doctor–patient relationship depends on open, frank dialogue. This also allows the doctor to discuss with the patient which specific risks may be important to them. A consequentialist may argue that better outcomes are achieved by advancing patient choices in healthcare decision making. It is important to be aware that for some patients, discussion about a large number of serious risks can be so overwhelming that the patient becomes too scared to make any decision. Time should be given for reflection and discussion of these fears. In practice, how and where information is discussed is as important as the information itself.

Key Points
• Dialogue with patients is key in order to gain some understanding of the issues which are important to them. • The setting and manner of information provision are important factors. • The discussion and outcome must be clearly documented in the medical notes and on the consent form.

CASE 43: OUT OF YOUR DEPTH

Osman is an FY1 doctor currently on call on a night shift in a busy London hospital. An FY2 and a registrar are working alongside him. Osman is midway through his shift when he receives a bleep saying that he is required to take an arterial blood gas (ABG) from a new admission. The patient is a 55-year-old gentleman who has suffered from chronic obstructive pulmonary disease for 10 years. It is believed that he is suffering from type 2 respiratory failure. Osman tells the patient that he has to take blood to confirm the diagnosis; however, the patient is anxious and agitated. Furthermore, the patient reveals that he has a phobia of needles and does not want the ABG to be done. Osman states that there is no other option and the ABG is essential; however, the patient is becoming more hysterical. Osman is unsure of what to do. He is worried about asking the registrar for help, as the registrar stated during the handover meeting at the start of the shift to only bleep him if it is an emergency. Furthermore, the registrar has a reputation for being an intimidating figure.

Questions
- What should Osman do in this situation?
- Who would be held accountable if there were complications from the procedure?
- Are junior doctors held to the same legal standard of care as consultants?

ANSWER 43

Feeling out of depth is a very common problem for many in the medical profession, ranging from medical students to senior doctors. In 2014, 31% of FY1 doctors said that they had felt forced to cope with clinical problems beyond their competence or experience (General Medical Council, The State of Medical Education and Practice in the UK, 2014).

It is imperative to remember that the doctor must put the patient's safety first at all times. Doctors may feel pressured into doing a task and that there is no other option but to do it; however, they must always consider the potential risks to their patient. This is exemplified by GMC's Good Medical Practice (2013), which states that 'good doctors make the care of their patient their first concern'. Furthermore, they must recognise and work within the limits of their competence.

In this scenario, Osman clearly feels that he is not competent to take an ABG from a patient who is needle phobic and may become aggressive. Osman should therefore not attempt the procedure. The risk of an adverse event causing the patient harm, and potentially causing Osman harm, is much more important than Osman being reprimanded by the registrar. At the same time, it is imperative that an ABG is taken urgently. Therefore, Osman should ask for help. If he feels uncomfortable asking the registrar, he could ask the FY2 to perform the procedure. If Osman is intimidated by the registrar it may help to remember that it is the duty of a senior colleague to provide appropriate supervision (GMC, Good Medical Practice, 2013).

Osman is accountable for his actions. If he undertakes a procedure he does not feel competent to perform and it goes wrong, this could potentially lead to disciplinary action and in more serious situations may result in a claim of negligence.

The standard of care is not reduced just because of inexperience.

> The law requires the trainee or learner to be judged by the same standard as his more experienced colleagues. If it did not, inexperience would frequently be urged as a defence to an action for professional negligence.
>
> *Wilsher v Essex Area Health Authority* (1988)

However, the inexperienced doctor will not be liable for making a mistake, provided he sought the help of a senior colleague. Therefore, it is important that the limits of competency are recognised. Assistance and supervision should be sought if the individual does not feel confident in doing the procedure alone.

 Key Points

- Patient safety is paramount.
- Doctors must work within the limits of their competence or ask for assistance from a senior if they feel out of their depth.
- If a doctor performs a procedure they are not confident doing, they may be legally accountable for their actions.

CASE 44: REPORTING CONCERNS

Jessica is an FY1 doctor on her orthopaedic surgery rotation. Over the past week, Jessica has noticed that her registrar frequently turns up late and has often not shaved. He has a reputation for enjoying a good night out and has occasionally turned up with a hangover. However, Jessica is concerned that there are incidents where he appears drunk and that this is beginning to affect his concentration and the level of care he is providing to his patients. He often rushes or neglects his bedside care of patients.

Jessica asks the registrar if he is feeling OK, but he irritably brushes her aside and says that it is none of her business. Jessica is unsure what to do next.

Questions

- What is whistleblowing?
- What are the legal protections for a whistleblower?
- Does Jessica have a professional duty to report?

ANSWER 44

'*Whistleblowing*' is the term applied to a situation where an employee, former employee or member of an organisation raises concerns to people who have the power to take corrective action. This term had developed negative connotations toward the individual raising concerns, and 'whistleblowers' have been highly stigmatised and in some cases even lost their jobs. More recently there has been a culture change toward reporting concerns where patient safety or well-being is at risk. Healthcare professionals are beginning to recognise that this is something that should be promoted and encouraged.

The Public Interest Disclosure Act 1998 (PIDA) aims to protect whistleblowers who have disclosed information in the public interest from victimisation and dismissal. However, in 2015, Sir Francis in launching his 'Freedom to Speak Up Review' stated that 30% of people who had raised a concern said they felt unsafe after they had done so. Eighteen per cent of staff said they did not trust the system so they would not speak out, and 15% feared being victimised if they did so (Freedom to Speak Up Review 2015).

Doctors and medical students have professional duties to take steps to raise concerns about another colleague's behaviour, health or performance to an appropriate person. GMC, Good Medical Practice, 2013 states there should be 'a culture that allows all staff to raise concerns openly and safely'.

It is imperative to recognise that doctors have a duty to put patients' interests first, which overrides any personal and professional loyalties. Additionally, a doctor does not have to wait for proof of their concern. Raising a concern can be justified if it is done honestly, on the basis of reasonable belief and through appropriate channels. When reporting a concern, the focus should be on providing as much factual information as possible. Written records of concerns and any steps taken should be kept.

Jessica has significant and justifiable concerns. In the first instance she should discuss this with her consultant or clinical supervisor. More senior professionals may need to discuss concerns with the medical director or the clinical governance lead. Concerns should not be discussed with other junior colleagues or gossiped about with colleagues.

 Key Points

- Doctors have a duty to protect the patients under their care.
- Doctors have a professional duty to raise any concerns they have regarding colleagues, systems or policies to a higher authority.
- There is statutory protection under the Public Interest Disclosure Act.

CASE 45: MAKING MISTAKES AND INCIDENT FORMS

You are an FY2 doctor on your 4-month cardiology rotation. You are coming to the end of a long day shift on the ward. One of your patients, Taz, is a diabetic suffering from heart failure. As listed on the drug chart, you give Taz his evening dose of insulin, but you forget to record this on the drug chart. You hand over to the night team. During the night shift the patient receives another insulin dose as the night staff thought this had not been done. The following day Taz complains to you that he had a terrible night. He explains how he sweated profusely, felt dizzy and endured headaches, all of which are signs of hypoglycaemia. You realise your error when you look at the drug chart. You tell your consultant, who advises that you should fill out an incident form.

Questions

- What should you tell Taz?
- Are NHS trusts under any obligations to be open and honest when mistakes are made?
- What is the purpose of an incident form?
- What happens to the form once it has been completed?

ANSWER 45

All doctors have made a mistake at some point during their career. Human error is common, with an estimated 10% of hospital admissions resulting in an adverse event. It is often the handling of the mistake rather than the mistake occurring that causes problems. Patients often blame doctors more for a lack of openness rather than for the original mistake, thus good communication is imperative. It has also been shown that honesty and openness decrease the chance of a formal complaint being made.

Doctors have a professional duty to be transparent and truthful with patients if things go wrong. If possible they must put matters right, offer an apology and give a full explanation of what occurred (GMC, Good Medical Practice, 2013). Where a mistake results in moderate harm, severe harm or death, there is also a statutory duty of candour.

The National Patient Safety Agency gives definitions of harm:

- *No harm*: Any incident that had the potential to cause harm but was prevented OR any incident that occurred but did not result in any harm.
- *Low harm*: Any incident that resulted in the patient requiring minor treatment.
- *Moderate harm*: Harm that requires a moderate increase in treatment and is significant but not permanent harm. This includes unplanned return to surgery, unplanned readmission to hospital or a prolonged episode of care.
- *Severe harm*: A permanent lessening of bodily, sensory, motor, physiologic or intellectual functions, including removal of the wrong limb or organ or brain damage, that is related directly to the incident. Severe harm also includes prolonged psychological harm which the patient experiences for a continuous period of at least 28 days.
- *Death*: Any patient safety incident that directly resulted in the death of the patient.

There is a legal duty for all employers to comply with the Reporting of Injuries, Diseases and Dangerous Occurrences Regulations 2013 (RIDDOR) and for employers to provide incident forms, which should be available to all staff.

The purpose of incident reporting is multifaceted and includes early identification of potential hazards, pre-empting complaints and changing procedures so that a similar mistake should not occur in the future. In practice, the majority of clinical incidents are analysed and dealt with at a local level. Each hospital will have a designated senior staff member who has overall responsibility for ensuring incident reporting and follow-up.

An incident report should be objective and contain fact, not opinion. Submitting an incident form is not an admission of liability. An open and fair culture is encouraged so that members of staff feel able to report problems without fear of reprisal. Disciplinary action will rarely need to be taken as a result of incident reporting.

 Key Points

- Doctors are under a professional duty to be open and honest with patients when things go wrong.
- The purpose of an incident form is to identify, document and manage incidents.
- Submitting an incident form and apologising to a patient are not admissions of liability.

CASE 46: COMPLAINTS

You are doing a home visit with the hospice nurse to a patient, Rosamund, who has advanced metastatic pancreatic cancer. You have been asked to visit with the hospice nurse to provide support to the patient whilst difficult decisions are discussed. You are aware that the patient has recently refused to see both the gastroenterology consultant and the oncologist as she feels that they were very abrupt and dismissive of her feelings when discussing completion of a Do Not Attempt Resuscitation form. The patient is evidently distressed and angry at both of the professionals. You suspect that she is subconsciously pushing the professionals away as she is having difficulty coming to terms with her prognosis.

When you arrive the first thing Rosamund asks is how she can go about making a formal complaint about her gastroenterologist and oncologist.

Questions
- How can patients make a complaint?
- What is the most common reason for complaints occurring?
- What should you do if a complaint is made against you?

ANSWER 46

It is inevitable that every doctor will receive a complaint at some point throughout their career. Complaints are usually made following a breakdown in communication between medical staff and the patient or their families, rather than as a result of a clinical mistake. The breakdown in communication can happen for many reasons, including fear, pain and lack of explanation or empathy. Illness can be a frightening experience, and hospitals, medical investigations and procedures are often mysterious to lay people. Sometimes complaints are not directed against a specific individual but rather due to frustrations over waiting lists, poor facilities or refusal to fund treatment.

The NHS has a very transparent complaints procedure which ensures that every patient knows they have a right to complain. Patients are first of all encouraged to complain at the local level to the practice manager of a GP practice or the Patient Advice and Liaison Service (PALS) within a hospital to see whether their grievance can be resolved locally. Every complainant has the right to

> - Have the complaint dealt with efficiently, and be properly investigated
> - Know the outcome of any investigation into the complaint
> - Receive compensation if harm has occurred
>
> NHS Complaints Procedure (2014)

If a patient is not satisfied with the outcome of a local investigation, the next step in the process is to ask the Parliamentary and Health Service Ombudsman to open an investigation. This is an independent organisation.

Where there are concerns about professional misconduct, patients are advised to contact the regulatory body for that healthcare professional; for example the GMC or General Nursing Council (GNC). More significant complaints where a patient is seeking judicial review or financial compensation should be handled through a solicitor.

In the first instance, doctors who receive a complaint should seek advice from their consultant or practice complaints lead. Receipt of the complaint should be acknowledged within 48 hours to give the patient assurance that their complaint has been received and is being investigated. A more formal response should then be given as soon as possible. This should include objective details of what happened, and where feasible, the patient should be invited to have a face-to-face discussion. An apology to the patient is not seen as an admission of liability but is important and should be given whenever appropriate. The doctor's medical defence organisation can be contacted for advice and is also able to review written responses to complaints and provide legal and emotional support to doctors involved in the complaint.

 Key Points

- Most complaints are due to a breakdown in communication.
- All doctors need to be registered with a medical defence organisation in case they make a mistake.
- Senior colleagues, GP practice complaint leads and medical defence organisations can provide practical and emotional support.

SECTION 8

ETHICS AND LAW IN CLINICAL PRACTICE: MENTAL HEALTH

CASE 47: WHEN TO SECTION A PATIENT UNDER THE MENTAL HEALTH ACT

Kate is 27 and lives at home with her parents and younger brother. She studied anthropology at university and had been in a long-term relationship. After leaving university with a good degree, she struggled to get a job. She eventually found work in a restaurant, which she seemed to enjoy. Last year her boyfriend moved out and she decided to quit her job and move back home. Over the past year her family has become increasingly worried about her health and behaviour. Her personal care has deteriorated and she has slowly withdrawn from interacting with her family. She has not bothered to find a job locally and only leaves her bedroom to wash and get food from the kitchen. Kate has also begun to clean her hands obsessively although otherwise she does not seem to wash. Her room smells stale and she has refused to let her mum change her bedding. She does not seem to change her clothes and does not allow them to be washed with the family clothes. Her mother has noticed that Kate's hands are raw and that she has sores on her back and her legs. She refused to speak to a GP about her mood, and in desperation Kate's parents have spoken to their GP about what can be done. The GP was concerned enough to attempt a home visit, but on arrival Kate refused to come out of her room, saying that she was just having a break from the stresses of living.

Questions
- Could Kate be detained for assessment or treatment under the Mental Health Act?
- Should Kate be detained for assessment or treatment under the Mental Health Act?

ANSWER 47

The Mental Health Act 1983, amended in 2007, (MHA) enables a person to be detained for assessment of a mental disorder (Section 2) and, if a diagnosis has been made, to be detained for treatment (Section 3). Section 2 is generally used for first admissions, and if Kate had a known diagnosis she could be detained under Section 3. An admission for assessment lasts for a maximum of 28 days and it cannot be renewed, although a patient can at any time be detained under Section 3 instead. The application is usually made by an approved mental health professional (AMHP), and the person must be seen by two separate doctors, one of whom must have had specialist training.

Mental disorder is defined as 'any disorder or disability of the mind' and this is determined by relevant professionals in accordance with good clinical practice and accepted standards. There is a broad spectrum of clinically recognised conditions including schizophrenia, bipolar disorder, severe depression, anxiety and obsessive compulsive disorders. Someone with a learning disability and no other form of mental disorder may not be detained for treatment unless their learning disability is accompanied by abnormally aggressive or seriously irresponsible conduct. The aggressive behaviour must relate to the learning disability and not be attributable to other factors.

The purpose of the detention for assessment under Section 2 is to evaluate whether the person has a mental disorder and whether treatment is necessary. It can be authorised if the person

- is suffering from a mental disorder of a nature or degree which warrants her detention in hospital *and*
- ought to be detained in the interests of her own health or safety or with a view to the protection of others.

Consideration must be given to both the nature and degree of a person's mental disorder.

Kate is not a risk to others, but her current obsessive and compulsive behaviours do seem to pose a risk to her health and well-being. There is a suggestion of self-neglect and self-harm, and her condition might deteriorate without treatment. Nevertheless there can be significant harms of detaining someone against their will. Kate may be very frightened and anxious and feel a real lack of control over her situation. She may distrust those who are seeking to help her, which could have adverse long-term consequences. Consideration should be given to alternative means of providing care and treatment which she would accept. A psychiatric outreach team may be able to become involved.

Compulsory detention and treatment is an infringement of personal autonomy. However, severe compulsive obsessive disorder would impair Kate's ability to make an autonomous choice about how she behaves and the care and treatment she requires. If she can get effective treatment to ameliorate her distress and harmful effects of her disorder, and which thus may ultimately enhance her autonomy, then the harms of detention may be justified.

 Key Points

- Mental health legislation enables compulsory detention for assessment and treatment of a mental disorder.
- Whether someone should be detained against their wishes depends on the benefits to be achieved balanced against the harms of detention.
- The aim should be to minimise the undesirable effects of mental disorder and maximise the safety and well-being of patients.

CASE 48: APPROPRIATE AND EFFECTIVE TREATMENT UNDER THE MENTAL HEALTH ACT

Robson is in his 40s and has paranoid schizophrenia. He has been assessed to lack capacity with respect to decision making about treatment for his condition. Over the past 20 years he has been detained under Section 3 of the Mental Health Act (MHA 1983, as amended 2007) many times but has never gained insight into his illness and has not engaged with treatment. He is currently detained at an inpatient unit. In the past and during his current admission he has been treated with a depot antipsychotic medication which is administered by an injection every 2 weeks, but because he resists, he needs to be restrained to administer the injection.

The treating team considers that the current depot medication prevents his mental state from deteriorating. However, they are now considering whether to try clozapine, which is recommended by the National Institute for Health and Care Excellence (NICE) to treat patients with 'treatment-resistant' schizophrenia, i.e., if they have not responded to two different antipsychotic medications. Clozapine would have to be administered orally, and Robson would have to have regular blood tests to monitor him as the treatment has serious and potentially fatal side effects. The team hopes that this new medication may result in an improvement in Robson's mental health and enables him to gain insight into his condition, thus promoting engagement with his treatment plan.

Question

- Should a person be compulsorily detained under the MHA if the treatment provided does not improve his mental condition?

ANSWER 48

Article 5 ECHR states that 'everyone has the right to liberty'; however, a person can be lawfully deprived of his liberty if conditions of the MHA are met. Detention for treatment under Section 3 requires that

- the person is suffering from a mental disorder of a nature or degree which warrants detention *and*
- appropriate medical treatment is available *and*
- detention is necessary for the health and safety of the person detained or for the protection of others *and*
- treatment cannot be provided unless detained.

Medical treatment is defined widely and includes nursing, psychological intervention and rehabilitation (Section 145 MHA 1983). It must be given for the purpose of alleviating or preventing a worsening of a mental disorder or one or more of its symptoms or manifestations. Whether medical treatment available to the patient is 'appropriate' requires a balanced and holistic judgement and factors such as the patient's physical health, age, culture and ethnicity, religious beliefs, the location of the available treatment and the patient's views about what treatment works and does not, should be considered (MHA Code of Practice 2015).

Robson has been detained in order that medical treatment can be given to treat his schizophrenia. But is it appropriate to detain him to treat him either with medication which does not seem to improve his mental disorder, or to try new medication with potentially harmful side effects?

Robson cannot make an informed choice about treatment because he lacks insight. The current treatment regime has not improved his mental disorder and there are clear harms of detaining and restraining him against his will. Nevertheless the depot medication could be considered effective since it seems to have prevented his condition from getting worse and avoids future harms through his disengagement with services and self-neglect. There may be an argument for trialling clozapine since it may improve his mental disorder rather than merely prevent deterioration. However, the potential benefits of clozapine need to be balanced against the harmful side effects of this medication and restraining Robson to enable treatment. If Robson makes some improvement and is compliant with the medication, he could then be treated in the community with close monitoring from a specialist outreach team.

Detention for treatment is a significant threat to individual autonomy, liberty and dignity, and it could be argued that there is no justification to detain someone for treatment for the mental disorder unless that treatment improves the mental disorder. However, 'purpose is not the same as likelihood' (MHA Code of Practice 2015, paragraph 23.4). The Code of Practice states that medical treatment which aims merely to prevent a disorder from worsening is unlikely to be appropriate in cases where normal treatment approaches would aim to alleviate the patient's condition significantly. However, for some patients with persistent and severe mental disorders, management of the undesirable effects of their disorder may be the most that can realistically be hoped for.

 Key Points

- Appropriate medical treatment must be available for a person detained under Section 3 MHA.
- The purpose of medical treatment is to alleviate, or prevent a worsening of, a mental disorder or one or more of its symptoms or manifestations.

CASE 49: MEDICAL TREATMENT FOR PATIENTS WITH A MENTAL HEALTH DISORDER

Simon, a 27-year-old man with schizophrenia, is admitted with severe psychosis which is manifested by auditory hallucinations telling him to harm himself. He has refused antipsychotic medication in the community and has been sectioned for treatment of his mental disorder under Section 3 of the Mental Health Act (MHA).

During his admission he develops pneumonia, requiring intravenous antibiotics, which he refuses, stating he 'does not want a drip because it might be poisoned'.

The team has a dilemma – although they can treat his psychosis without his consent under the MHA, how should they address his refusal of treatment for his pneumonia?

Questions

- In what circumstances can physical problems be treated under the MHA?
- How does the Mental Capacity Act (MCA) apply to patients under section?

ANSWER 49

The challenge in this case is that Simon is refusing treatments for two distinct problems – a mental health problem and a physical problem. There are two relevant pieces of legislation – the Mental Health Act 1983 (amended 2007) and the Mental Capacity Act 2005.

Mental Health Act 1983, as amended 2007

Simon has a 'disorder or disability of the mind' which appears to impair his ability to make decisions regarding treatment of his psychosis, and his thoughts of self-harm pose a risk to him. Therefore, it would be appropriate for him to be detained under Section 3 MHA to receive treatment for his psychosis. The MHA (Section 63) provides that medical treatment (apart from some treatments like electroconvulsive therapy) for the mental disorder can be given without consent if necessary. Approval by a second opinion appointed doctor (SOAD) is required after 3 months.

The MHA also permits treatment of physical problems without consent but only if the 'treatment is part of, or ancillary to, treatment for mental disorder' (MHA Code of Practice 2015, 13.37). Examples include treating wounds self-inflicted as a result of mental disorder, or treating side effects of antipsychotic medications.

However, in Simon's case his infection is not a result of his mental illness. Given that his psychosis preceded his infection, it is unlikely that antibiotics would significantly alter the course of his psychosis. Therefore, antibiotics are neither part of, nor ancillary to, the treatment for his mental illness, and it would not be lawful to administer antibiotics under the MHA.

Mental Capacity Act 2005

Despite Simon's diagnosis of schizophrenia he may still have capacity to refuse intravenous treatment for his infection. As with any patient refusing treatment, Simon should be assessed according to the MCA to establish whether he has capacity to make such a decision (Case 26). The fact that he has a mental disorder and is sectioned under the MHA does not automatically mean he lacks capacity, since all patients (16 and over) should be assumed to have capacity unless it can be demonstrated otherwise (*Re C (Adult: refusal of treatment)* 1994).

In this case, Simon's psychotic belief that his drip might be poisoned suggests he may not be able to understand and weigh up the information being given to him because his decision is unfounded and due to psychosis. This is in contrast to someone who may make an unwise decision to refuse treatment based on his values. This should be further explored. If he is considered to lack capacity to refuse antibiotics he should be treated in accordance with his best interests. The authority for treatment is the Mental Capacity Act not the Mental Health Act.

Determining whether intravenous antibiotics would be in Simon's best interests may be challenging, as best interests extend beyond medical interests and include social, psychological and religious factors. Practical issues might also warrant consideration, for example whether he would require restraint to insert a cannula for antibiotics. It may be decided that in Simon's case although intravenous antibiotics would be more effective, restraining him and repeatedly inserting cannulas might not be in his best interests, and so an oral antibiotic would be a less invasive (albeit less effective) suitable alternative.

🔑	Key Points

- If a patient is formally detained under the MHA, treatment may be given without consent for their mental disorder and for physical problems where the treatment is part of or ancillary to the treatment for their mental disorder.
- If a patient is refusing treatment for a physical problem unrelated to their mental disorder, their capacity to make such a refusal should be assessed according to the MCA.
- If they are deemed to have capacity their refusal should be respected, and if they lack capacity they should be treated in accordance with their best interests.

CASE 50: CONFLICT IN TREATMENT AIMS

John is a 56-year-old university lecturer. He has been diagnosed with inoperable lung cancer and has been admitted to an oncology ward to receive intensive radiotherapy. John also had an episode of psychosis in his 20s which required him to be sectioned under the Mental Health Act. Fortunately, following this episode he has remained well and has had a very successful career. His main concern when learning of his cancer diagnosis was that he would not get a chance to finish the current projects he was currently involved with at the university, including setting up a bursary.

Shortly after arriving on the oncology ward to commence radiotherapy he began displaying signs of psychosis. He had flight of ideas and pressured speech and was quite agitated. Multiple investigations ruled out a physical cause for these new symptoms, and in light of his previous medical history oral antipsychotic medication was started.

Over the next few days his mental state worsened. He began making abusive phone calls to his family, removing his oxygen, telling ward staff he was cured of his cancer and that he was being awarded a Nobel prize. Whilst happy to continue with his radiotherapy, John stopped taking the antipsychotic medication prescribed by the psychiatrist. He was aware of some of the detrimental effects of his psychosis, but denied he needed medicine to resolve it and was adamant he just needed to be left in peace so that he could focus on his university work.

As an articulate, intelligent man, John had insight that some of his beliefs and behaviours were characteristic of psychosis and hid them from the doctors; he denied saying he was cured of cancer when confronted by the consultant looking after him. His consultant is concerned – he is reluctant to continue giving radiotherapy in light of his worsening mental health, but delaying treatment for his cancer may ultimately hasten disease progression.

Questions

- Is it more important for John to stay on the oncology ward and receive radiotherapy or be sectioned and treated for his psychosis?
- Who should be involved in this decision?

ANSWER 50

If John is detained under the Mental Health Act and moved to a specialist psychiatric hospital, he would not be able to continue his life-prolonging radiotherapy treatment, which can be administered only by specialist trained nurses within an oncology department. Due to the nature of psychosis, if he is sectioned it would be most likely that he would then spend the last period of his life in a mental health ward.

In contrast to Case 49 where a patient detained under the Mental Health Act was refusing treatment for a physical condition, John is not yet sectioned and despite his psychosis and refusal of treatment for his mental health disorder he has not yet refused treatment for his physical disorder. Because of this there would currently not be an indication for detention as he is not considered a risk to himself or others.

However, without effective treatment for his psychosis there is a good chance that his mental health will deteriorate significantly. Risks with this include the possibility that he would be unable to understand information provided about physical treatments (although his capacity would need to be assessed separately from his mental health) or that his belief that he is cured from cancer becomes more fixed and he could subsequently refuse radiotherapy.

The conflict in treatment would arise if John's mental health prevented him from engaging with treatment for his lung cancer, which could ultimately be fatal. If this occurred then it would seem reasonable to section him for treatment of the psychosis, as he would then be considered a harm to himself due to his refusal of radiotherapy. Being sectioned and treated for his mental health disorder may lead to an amelioration of his psychosis, but could be a traumatic experience and would still result in a potentially fatal delay in radiotherapy.

Ethical issues

Sectioning John under the Mental Health Act could disrupt the therapeutic relationship that exists with John's oncology team. As treatment reduces his psychosis he would be able to take some pleasure in finishing the projects important to him, even if not receiving radiotherapy would result in an untimely death. Remaining psychotic would undoubtedly prevent this from happening.

 Key Points

- Mental disorder may impact on a person's ability to understand a physical health issue and the need for treatment.
- There may be conflict when deciding whether treatment for a physical disorder or a mental disorder should take priority.
- The decision whether to detain a patient to treat a mental health disorder in the context of a terminal illness can be ethically challenging.

CASE 51: TREATMENT FOR EATING DISORDERS

Samantha is a 27-year-old who has suffered with anorexia nervosa since her teenage years. She has had recurrent admissions to specialist eating-disorders units under Section 3 MHA, and on a number of occasions has required feeding with a nasogastric tube against her wishes. During each admission her weight would improve slightly, she would be discharged, attend outpatient psychotherapy sessions, but subsequently relapse, lose weight and require readmission.

On this occasion she has been admitted with dangerously low electrolyte and glucose levels due to her anorexia. She has a body mass index of just 13 and is critically unwell. She has refused all treatment and therefore is being treated under Section 63 MHA. She initially had a nasogastric tube inserted (requiring restraint and sedation for the insertion) but has subsequently pulled it out and is currently refusing further nasogastric feeding.

The team is seeking advice as to whether they should continue to attempt nasogastric feeding in her case.

Questions
- What is the justification for providing nasogastric feeding to patients with anorexia without their consent?
- What factors should be taken into account when making decisions around appropriateness of treatment in such cases?

ANSWER 51

Samantha has been admitted under Section 3 MHA. Her anorexia constitutes a 'disorder or disability of the mind' and appropriate medical treatment is necessary for her own health and safety. As she is refusing treatment (and such treatment can be provided only if she is detained), an admission under Section 3 is necessary.

Appropriate treatment which could be given to Samantha without her consent could include psychotherapy and psychiatric medications but may also extend to nasogastric feeding. 'Treatment' as referred to in the MHA can include medical treatment for 'alleviating, or preventing a worsening of, a mental disorder or one or more of its symptoms or manifestations' (MHA Code of Practice 2015). Nasogastric feeding in anorexic patients treats the physical manifestations of their mental disorder (i.e., treats the malnutrition which results from the patient's lack of food intake). It may also maintain and improve their physical health enough to allow them to gain the cognitive ability to participate in psychological therapies, and weight gain may even be psychologically therapeutic in itself.

Samantha should be treated in accordance with her best interests. However, these are difficult to determine. Both possible courses of action here – deciding not to give Samantha nasogastric feeding, or alternatively forcing her to have nasogastric feeding against her will – have the potential to result in harm. Deciding not to provide feeding could result in her death, which would fail to give appropriate weight to the sanctity of life principle. On the other hand, forcing Samantha to have nasogastric feeding fails to respect her autonomy, and whilst her ability to make autonomous decisions may be adversely affected by her mental illness, there is still an inherent moral good in taking into account her wishes. Additionally, the need for physical restraint could amount to inhuman and degrading treatment contravening Article 3 ECHR, although this is unlikely if it can be convincingly shown to be a therapeutic necessity.

Although Samantha has a mental illness, it is important that the doctors still involve her in decisions regarding her care as much as possible. The views of her family and friends may be valuable, particularly given the support she may require from them during her treatment. Furthermore, the likely success of the various treatment options should be considered, as this will be important in assessing whether the proposed benefits are sufficiently great to justify the potential harms that may be associated with each treatment option.

 Key Points

- Nasogastric feeding is recognised as a potential treatment that may be enforced under Section 63 MHA for patients with eating disorders.
- The appropriateness of enforced nasogastric feeding must be considered. Factors such as the patient's wishes, previous treatments, the need for restraint and the patient's prognosis should be taken into account.

CASE 52: PERSONAL IDENTITY

Melissa, a 30-year-old woman, had always been hard-working and conscientious but had often doubted her abilities and worried about her performance at school, university and work. She was shy and nervous in new situations. She had suffered from depressive episodes since her final year at university and had counselling on various occasions, which she found helpful. Recently, in the space of a few months, she was promoted to a stressful position at work, her mother died unexpectedly, and her boyfriend of 4 years left her having met someone else. She felt permanently tired, lacking in motivation and enthusiasm, and was apt to burst into tears at the slightest provocation. She sought psychiatric help, was diagnosed with depression and was prescribed a course of antidepressant medication. Melissa responded well to the medication and stopped feeling tired and unhappy and unable to cope. She stopped worrying about her abilities and her performance at work and found her job much more enjoyable. Where previously she had felt shy or nervous in new situations, she felt more confident and convinced of her own ability to contribute.

Sometime after the course of medication finished, Melissa found herself returning to her previous state. She was less self-confident and more concerned about whether her abilities were adequate for the job she had to do. She was not prone to crying or permanently tired as she had been when the medication was prescribed, but she felt shy and nervous and unable to express herself as fully as she had done when on the medication. She felt lacking in motivation and 'flat'.

Eventually, Melissa asked her psychiatrist whether she could be prescribed the medication again, saying that it was only when on the medication that she had felt her true self. She now realised that the shy, nervous worrier she had previously been was not really her at all, and she wanted to give her real self the chance to come through again.

Questions

- Should Melissa have been given medication in the first instance, given that she had previously found non-pharmacological treatment for her depressive episodes to be successful?
- Should she be prescribed the medication again?
- What does it mean to say that one has a 'true' or 'real' self, and to say that one's real self can only be expressed with the aid of medication?

ANSWER 52

The simple answer to this case is that antidepressant medication should be prescribed when someone meets the clinical requirements for a diagnosis of depression, and not otherwise. Clearly there are degrees of depression and scope for differences of opinion between health professionals about when treatment is required and what type of treatment should be given. If the medication does more than simply relieve the psychiatric condition, by improving Melissa's normal functioning, is it fair to deprive her of this additional effect which she sees as essential?

This case raises difficult and fundamental questions about the nature of personal identity. The idea of a real or true self is one that we are all familiar with but is hard to explain.

- Are there some core personality traits that define us?
- What happens if they change?
- Do I become a different person?
- Who decides what is our 'real' self?
- Is it something that only we can know or is it something that other people could decide?
- Would Melissa's friends and family say that she had become a different person when on medication, or would they say that she was still Melissa, just more outgoing and self-confident than she had previously been?

The question of who decides what is an individual's real self is clearly important in clinical decision making. On what moral basis can a health professional override someone's personal view of themselves? Is an integral part of respect for autonomy an acceptance that all individuals should be able to determine what kind of a person they are or should be?

Another important point that could affect the way an individual is judged is whether it matters what means are used to change personality. Some people may instinctively feel that changing personality traits using chemical means is wrong. It might seem that although Melissa thinks she is her true self when on medication, this cannot be correct. The medication is creating an artificial effect, which masks Melissa's true self. But now imagine that Melissa gets a new boyfriend, achieves success at work, and makes use of behavioural therapies aimed at improving self-esteem. She might end up feeling the same as she did on medication. How is it different from taking the medication if the end result is the same? If it is possible for Melissa to be her true self without medication, why should she be made to take a longer, harder route, which might have less chance of succeeding? The potential for changing personality through medication also has implications for cases where individuals make decisions about their future treatment. If Melissa would make a different decision on medication than off it, which of these decisions should be respected?

There are no straightforward answers to any of the myriad questions raised by this case, nor does recourse to generic ethical principles assist. In considering the problems identified, readers should be alert to their intuitive response, attempt to analyse the basis for it and monitor it for inconsistency.

 Key Points

- Personal identity can be affected by many different things, e.g., medication and alcohol. It can also change throughout life.
- It can be difficult to assess whether a person's 'true' self changes with psychiatric illness.

CASE 53: SELF-HARM

While you are working in Accident and Emergency (A&E) on a Sunday afternoon you are asked to see Naomi, a 15-year-old 'regular attendee'. No one else wants to see her. Naomi is very subdued and has a deep cut along the top of her thigh. Her legs and arms are criss-crossed with scars. She asks you to just hurry up and 'practise your suturing' so that she can get home in time for a family roast. You are concerned about her blasé attitude to her injuries. Looking through the notes you discover this is her 18th attendance to A&E in the past 6 months for similar treatment. You try to talk to Naomi about why she self-harms. Naomi is surprised, as no one has asked her this before.

Questions

- How should patients who self-harm be managed?
- What can be done to prevent a 'revolving door' system of hospital admissions?

ANSWER 53

Health and Social Care Information Centre data shows that the number of hospital admissions due to self-harm has risen from 16,417 in 2010 to 25,580 in 2014. The prevalence of self-harm is actually estimated to be much higher since many patients will not require medical treatment for their injuries. Despite this the amount of government spending on adolescent mental health has decreased. Self-harm is different from attempted suicide as there is no desire to die. It is a phenomenon found mainly among 12–25-year-olds and is often an indication of underlying mental illness or emotional instability and is regarded as a maladaptive coping mechanism. The tangible physical pain of self-harm is often easier to cope with than emotional distress. Some of the reasons thought to be involved in the rise of self-harm are the increased pressure on adolescents to fit in and succeed, the use of social media and constant pressure to achieve good exam results.

> **!** **Examples of self-harm include**
>
> - Cutting and scratching
> - Burning and scalding
> - Ingestion of toxic substances

It can be difficult to know how to help effectively young people who present to A&E or their GP with self-inflicted wounds. Many injuries will be superficial and require only minimal medical input, yet these patients will often become regular attendees at hospitals and will undoubtedly benefit from psychological support.

There is a wide range of services across the UK for people who self-harm, but there is no significant data on the efficacy of the different therapies. It is understood that good communication between the patient and their doctor is paramount in developing a rapport to ensure that the patient feels comfortable engaging with ongoing support, which might include psychological or psychiatric services. The patient should be encouraged to tell their family and school teacher about the difficulties they are having with coping.

Health professionals need to have a greater understanding of the cause and prevalence of self-harm to prevent a revolving door into A&E. Promoting trust between the doctor and patient will enable individuals to feel valued and help them make autonomous decisions regarding their own health. This in turn should make them feel more in control of their situation and emotions. Listening to them empathetically can help them feel that they are understood and so prevent the need to release their psychological pain through physical outlets. People who self-harm have a right to be treated with respect and not be discriminated against.

The report 'Truth Hurts: The Report of the National Enquiry into Self Harm amongst Young People' (2006) recommended that health professionals should 're-connect to their core professional skills and values: empathy, understanding, non-judgemental listening and respect for individuals'.

> **🔑** **Key Points**
>
> - Patients who self-harm need to be treated sensitively. They are vulnerable patients who require understanding, confidentiality and care.
> - Patients who self-harm are entitled to the same level of care for their physical wounds as any other individual. Their refusal of psychological help should not impact on provision of any other necessary treatment.

CASE 54: COVERT MEDICATION

As a newly qualified GP you have taken over the responsibility of looking after the four local care homes in your area. Having one person from the practice doing this ensures that there is good continuity of care for patients with complex needs. The GP can also get to know their patients, the relatives and the care home staff well.

During your weekly visit to Rosemary Cottage Care Home you are asked to rewrite and sign a letter stating that the staff can continue giving Doris her anti-psychotic medication covertly. In the past Doris had suffered with schizophrenia, and although her hallucinations have not been evident for many years, she is still prone to periods of increased agitation and paranoia. These seem to have improved since starting a small dose of risperidone every night which was initiated by her previous GP.

Although you had known that Doris was receiving this medication you had not been aware that it was being crushed up and given with her evening cocoa. On the few occasions you had seen Doris for other reasons she had always come across as calm and able to make her own decisions.

Questions

- Is covert medication ever justifiable?
- Should Doris be told that she has been given medication with a view to negotiating informed consent?

ANSWER 54

Legal issues

Covert medication may be justifiable for a patient who *lacks capacity*, in his best interests, because it may help improve both physical and mental health. The Mental Capacity Act 2005 emphasises the need for facilitation and enhancement of capacity, and covert medication might be seen to help achieve those objectives. Neither the Royal College of Psychiatrists nor the Nursing and Midwifery Council rules out covert medication as an option. Mental Welfare Commission for Scotland has also drawn up specific criteria for the administration of covert medication.[*]

The Royal College of Psychiatrists statement on covert administration of medicines recognises that there are times when severely incapacitated patients can neither consent nor refuse treatment. In these circumstances, treatment should be made available according to the patient's best interests and administered in the least restrictive fashion, which may, in exceptional situations, require administration of medicines within food without the patient's awareness of this being done.[†]

Ethical issues

Administering covert medication to patients who have the capacity to make healthcare decisions fails to respect their autonomy. It deprives them of the ability to decide whether or not to take the medication and is unjustifiably paternalistic. Although Doris is no doubt calmer and happier with the medication, the issue of whether she has capacity to make this particular decision regarding medication needs to be further explored. The fact that Doris is unaware that she is taking risperidone inevitably compromises the assessment of her capacity because the purpose, relative benefits and harms of either taking medication or refusing it cannot be explored adequately. To assess her capacity properly necessitates disclosure that she is already taking risperidone.

The benefits of disclosing include the following:

- Maximising autonomy. Healthcare professionals have a duty to empower patients to make informed decisions about their care.
- Continuing with covert medication may be denying Doris the opportunity for better treatment after re-assessment by a mental health specialist.
- The side effects of medication could be monitored better.
- Continuing with covert medication may compromise her relationship with professionals in the future if she were to discover that she was being given medication without her knowledge.

The harms of disclosing include the following:

- Disclosure may lead to refusal of medication with detrimental consequences to Doris's mental state and possible risk of harm to others.
- Disclosure would potentially put the medical practice and care home in conflict with services and lead to distrust by the families of other residents.
- The upset and disruption of a situation that is being managed at present, albeit imperfectly. For example, if Doris then refused medication and deteriorated this may lead to hospital admission and a worsening of her mental health.

---

[*] http://www.mwcscot.org.uk/media/140485/covert_medication_finalnov_13.pdf
[†] https://www.rcpsych.ac.uk/pdf/covertmedicine.full.pdf

From the GP's perspective, merely continuing with the collusion without reassessment would impact on their professional integrity.

 Key Points

- Honesty is the basis of an effective therapeutic relationship.
- Covert medication should not be given to anyone who has capacity, even if they are detained under the Mental Health Act.
- Those giving covert medication should ensure that it is still pharmacologically effective in its altered form.

SECTION 9

ETHICS AND LAW IN CLINICAL PRACTICE: PUBLIC HEALTH

CASE 55: PATIENTS' RESPONSIBILITY FOR HEALTH AND RESOURCE ALLOCATION

Imagine there are three patients in your clinic. They all need coronary artery bypass surgery, but only one of them can have it due to limited resources.

Patient 1

Aziz is a fellow doctor with special skills in neonatology. He is 50 years old and has a wife and three small children. He has been taking his medication sensibly for the past 5 years. However, he is still a heavy smoker and has two pints of Guinness a day.

Patient 2

Bertie is an 80-year-old man who served in the Second World War and was commended for his bravery. His wife recently died and he does not have any children. He has also been compliant with his medication. He has never smoked and only has the occasional whiskey.

Patient 3

Chloe is a 30-year-old woman with a genetic disorder that has caused a learning disability and early heart disease. She lives in a care home and is visited often by her family. She is much loved by everyone who knows her and is often seen in her local village selling cakes for charity.

Questions

- Who should you prioritise to receive the surgery?
- What are the ethics behind resource allocation in the NHS?
- Should priority be given to patients who are not to blame for their illness?

ANSWER 55

With ever-increasing frequency the media are highlighting inequalities in the modern-day NHS: newly licensed drugs are available according to a postcode lottery, waiting lists for hip operations vary from area to area and potential life-prolonging treatments are being denied on the basis that they are not cost-effective. When the NHS was created in 1948, the Beveridge Report stated that the ideal plan would be 'a health service providing full preventative and curative treatment of every kind to every citizen without exceptions, without remuneration limit and without an economic barrier at any point to delay recourse to it'. In an ideal world access to healthcare would be available to everyone and it would be free. As this is not the case there has to be a compromise between providing an adequate level of healthcare at a cost that consumers find acceptable, and therefore 'rationing' has to be implemented. Rationing has been defined as when 'anyone is denied an intervention that everyone would agree would do them good and which they would like to have'.

The way in which healthcare resources should be rationed is a topic of constant debate and multiple theories. It is an extremely complex area of medical ethics and this answer shall only address the basics. The NHS is continuously underfunded, and hospital managers have to find ways of implementing money-saving strategies. Deciding who should receive medical treatment is a difficult ethical quandary. Doctors take an oath to do the best they can for the patients they care for. Healthcare, as with most things in life, is not inexhaustible. How then is it best to judge who should receive healthcare and who must wait? Which illnesses are more deserving of the newest drugs? Which patients? There are several ethical theories regarding resource allocation and healthcare funding.

Ethical issues

Consequentialism advocates the provision of medical treatment which produces the best overall consequences, and perhaps this would include taking into account the benefits that an individual would give to society by having treatment. In this case, Aziz may go on to save the lives of lots of babies, and he also has a wife and children to support. On the other hand, it could be argued that Bertie is most deserving of the surgery since he has looked after his health, has been a responsible member of the public and has previously risked his life to save his country. But he is 80 and unlikely to live much longer even with the operation.

The most common way of rationing is based on whether treatment is more or less beneficial to the person receiving it – QALY theory.

> **! Quality adjusted life-years (QALYs)**
>
> The QALY is a measurement designed to assess the number of years and the quality of those years that a treatment would give a patient. A year of life with perfect health is given the value 1, and years of life with imperfect health are given a value between 0 and 1. Treatment is considered beneficial if it improves the number of good-quality life-years a person or population has. Each given treatment will have a financial cost which can then be calculated as cost per quality life-years gained.

QALY theory has several problems. QALYs can be inherently ageist since an older person will have fewer quality life-years to gain. They do not take multiple comorbidities into account. A QALY is extremely subjective – what one person may experience as an increase in quality of life, another person will not. It also denies treatment to people who are suffering greatly but in whom treatment will only marginally improve suffering. It denies good-quality care for terminally ill people since they will not have any years left to benefit from the treatment. In the scenarios, Bertie would not be favoured for treatment due to his age. John Harris would say that this patient has had his 'fair innings'.

Another theory of how to allocate medical treatment is based on taking the patient's lifestyle and social worth into consideration. This implies that a patient who is responsible for their own ill health is less worthy of receiving treatment than someone who is blameless. Suggested ideas include denying operations to patients who are clinically obese or who are still smoking, factors that some consider patients should be able to control. Aziz would therefore be less likely to be allocated the surgery since his need for it stems from his drinking and smoking. Chloe, in contrast, requires the surgery due to her genetic makeup, which is no fault of her own.

But is it justifiable to limit resource allocation based on patient-related factors? Should the obese patient who has not dieted or taken exercise be entitled to their new hips and knees on the NHS? Is the smoker with cardiac disease entitled to his angioplasty, and should former alcoholics be allowed new livers? To what extent should patients be held responsible for their own health and be made to be morally responsible for the mistakes they make? Should a doctor continue to treat the patient who misses hospital appointments and is non-compliant with medication? The GMC has stated that it is unethical to withhold or otherwise change the treatment a patient receives as a result of their 'lifestyle'.

Is it fair to ask doctors to assess a patient's 'social worth'? Many argue that doctors should assess patients merely on clinical need. There is an argument about whether it is justifiable to treat the identifiable patient rather than reserving resources for potential future patients. Certainly for doctors it is easier to prescribe expensive medication to the person in pain and suffering sitting in front of them than to refuse them treatment on the premise that another unidentifiable individual will require it.

> If you have a management role or responsibility, you will often have to make judgements about competing demands on available resources. When making these decisions, you must consider your primary duty for the care and safety of patients. You must take account of any local or national policies which set out agreed criteria for access to particular treatments and allocating resources.
>
> General Medical Council, Leadership and Management for All Doctors (2012)

 Key Points

- Need, benefit and justice may lead to different results as to which patient should be prioritised for treatment.
- A QALY is one of the most commonly used methods of assessing whether treatment is cost-effective. It compares the improvement in quality of life and the number of life-years gained after giving a specific treatment.
- More often patients are encouraged to take responsibility for their own health.

CASE 56: MANAGING PATIENT EXPECTATIONS

Pippa is a 33-year-old barrister. She has had asthma since she was a child. Over the past few days she has developed a viral illness. She is now wheezy and short of breath. It is Saturday afternoon and her local GP surgery is closed until Monday. She is worried that she has a big case to prepare for court on Monday. She does not want to attend A&E as her symptoms are not serious enough yet. However, she does feel it would be useful to be able to book a GP appointment at her local surgery so she can be assessed properly.

Mabel is 89. She is housebound and relies on a relative to take her to the surgery. She has a history of Parkinson's disease, ischaemic heart disease and diabetes. Each day she takes 14 different medicines which her local chemist puts into blister packs for her and delivers once a month. She has seen the same GP at her surgery for the last 15 years. Due to her complex needs her GP always allows extra time to see her.

Questions

- Should GP surgeries provide appointments 7 days a week?
- Why has there been an increase in demand for primary healthcare services?

ANSWER 56

A recent report by the King's Fund has shown an unprecedented slowdown in spending on the NHS over the last 2 years. Sadly, cracks are beginning to appear in terms of financial deficit and consequently patient care. The media headlines over the last few years have also helped promulgate a growing public dissatisfaction with the NHS as waiting lists for hospital services grow ever longer and the ability to book a GP appointment within a week becomes increasingly difficult. There are myriad different reasons for an increase in demand for care, including an aging population, advances in medical technologies and available treatments. Combined with financial cuts to health and social care and government propaganda on 'patients' rights' to healthcare, this has created a demand which is unable to be met.

Recently the debate over 24/7 access to primary care services has fuelled many hours of political hyperbole and reels of newspaper print. However, the simple truth of the matter is that there are insufficient healthcare professionals to staff a fully functional primary care service 24 hours a day. Despite promises to spend money on providing more GPs, in 2015 one-third of GP trainee positions remain unfilled across the UK following the first round of recruitment (*Pulse*, April 2015). Being a GP is currently not a desirable career path for junior doctors and others in the profession are either taking early retirement or emigrating due to the increased workload and job pressures. Since the number of GPs available is unlikely to improve, the question posed by government should be whether it is preferable to have increased access to a doctor by enforcing extended opening hours or to try and improve patient care and continuity by keeping as many doctors as possible working core opening hours.

There are good reasons for these decisions to be made on an individual area basis. For example, a GP practice providing care to a high proportion of university students and young professionals may best be able to serve their specific population by being open later and at the weekends. This makes healthcare more accessible around working hours and in general a young population are going to present with more acute problems and have less complex needs. In contrast a GP practice with a primarily elderly population will benefit from more staff being available during core opening hours so that the patients can have better access to a specific doctor who will understand them and their medical history. The difficulty with this as a model is that acute illness or sudden deterioration in a chronic disease does not fit into a '9–5' model.

Other ways to improve access to general practice and urgent care are also being explored by NHS England in their document 'Putting Patients First'. It highlights core aims as being to

- Provide better support for people to self-care
- Help people with urgent care needs to get the right advice in the right place, the first time
- Provide highly responsive urgent care services outside of hospital so people no longer choose to queue in A&E
- Ensure that those people with more serious or life-threatening emergency needs receive treatment in centres with the right facilities and expertise in order to maximise chances of survival and a good recovery*

Recent articles in the *Daily Telegraph* and the *Guardian* listed some of the more bizarre reasons why people book GP appointments, including asking how to stop their cat from

---

* http://www.england.nhs.uk/wp-content/uploads/2014/04/ppf-1415-1617-wa.pdf

scratching their furniture, complaining that their skin is too soft, requesting a prescription for shampoo to make hair shiny and asking for help to write their CV. Although most of the examples given were extreme, they highlight the ever-increasing demands being put upon general practice for non-medical issues. One of the more optimistic ways of looking at this is that the GP is a trusted member of the community who is able to give pastoral care and advice on a wide range of topics. A more pessimistic view is that the GP is free at the 'point of abuse' for both patients and organisations such as schools who may require proof of illness for childhood absence.

Greater patient responsibility for health and the provision of healthcare services based on public need rather than want is one way to address unrealistic demands on general practice. This will ensure that the people who do need to see a GP can access a timely appointment and could therefore prevent an ongoing increase in A&E attendances.

Key Points
• Increasing demands on GP services which cannot be met has a knock-on effect on A&E attendances. • Local provision of appropriate alternative pastoral services is required to address non-medical needs.

CASE 57: REQUESTS FOR EXPENSIVE MEDICAL TREATMENT

Harriet, a 45-year-old nursery school teacher with two young children, has ovarian cancer. She has had two courses of chemotherapy and a total hysterectomy and bilateral oophorectomy. She found the chemotherapy really tiring and had a lot of side effects. Since she was diagnosed 18 months ago she has not been able to work. A follow-up positron emission tomography (PET) scan demonstrated that she had a further lesion in her breast. A biopsy confirmed this to be a primary breast cancer. Her oncologist suggests a third course of chemotherapy. Harriet has heard about a new wonder drug which has been discussed on the news. The drug is reported to increase the curative rates of breast cancer in women under 50. However, there are few randomised drug trial data on the drug. It is also extremely expensive. Harriet wants to know more about it and whether or not her doctor will prescribe it for her.

Questions

- Is there a legal requirement to provide treatment on the National Health Service (NHS)?
- How is the NHS funded?
- What is the role of the National Institute for Health and Care Excellence (NICE)?
- Should doctors be the gatekeepers of resource allocation?

ANSWER 57

On 5 July 1948, the NHS changed from a vision into a reality. The founding principles were that it would provide free healthcare to everyone resident in the UK: from preventative to curative to palliative medicine. The NHS was, and still is, financed from central taxation. However, with the increase in life expectancy, advances in medical technologies and increased cost of drugs, the NHS is struggling to fulfil its original principles. To what extent, however, is the NHS obliged by law to provide healthcare?

The National Health Service Act 2006 imposes a duty on the Secretary of State for Health to 'continue the promotion in England of a comprehensive health service designed to secure improvement (a) in the physical and mental health of the people of England, and (b) in the prevention, diagnosis and treatment of illness'. The statutory duty is to promote a comprehensive health service rather than to provide one, and human and resource limitations mean that a comprehensive health service may never be achievable.

With the introduction of the Human Rights Act 1998, there have been a number of cases which have questioned whether the NHS contravenes patients' human rights by failing to provide them with a specific treatment or by making them wait too long for treatment. Although Article 2 ECHR provides a right to life, this does not equate to a right to medical treatment, although the State must act reasonably in how it allocates resources.

The National Institute for Health and Care Excellence (NICE) was founded in 1999. Its role, as an independent organisation, is to give guidance to the public and to healthcare professionals on the use of new and existing treatments and procedures within the NHS. It examines the clinical benefits of new and expensive treatments and advises NHS funding bodies under what conditions and in which circumstances these drugs should be prescribed.

Local clinical commissioning groups (CCGs) allocate funding for their area, and this explains why some treatments may be better funded in some areas rather than others. Where funding is not routinely offered, individual funding requests may be made by the relevant clinician to a patient individual needs (PIN) panel comprising clinicians and lay people. They must be able to demonstrate that their case is unique or exceptional to justify funding. Due to the present financial state of the NHS, most of these requests are denied. The only exception to this method of funding is for specialist cancer drugs where an application is made to a national funding body.

Deciding which patients should be provided with expensive treatment is an ethical minefield, particularly when there is a limited budget. An expensive treatment for one person may be considered unethical if the money could be spent on less expensive treatment for more people.

In contrast, the law provides that a particular treatment does not have to be provided if it can be rationally argued that it is not cost-effective or of proven clinical benefit.

 Key Points

- Not all treatments can be provided, even if clinically indicated, due to limited NHS resources.
- Treatment and medication prescribed should be cost-effective.
- NICE is an organisation which provides information about the cost-effectiveness of new and existing medication.

CASE 58: PROPHYLACTIC SURGERY

Diane is a 34-year-old police officer. She has been referred to your surgical clinic by her GP as recent genetic tests have revealed that Diane carries the BRCA 1 gene. These were performed by the local genetics department as her mum and older sister had both developed breast cancer in their 40s. Diane has come to request that you list her for surgery to remove both breasts in an attempt to prevent her from developing breast cancer.

You have never come across someone asking for their breasts to be removed but have heard several stories in the media where this has been performed in similar circumstances. You are uncertain about some of the ethical issues regarding her case and tell the patient that you will consider her request but that you are unable to give her a definite answer yet. You arrange to see her again in 2 weeks after you have had a chance to discuss her request with your colleagues and the hospital's clinical ethics committee.

Question

- Is removal of healthy tissue ever appropriate to prevent disease?

ANSWER 58

The practice of prophylactic mastectomy is not a new medical procedure. However, there has been a sharp rise in the number of women (and some men) that are opting to undergo surgery in order to decrease the chances of them developing breast cancer in the future. One potential reason for this is that genetic screening is becoming more advanced so that more people are able to discover whether they are at increased risk. Another reason is that several high-profile celebrities have spoken out about their surgery and the reasons behind it and highlighted surgery as an option to other people.

Prophylactic mastectomy is the removal of *completely* healthy breast tissue in someone who is perceived to have an increased risk of developing cancerous tissue at some point in the future. This usually applies to individuals who have tested positive for BRCA 1 or BRCA 2 genes but can also include women who have a strong family history or who choose to remove both breasts if a tumour has been discovered in one breast. Although the statistical evidence for reducing the risk of breast cancer is strong – up to 90% reduction in risk in some women – it is still just this: a reduction in risk. A positive genetic test for one of the BRCA genes will give an increased predisposition to developing cancer, but that does not mean that the individual will definitely develop cancer. There is also still a risk of developing cancer even in those who undergo surgery since not all of the tissue can be removed.

Prophylactic breast surgery is no doubt a difficult decision to make. The breast conjures up not only images of womanhood and sexuality but also of motherhood and nurturing. There can be huge psychological sequelae for women who lose their breasts due to cancer and this loss should not be underestimated even if the woman has chosen to have her breasts removed. Prophylactic surgery also poses considerable ethical dilemmas for the medical profession. The principle of non-maleficence makes prophylactic surgery hard to justify. Any surgery comes with inherent risks, so the removal of healthy tissue should be carefully considered and the patient needs to be fully informed as part of the consent process to the risks of removal compared with the risks of a future cancer. Interestingly, although evidence has shown that prophylactic mastectomy reduces the risk of cancer, this does not correlate with an increase in life expectancy – one of the reasons for this may lie in the fact that breast cancer is potentially much more manageable with new hormonal therapy.

If prophylactic mastectomy becomes the norm, does this pave the way for more extreme surgeries to remove healthy tissue? For example, surgery performed merely due to patient anxiety and fear of developing cancer in the absence of evidence of other risk factors, or removal of both legs in someone with diabetic neuropathy who did not want to risk getting gangrenous infections. In extreme circumstances surgery to remove healthy limbs could be seen as an appropriate *treatment* for body dysmorphic syndrome. But can prophylactic mastectomy be considered treatment for a potential medical condition?

 Key Points

- Prophylactic surgery can be justified to prevent potential harm if it is considered sufficiently serious.
- Respect for patient autonomy requires sufficient information and discussion about the risks and benefits of surgery versus non-surgery.

CASE 59: SCREENING PROGRAMMES

The NHS Breast Screening Programme (NHSBSP) has invited Margie, age 71, and Pam, age 52, for screening at their local hospitals. Neither woman has a family history of breast cancer nor have they noticed anything unusual about their breasts. They have not spoken to their GPs about the screening programme and wonder if they have to attend.

Question

- What legal and ethical issues arise through screening programmes?

ANSWER 59

Screening is a process of identifying apparently healthy people who may be at increased risk of a disease or condition. Screening programmes are aimed at population groups who do not have symptoms of disease but may be at risk. A person who shows symptoms of a disease should be referred to a specialist and screening is not appropriate.

Public screening programmes are based on certain criteria pertaining to the *condition*, the *test* and *treatment* and these include the following:

- The condition should be an important health problem.
- The natural history of the condition should be adequately understood.
- There should be a simple, safe, precise and validated screening test.
- The test should be acceptable to the population.
- There should be an accepted treatment or intervention.
- There should be agreed evidence-based policies covering which individuals should be offered treatment and the appropriate treatment to be offered.[*]

There are a number of screening programmes run across the UK as part of a public health service. They include Down's syndrome, infectious disease in pregnancy, antenatal sickle cell and thalassemia and for adults; abdominal aortic aneurism, diabetic retinopathy and breast, cervical and bowel cancer screening programmes. The UK National Screening Committee makes UK-wide policies but each part of the UK determines when and how to put those policies into practice.

Screening identifies whether asymptomatic individuals are at increased risk of a disease or condition. They can then be offered information, further tests and appropriate treatment to reduce their risk and/or any complications arising from the disease or condition.

Informed consent

Consent or lawful authority (i.e., it is in the best interests of a patient lacking capacity to consent) is required before any examination or investigation is undertaken. Individuals invited for screening are provided with a leaflet, but do not have an opportunity to speak to a healthcare professional about the procedure beforehand unless they arrange to speak to their GP. An information leaflet *may* be an appropriate way of providing information about a procedure (*Al Hamwi v Johnston* 2005) but it is only part of the consent process and there is no guarantee the person has read it or understood the information given. Information provided in leaflets is variable and there have been criticisms that the NHSBSP leaflet[†] emphasises the benefits of screening and does not provide adequate information about the potential harms of screening. Individuals may not understand that they are being 'invited' for screening and can refuse. Reminder letters are sent to those who do not respond to the initial invitation.

Harms and benefits

Screening programmes benefit populations, but individuals may not benefit and indeed may be harmed. A positive screening means the asymptomatic individual is transformed into a potential patient, with no guarantee that treatment will reduce mortality. Screening programmes have different rates of 'false positive' and 'false negative' results. A false positive

---

[*] UK National Screening Committee, UK Screening Portal; Criteria for appraising the viability, effectiveness and appropriateness of a screening programme.

[†] NHS Breast Screening, Helping You Decide, 2013, http://www.cancerscreening.nhs.uk/breastscreen/publications/nhsbsp.pdf.

result means the person does not in fact have the condition but will nevertheless receive treatment causing unnecessary anxiety and distress. Those with a false negative screening test result do in fact have the condition and therefore will not receive the treatment they need. Those who consent to screening may not be aware of or understand the risk of false negative/positive results until they have undergone further invasive investigations.

Cost-effectiveness

A publicly funded screening programme should be cost-effective compared to not screening. Public Health England Guidance: Criteria for appraising the viability, effectiveness and appropriateness of a screening programme, 2013 states that 'the opportunity cost of the screening programme (including testing, diagnosis and treatment, administration, training and quality assurance) should be economically balanced in relation to expenditure on medical care as a whole (i.e., value for money)'. Thus the monetary costs as well as health benefits are relevant in assessing the overall benefits of a screening programme.

Breast screening programme

The NHS breast screening programme (NHSBSP) invites all women aged 50 to 70 for breast screening every 3 years. As part of Improving Outcomes: A Strategy for Cancer, women aged 47–49 and 71–73 are invited for screening in a randomised control trial which aims to see if extending the age range of breast screening reduces deaths from breast cancer. The NHSBSP annual review 2012 states that 2,862,370 women were invited for breast screening and 73.4% accepted the invitation, resulting in detection of 17,000 cancers.

Breast screening (mammogram) involves placing the breast on a mammogram machine, lowering a plastic plate to flatten the breast and then taking two X-rays. Women may find this uncomfortable. There have been arguments that breast screening results in over-diagnosis and thus women are exposed to the physical and psychosocial harms of unnecessary treatment. A study in Norway found that 15–25% of cases of breast cancer detected by screening are over-diagnosed (Kalager et al. 2012).

The Swiss Medical Board review noted that mammography screening might prevent one death attributed to breast cancer for every 1000 women screened and recognised the risk of over-diagnosis. It concluded that 'it is difficult to justify continuance of a public screening programme if the overall benefits do not outweigh the harms'. It recommended that the breast screening programme there be discontinued (Biller-Andorno and Jüni 2014).

 Key Points

- NHS screening programmes identify individuals at risk of certain diseases/conditions.
- Individuals are invited to attend but they can refuse to do so.
- Individuals should be adequately informed about the risks and benefits to them.

CASE 60: CHILDHOOD IMMUNISATION

Sophie's first child, Alfie, is 3 months old. She had an easy pregnancy and uncomplicated birth. Alfie is happy and thriving. Sophie regularly takes him to meet with other mums from her antenatal group. A few of those mothers have said that they are not going to take their children to the GP to have the measles, mumps and rubella (MMR) vaccine because they are worried about the side effects. Sophie is concerned to hear this. She and her husband had intended to take Alfie for all the routine immunisations because they want to do what is best for him. The mothers' talk is making Sophie doubt if this is the case.

Questions

- Are childhood immunisations compulsory?
- Can parents legally refuse to have their child immunised? What if they disagree?
- Are there any ethical justifications for non-immunisation?

ANSWER 60

A range of routine vaccinations are offered on the NHS to all babies and children in the UK. Immunisation programmes provide protection to individuals who have received them, as well as the wider unvaccinated population through 'herd immunity'. This is the level at which the population of those non-immunised is sufficiently small that the chance of catching the disease amongst that group is negligible. Effective immunisation programmes may eradicate the disease for future generations, e.g., as is the case for smallpox and polio. The level of immunity necessary to eliminate measles is 94–96%. In the United States immunisation is required for children entering public schools, and compulsory immunisation laws exist in Eastern European and countries in South America. Immunisation in the UK is voluntary and consent is given by a person with 'parental responsibility' (Case 17) – the parent taking the child to clinic for immunisation.

While most vaccines are effective and safe, there are side effects such as fever, rash, local soreness and, more rarely, febrile convulsion. The Vaccine Damage Payments Act 1979 provides for payments to be made to children severely disabled as a result of vaccination. Some parents take the view that as immunisation is a preventative measure and as there is no certainty that their child will ever catch the disease, they do not wish to subject their own child to the risks of vaccination but rather take advantage of herd immunity.

If a child is to *benefit* from herd immunity then to what extent should parents be at liberty to decline immunisation because they do not consider it to be in their child's best interests?

In clear instances of harm, State interference in parental decisions may be justified, but the utility that is gained from such interference should be balanced against the harms of coercion. There is a difference between parental refusal of *treatment* that is proposed to benefit *this child* and immunisation programmes which aim to benefit all children in an age range, although a few may suffer incidental, and potentially serious, harm. Dare argues that mass immunisation programmes can tolerate small numbers of parents who refuse immunisation as there is no significant reduction in overall benefit* and so no real harm ensues from respecting their autonomy. However, the low uptake of MMR vaccine in the UK due to discredited research has resulted in an increase in the incidence of measles. In a small number of cases this might result in the death of the child (or anyone else who has not been immunised) or other health sequelae such as infertility and deafness.

Although there have been calls for childhood immunisation to be mandatory, others argue that parents should be free to determine the best interests of their child without State interference.

If parents disagree about immunisation and the issue is referred to court, the judge will consider the best interests of the child. Recent case law indicates weight is attributed to the medical benefits, and so MMR vaccination is considered to be in the best interests of the child.† However, a decision by both parents to refuse immunisation would come within the range of decisions where their autonomy is upheld, given that the risks arising from refusal are not incompatible with child welfare.

 Key Points

- Immunisations for children in the UK are not mandatory.
- The aim of the immunisation programme is to benefit a population, although some children who are immunised may experience harmful side effects.

---

* Dare, T. Mass immunisation programmes: Some philosophical issues, *Bioethics* 1998; 12, 125–149, 146.
† *F v F* [2013] EWHC 2683 (Fam).

CASE 61: PROFESSIONAL RESPONSIBILITY TO DISCUSS OBESITY

You are a medical student observing consultations in a paediatric outpatient department. The last patient of the day is a 12-year-old boy who has been brought in by his mother. He has had a recent inpatient stay with abdominal pain and has come for the results of some further investigations he has had as an outpatient. No cause for his pain was found at the time and it has not returned. The consultant is also able to reassure the child and his mother that all the other tests have been normal too. The consultant then goes on to bring up the thorny subject of the child's weight. Although his mother is very slender, it is obvious that Daniel is obese. Unfortunately, at the mere mention of his weight, Daniel becomes tearful, and as the consultant pushes on to discuss it further, he gets very distressed and leaves the room.

Questions
- Should the consultant have raised this subject?
- Would it have made a difference if the consultation was with an adult?
- What other lifestyle choices should healthcare professionals discuss with their patients?

ANSWER 61

Obesity is fast becoming the UK's biggest risk factor for significant and severe chronic disease. Over the past few decades society has had increased access to calorie-rich food, and advances in technology and transportation have led to much more sedentary employment and lifestyles. Statistics demonstrate that at present 25% of adults are classified as obese (BMI > 30). This number is expected to double by 2050. This will have enormous implications on healthcare.

In 2014, NICE published guidance on how healthcare professionals and clinical commissioning groups should be tackling the obesity epidemic. It is clear in their guidance that GPs and other healthcare professionals have a responsibility to raise the issue of weight with obese patients at every conceivable opportunity. Research demonstrates that obese individuals are often too embarrassed to raise the subject themselves but that many are grateful for the input if done in a supportive and non-judgemental way.

NICE key recommendations include the following:

- Adopt an integrated approach to preventing and managing obesity
- Ensure that services cause no harm
- Raise awareness of lifestyle weight management services among health and social care professionals
- Raise awareness of lifestyle weight management services among the local population
- Commission programmes that include the core components for effective weight loss *and* prevent weight regain
- Provide continuing professional development on lifestyle weight management for health and social care professionals[*]

Several clinical trials have demonstrated an improvement in health even with only losing 3% of baseline body weight. However, there is a paucity of long-term outcomes with these studies, so it is impossible to determine any long-term clinical effect. The main difficulty with any weight loss programme is ensuring that the weight loss is maintained.

The Foresight Project was a government-funded project looking at the long-term societal effects on obesity. It makes for interesting reading as it challenges the idea that obesity is an individual problem as a result of gluttony and raises awareness that instead it should be perceived as a societal problem.

> 'Tackling obesity requires far greater change than anything tried so far, and at multiple levels: personal, family, community and national. Preventing obesity is a societal challenge, similar to climate change. It requires partnership between government, science, business and civil society.'[†]

In the case scenario the consultant was taking advantage of a clinic appointment to address the issue of Daniel's obesity. However, his communication skills were evidently lacking in that he made Daniel feel judged. Bringing up the issue of obesity is going to be a sensitive subject for many, which is why so many professionals avoid the 'elephant in the room'.

---

[*] http://www.nice.org.uk/guidance/ph53/chapter/1-recommendations.
[†] Tackling obesities: Future choices – project report (2nd edition) www.gov.uk.

Other health promotional subjects such as smoking, alcohol and screening programmes are often easier to address.

 Key Points

- Obesity is a public health concern.
- Professionals should address the issue of obesity with patients routinely but sensitively.

CASE 62: INCENTIVES FOR TREATMENT AND HEALTH PROMOTION

Claudia has just given birth to her first child. She is surprised when the health visitor says that she will be given food vouchers if she tries to breastfeed her baby for 3 months.

James has had schizophrenia for 15 years. His compliance with medication is variable. He is offered a chance to take part in a programme whereby he will be paid £10 for each injection of depot antipsychotic.

A council-run weight loss programme is offering reduced membership to the local gym for people who have a BMI of more than 35 and who commit to a weight loss and fitness programme for 6 months.

Roger is a sexual health consultant with responsibility for a local hostel for women who are sex workers. A number of them do not use contraception effectively, which results in pregnancy and increased abortion rates. Roger wants to encourage the women to come to a talk about depot contraception which he thinks would be an effective strategy to prevent pregnancy, in addition to using barrier methods. He offers lunch vouchers and toiletries to encourage their attendance at the talk.

Ewan is a heroin addict and is enrolled in a drug rehabilitation programme where he is being prescribed Subutex. His local drugs clinic is offering him a £10 shopping voucher if he can provide a clean urine sample at a weekly meeting with his key worker.

Questions
- What are the ethical concerns if incentives are offered to encourage healthy lifestyle choices and compliance with medical treatments?
- Do incentives effectively coerce consent?

ANSWER 62

Incentives are positive reinforcements given for completion of tasks or improvements in behaviour.[*]

As part of health promotion, patients can be incentivised and rewarded for positive behaviours through payment of money or receipt of other benefits such as gym membership. 'Money is the most tangible motivating factor for many people.'[†] If incentives provide what the patient, doctor and society want through achievement of improved health or adherence to medication, is there anything wrong with incentivising patients? After all, GP practices receive financial incentives if they meet certain targets for health promotion such as childhood immunisations, and individuals are paid to take part in research trials.

One ethical objection to the use of incentives is that they interfere with patients' autonomous choices. Patients should exercise unfettered choice to improve their health, and if they have decided not to take medication or lose weight, that should be respected. This objection against incentives assumes an individual's self-determination is corrupted by incentivisation. However, illness and vulnerability may also reduce autonomous choice. Incentives could be considered to be in a patient's best interests; for example, by encouraging compliance with a drug rehabilitation programme, the chains of addiction are broken and autonomy is thus promoted.

Some argue that an incentive is a form of bribery which coerces the patient into making decisions and this undermines the therapeutic relationship. Patients should be intrinsically motivated to adhere to a healthy lifestyle and/or take necessary medications because ultimately they will feel better and the goal is the reward. However, providing information about benefits does not seem to be a sufficient trigger. Twenty-five per cent of the population is obese, and despite health promotion campaigns many do not make the necessary lifestyle changes needed to lose weight.

Some argue that incentives reward those who have not behaved well so far, rather than those who have. There is no cost benefit for those who do adhere to medication/do not smoke/do not take illegal drugs although there are clear health benefits. As a consequence, patients who would otherwise have complied with medication may demand incentives to now do so.

Cost/benefit

The costs of obesity to the UK economy exceed £3 billion per year[‡] whereas the cost of incentives is merely symbolic. If delivery of the incentive depends on physical consumption (taking medication, not using heroin) then costs will be incurred to supervise administration of the medication or check urine samples to ensure the individual is drug free. It is not feasible to check how individuals spend financial payments received to reward compliance with a programme, and they may spend the money unwisely. Some studies have shown that incentives are effective, for example in changing the behaviour of people

---

[*] Michalczuk R. and Mitchell A. Monetary incentives for schizophrenia (review), 2010, The Cochrane Collaboration, John Wiley & Sons Ltd.

[†] Guidelines on the practice of ethics committees in medical research with human participants, RCOP, 4th edition, 2007, para 10.4, https://www.rcplondon.ac.uk/sites/default/files/documents/guidelines-practice-ethics-committees-medical-research.pdf.

[‡] http://www.birmingham.ac.uk/research/activity/mds/centres/obesity/obesity-uk/index.aspx.

with severe mental health problems and improving adherence to treatment (Kendall 2013; Priebe et al. 2013).

 Key Points

- Incentivising behaviours in healthcare is controversial.
- Incentives for compliance with medication may undermine patient autonomy and harm the therapeutic relationship.

CASE 63: FRONT-LINE STAFF AND FLU IMMUNISATION

Claire is a healthcare assistant (HCA) on the cardiology ward. She is approached by a member of the occupational health team who asks if she would like to have her annual winter flu immunisation, stating that 'all the other staff are having it' and that she will get a 'flu fighter' badge if she does. Claire is not sure if she wants to have it; she has heard people often get ill after the injection and she has never had the flu anyway.

Question

- Is there a moral obligation for front-line NHS staff to have the flu immunisation?

ANSWER 63

Front-line healthcare workers are offered the flu vaccine annually. Advertising targets front-line staff. Occupational health staff visit wards to easily facilitate immunisations, and sometimes incentives, such as chocolate and pens, are given to those who take up immunisation. Whilst strongly encouraged, it is not currently compulsory for front-line staff to have the flu vaccine.

The main proposed benefits of flu immunisation are that it may:

- Prevent staff transmitting flu to, and then between, patients
- Protect healthcare workers themselves from contracting flu, thus reducing sick leave which can be particularly detrimental during winter pressures

The evidence regarding the effectiveness of the flu vaccine is disputed, and this has particularly come to light with new evolving strains of flu, against which immunisation may be less effective.

Some might argue that Claire has a moral obligation to be immunised. As a HCA, Claire has a duty of care to protect her vulnerable patients, and accepting immunisation could be considered part of this duty. The principle of non-maleficence requires that she does what she can to avoid harming patients, and flu immunisation, even if not fully effective, may be one way of doing this. The harms to Claire (for example, a sore arm, mild side effects or extremely rare serious effects) may be outweighed by the benefits to patients, providing a consequentialist justification for her consenting to immunisation. Furthermore, by accepting the risk of such harms for the benefit of her patients, she is acting as a 'virtuous' healthcare professional, displaying the virtues of selflessness, altruism, professionalism and commitment to her work.

Others may argue that Claire has no moral obligation to be immunised. Claire is an autonomous individual, and thus has the right to make decisions for herself in the same way that a patient would have the right to make a decision about whether or not to be immunised. This is particularly relevant in the case of flu immunisations, where the evidence supporting the effectiveness of immunisation is not fully established. Furthermore, the benefit of Claire being immunised is predominantly experienced by patients rather than by Claire herself, and so the evidence for effectiveness might have to be stronger to justify obliging her to have the immunisation. Incentivising the flu vaccine may also be problematic, as this could impact on Claire's ability to make a voluntary and autonomous choice. Claire should be provided with information about the risks and benefits of immunisation in an unbiased form, and her consent subsequently sought.

An interesting comparison may be made between the flu vaccine, which is currently not compulsory, and the hepatitis B virus vaccine, which is compulsory for certain healthcare workers. Whilst both the flu and hepatitis B immunisations have similar side effect profiles, hepatitis B generally results in a more serious disease than flu, and therefore the harms that are to be avoided through the hepatitis B immunisation may be greater. Furthermore, there is strong evidence that the hepatitis B vaccine is very effective against transmission of the virus, whereas the strength of evidence for flu immunisation is more disputed. By making hepatitis B immunisation compulsory, it can be inferred that the harms of overriding the rights and autonomy of the individual healthcare worker are outweighed by the benefits obtained through prevention of this disease.

Key Points

- There is no legal or professional obligation for healthcare workers to be immunised against flu.
- The moral argument for mandatory immunisation is stronger in circumstances where immunisation is increasingly effective at preventing transmission of the disease.

CASE 64: OVERSEAS VISITORS

Farida is a 32-year-old Indian lady who has travelled to the UK to have a holiday with her sister, who is ordinarily resident in London. Two days after her arrival she attends the Accident and Emergency department (A&E) with abdominal pain. Staff discover she is 9 months pregnant and that the baby has congenital heart problems. It later transpires that Farida knew this and chose to travel to the UK to receive the best care for her child. Although she is aware she will have to pay, she concealed her pregnancy so that the airline would allow her to fly.

Soloman is a 56-year-old gentleman who has also travelled to the UK for a holiday. He is visiting from Russia. Whilst on holiday he slips down an escalator and breaks his ankle in three places. The orthopaedic team feel he needs urgent surgery on his ankle.

Sheila is a 24-year-old Australian who has developed a urinary tract infection whilst travelling around the UK. She would like to make an appointment with a GP for assessment and treatment.

Questions
- What care are visitors entitled to on the NHS?
- What is the role of the healthcare professional in assessing entitlement to NHS care?
- How is the tension between the professional and moral duties of healthcare professionals to assist those in need, and to act as 'gatekeeper' to NHS treatment, resolved?

ANSWER 64

The NHS provides free treatment to anyone who is ordinarily resident in the UK. This means anyone who is lawfully living in the UK as part of the regular order of his or her life. It does not apply to UK citizens who have moved abroad even if they have previously lived and worked in the UK.

The NHS is also one of the only healthcare services in the world where emergency treatment is provided free of charge irrespective of residency. This includes immediate and necessary treatment provided in an A&E department or NHS walk-in clinic, treatment for specific infectious diseases, compulsory psychiatric treatment and family planning services.* Further care needed within the hospital even in an emergency is subject to a charge. It is the responsibility of the secondary care provider (management within the NHS Trust and not the individual doctor) to identify and appropriately charge overseas visitors.

There are reciprocal healthcare arrangements between the UK and some countries which entitle eligible residents of those countries to treatment which becomes medically necessary while temporarily staying in the UK. In return, eligible UK residents are entitled to receive free (or reduced cost) medical treatment while visiting these countries. It does not cover situations where individuals come to the UK to access treatment without an explicit referral. These people are colloquially known as 'health tourists'.

A similar situation applies to general practice. Visitors should not be charged if their condition is considered an emergency; this includes acute exacerbations of chronic conditions. For non-urgent treatment it is up to the individual GP practice to decide whether to refuse treatment or provide treatment on a private basis.

In reality it can be very difficult to expect medical staff to determine who should be entitled to free treatment and who needs to pay. Expecting doctors to act as 'gatekeepers' to NHS services could affect the standard of care that is given. Because of this many hospitals employ specific managers to act as gatekeepers.

Conversely health tourists should not always be deemed to be exploiting the NHS. Many are more than happy to pay for both private and NHS services in order to receive first-class care in internationally renowned hospitals.

In the above scenarios Farida will be able to receive excellent care for herself and her child but she will be liable to charges. The same is true of Soloman. Although his initial assessment and imaging would be free, he could well be charged for the operation and subsequent inpatient care. Sheila's case is a little more difficult. It could be argued that a urinary infection needs immediate care but it is also not considered life threatening. It would be up to the individual GP practice to decide whether to charge for her care.

	Key Points
	• Doctors should not be responsible for assessing eligibility for free care.
	• Some countries have reciprocal agreements for provision of healthcare.

---

* Overseas Visitors Policy. Department of Health, 2012.

ETHICS AND LAW IN CLINICAL PRACTICE: ORGAN DONATION

CASE 65: ORGAN DONATION

Abdul, a 41-year-old accountant, is married and has three young children. He was diagnosed with type 1 diabetes at the age of 24, which led to chronic kidney disease. Abdul's kidney function has deteriorated rapidly over the past several years, leaving him with end-stage renal disease. Six months ago he started dialysis treatment three times a week. Each session would last more than 4 hours, leaving Abdul feeling exhausted and drained.

Abdul's condition and medical treatment has impacted his work life; he can now only work part-time due to his regular hospital dialysis appointments and fatigue. This has implications on the family's financial situation, as his income is greatly reduced. Furthermore, he is spending less time with his children due to the hospital appointments and constant exhaustion. At his last renal appointment, the topic of kidney transplantation was discussed, however, the waiting list of around 3 years worried Abdul. When discussing this appointment with his family, his brother, Farhan, became concerned as to how his brother would cope with 3 more years of dialysis and part-time work. A week later, Farhan told Abdul that he wanted to donate a kidney to him.

Questions
- What is the Human Tissue Act 2004?
- How can consent be obtained for organ transplantation?
- How is organ transplantation governed?
- What are the different types of organ donation?

ANSWER 65

The Human Tissue Act and Authority

The law relating to organ donation in England, Wales and Northern Ireland is contained in the Human Tissue Act 2004. It replaced the Human Organ Transplants Act 1989, following scandals at Bristol Royal Infirmary and Alder Hey Children's Hospital during the late 1980s and '90s. It was discovered in the Kennedy and Redfern inquiries that children's organs had been removed and stored without parental knowledge and proper consent at these hospitals. Further reports, including the Isaacs Report (2003) indicated that this was a widespread problem. Therefore, statutory reform was required.

The Human Tissue Act 2004 sets out a new legal framework for 'the storage and use of tissue from the living and for the removal, storage and use of tissue and organs from the dead'. The central governing principle of the Act is appropriate consent.

The Human Tissue Authority (HTA) is the regulatory body for all matters concerning the removal, storage, use and disposal of human tissue (excluding embryos and gametes). Other responsibilities of the HTA include licensing establishments that carry out particular activities under the Act. The HTA also provides codes of practice on issues such as consent, examination of the body after death and the donation of organs, tissue and stem cells. These should be adhered to by anyone involved in these processes.

Lastly, the Human Tissue Act states that it is illegal to buy, sell, or have any commercial dealings in the sale of human organs. This offence carries a fine and up to 3 years' imprisonment.

Living donation

The Act describes two types of organ donation: deceased donation (Case 66) and living donation, which can be further subcategorised:

- Genetically/emotionally related donation – where the recipient is known to the donor. This is the most common form of organ donation.
- Paired/pooled donation – organ donation between more than two people due to relatives not being compatible.
- Altruistic nondirected donation – organ donation to a stranger.

All living organ donations must be approved by the HTA before donation can take place. Essentially, it must be evident that valid consent has been provided by the donor, there has been no coercion and that no reward will be given. For genetically or emotionally related donation, such as Abdul's case, the HTA transplant approvals team will make the final decision on the case. Paired/pooled donation and all altruistic nondirected donations will be assessed by an HTA panel of three authority members.

Where the potential living donor is a child or an adult lacking capacity, the donation must be approved by a court of law to ensure that it is in the donor's best interests to donate.

How to increase supply

Unfortunately, there is still a large number of people who die whilst awaiting a transplant due to a lack of donors. In England the current system is 'opt in' – individuals can choose to donate organs after death by joining the NHS Organ Donor Register. In 2008 the Organ Donation Task Force considered whether to change to an 'opt out' (or presumed consent) system for organ donation. Under this system all individuals are deemed to have given consent for organ donation unless they register otherwise. After examining the evidence, the task force reached a clear consensus in recommending that an opt-out system should not be introduced at that time (Organ Donation Taskforce, The potential impact of an opt out system for organ donation in the UK, 2008).

Specialist Nurses–Organ Donation (SN–ODs) are senior nurses from a clinical background, usually in intensive care or emergency medicine, who support doctors caring for someone who recently died and could be a potential organ donor. These specialists are highly trained to communicate with the next of kin about the benefits of organ donation.

In 2013 Wales became the first country in the UK to implement deemed consent legislation, the Human Transplantation (Wales) Act 2013. It creates a soft opt-out system, which means that a person who has not registered a decision to opt in or opt out of organ donation will be treated as having no objection to being an organ donor after their death – consent is presumed. This does not apply to children, people who lack capacity or those who do not live in Wales. Although this should, in theory, increase the number of organs available, as permission will still need to be obtained from the family, there needs to be an emphasis on counselling for families by a specialist organ transplant team.

Another idea to create the number of people registered to donate organs is to make it law that only people who have consented to donate an organ will be eligible to receive one if the need arises.

 Key Points

- The Human Tissue Act 2004 provides the legal framework for all organ and tissue donation in England, Wales and Northern Ireland.
- No organ can be obtained without appropriate consent.
- The Act sets up the Human Tissue Authority, which is the regulatory body concerning all tissue removal, storage, use and disposal.
- Living organ donation is permissible providing valid consent has been given and there is no coercion or reward.

CASE 66: POSTHUMOUS ORGAN DONATION

Mike is a 36-year-old banker with a passion for motorbikes. One winter evening when he is travelling back from a conference down the M1, his bike skids on a patch of black ice. He was driving at 90 mph. He hits the windscreen of an oncoming car and his helmet splits in half. An ambulance arrives at the scene within minutes and Mike is intubated and rushed to hospital. He has sustained severe injuries – he has fractured his pelvis and several vertebrae. At hospital he is assessed on the intensive care unit. Attempts to resuscitate him are unsuccessful, and when he is weaned off the ventilator he does not make any respiratory effort. Tests performed by two different consultants confirm that he has had massive brainstem injuries, and he is declared brainstem dead despite the ventilator continuing to keep his heart and lungs working and consequently the rest of his organs perfused. Mike is registered on the national organ donation database and was carrying an organ donor card on him. It is decided to keep him ventilated until his next of kin are traced and contacted, so that Mike's wish to donate his organs can be discussed with them.

Questions
- How can someone donate his or her organs after death?
- Can the next of kin prevent organ donation?

ANSWER 66

Legal issues

The Human Tissue Act 2004 sets out guidelines on the legality of obtaining organs after death. After someone has died, a healthcare professional should endeavour to find out whether the patient had expressed a wish as to what should happen to their organs after death. This can be done by checking medical records, looking for a donor card or checking the Organ Donor Register (ODR). If there is evidence of consent to organ donation by a competent adult, then legally organ donation can proceed. The relatives of the patient should be informed of the patient's prior consent to donation. If they object, every effort should be made to ask them to respect the wishes of the deceased, and they should sensitively be informed that they cannot legally veto the consent. However, in practice where there is real objection to organ donation, it would be unusual for donation to go ahead.

When no consent prior to death has been given, a person in a 'qualifying relationship' can give consent. The Human Tissue Act ranks persons in a qualifying relationship, for example, the wishes of a spouse take precedence over the wishes of a daughter. Children can consent to posthumous organ donation if they are Gillick competent. It is essential that their decision is discussed with the person who has parental responsibility and to take their wishes into account before proceeding. Where a child lacked capacity or no prior consent had been expressed, consent should be sought from the person with parental responsibility.

Ethical issues

Despite consent and respect for the individual being at the heart of the Human Tissue Act, it has a slightly utilitarian flavour by allowing the body of the recently deceased to be preserved while consent to donation can be established or refused. The concept that proxy-consent to posthumous organ donation can be given has interesting ethical arguments. In every other aspect of medicine consent to 'treatment' cannot be made by another adult, unless they have a lasting power of attorney. The Act also permits ventilation after death has been confirmed, e.g., after a cardiac arrest, to continue to perfuse organs – which leads us to the ethical question whether such 'treatment' is in the patient's best interests. Does a dead person have any interests? Can any harm be caused to a dead patient?

If the answer to these questions is no, it could be ethically justifiable that consent should not be an issue in posthumous organ donation and, therefore, all healthy organs should be removed and donated to living persons to maximise utility. Deontological theory would consider this morally unacceptable as no person should be used solely as a means to another's end.

 Key Points

- Relatives cannot veto posthumous organ donation if the deceased has given pre-mortem consent. However, in practice, the beliefs and views of the relatives will still be respected.
- It is legal to preserve bodies after confirmation of death to perfuse organs while consent is being established.
- There are complex ethical arguments about the need for consent for posthumous organ donation.

CASE 67: IS THERE A MARKET FOR LIVING ORGAN DONORS?

Dave, a 35-year-old healthy man, has been made redundant by the factory he used to work in. His wife has recently left him, as he cannot support her, and he has become depressed due to losing her respect. He is also still grieving the death of his son, who died from leukaemia at the age of 5. As he is wandering the streets, he notices an advertisement in a shop window.

One functioning kidney to save the life of a 15-year-old girl!
Potential donors will be morally and financially rewarded.

The advertisement makes Dave think. He has two kidneys and he is healthy. He knows that donating one of his kidneys will not be without risk, but he also knows that it could potentially save the life of a child and ease some of the guilt he feels following the death of his own son. It would also give him enough money to get back on his feet, try to win his wife back, and set up a business of his own. It seems that all parties in the transaction would benefit.

Questions
- What are the ethical implications of creating a market in organ donation?
- What other methods could be introduced to increase the availability of organs for transplant in the UK?

ANSWER 67

Despite a marked increase in living donations, there are currently more than 10,000 people awaiting a transplant in the UK (www.organdonation.nhs.uk). This number continues to rise every year due to advances in medical technology extending life and the number of potential donors declining.

The UK needs to re-examine its current opt-in protocol for organ donation and establish a method to increase the number of available organs, whether they are from living or dead donors. Various possibilities have been discussed and some are more feasible than others, such as making organ donation an opt-out system, or forcing all prisoners to donate organs. Another option is to reconsider the possibility of a market in organ donation.

Ethical issues

For many people the idea of buying or selling an organ is repulsive. Yet, on closer examination, the ethical reasons behind this typical gut reaction cannot be substantiated. It is often argued that to buy a kidney is to deny that person the natural dignity that should be given to all individuals. Cohen argues that, 'to sell an integral human body part is to corrupt the very meaning of human dignity' (Cohen 1999). The most common ethical principle usually ascribed to such sentiment is the Kantian philosophy of not using an individual simply as a means to another's end. Yet what if it was your loved one who could have their life saved for a small financial cost?

Another argument is that the promise of financial reward results in exploitation of the poor and vulnerable, and that the gift of donation should only have a purely altruistic motive. This is an imposition of others' moral sensibilities. Surely if a person can benefit the life of another from donating an organ and can better their own life as a result of it, they should be allowed. People should have a right to sell whatever is theirs. Denying them this infringes their autonomy.

Charles Erin and John Harris have proposed a model for a market in organ donation that they argue meets with all ethical standards.

> The market would be confined to a self-governing geopolitical area such as a nation-state … Only citizens resident within the union or state could sell into the system and they and their families would be equally eligible to receive organs. … There would be only one purchaser, an agency like the National Health Service (NHS), which would buy all organs and distribute according to some fair conception of medical priority. There would be no direct sales or purchases, no exploitation of low-income countries and their populations … There would be strict controls and penalties to prevent abuse.
>
> Erin and Harris (2003)

This concept does, in theory, protect all individuals from the harms associated with the traditional concept of a commercial market in organ donation.

 Key Points

- The current organ donation system is opt in. Due to a shortage of donors this needs to be reviewed.
- Selling organs gives rise to concerns about exploitation and is unlawful.

CASE 68: SOCIAL MEDIA AND ORGAN DONATION

Hi, my name is Sophie. I am 46 years old and a married mother of two lovely boys, Jake and Josh. Two years ago I developed renal failure after suffering from meningitis. I am very fortunate that the doctors and nurses managed to save my life, but unfortunately my kidneys did not recover and I need dialysis three times a week. I have been told that my life expectancy will be shortened unless I undergo a transplant, and so I am now looking for someone to donate a kidney. Are you that kind, generous person who could help save my life?

Questions

- Is it lawful for someone to advertise for an organ donor?
- Is it ethically appropriate for a stranger to donate an organ to someone they 'met' through social media?

ANSWER 68

End-stage renal failure is not curable, but individuals may receive life-prolonging treatment by dialysis. This is onerous and time-consuming. The NHS organ donation website shows that around 3000 kidney transplants are performed each year, but this still leaves 6000 people on the waiting list. The average waiting time for an adult kidney transplant is 1114 days. More than 350 people a year die while waiting for a kidney transplant (Kidney Research UK, https://www.kidneyresearchuk. org/about-us). Living donor kidney transplants are more successful than posthumous donation. They last longer and can be performed when the recipient is healthy, resulting in better outcomes for the recipient (Costello 2013). As a result of a shortage of organs, a pressing need and increased public awareness, potential recipients may advertise for a donor through social media or websites set up to facilitate linking those who need a kidney with those willing to donate.

Where there is no pre-existing relationship between donor and recipient prior to contact through social media the donation is termed *directed altruistic donation* (DAD). The Human Tissue Authority can give legal approval for DAD cases to proceed if it is satisfied that there is no evidence of coercion of, or reward for, the donor. The donation should be sufficiently autonomous and the medical and psychosocial risks and benefits should be considered. However, because of inherent uncertainty about coercion, the British Transplantation Society (BTS) has issued guidance (British Transplantation Society 2013) that transplant units should not accept cases for living donor assessment that arise from websites where potential transplant recipients pay a fee to register their need for an organ transplant. It is not illegal to place an advert, online or in a newspaper, seeking a living organ donor as long as there is no offer of reward, payment or material advantage to the potential donor.

Benefits

There is a benefit in recognising and giving effect to an altruistic act resulting in successful organ transplantation, and living altruistic organ donors are likely to be motivated by spiritual beliefs and a desire to help others. Finding a donor through websites prevents costly dialysis and reduces inequity arising from the mere chance of having a relative or family member who is a close enough genetic match.

Harms

Not all of those in need of a kidney will have the resources – time, Internet, know-how – to build a personal 'brand' which will attract potential donors. Some consider that online kidney solicitations will become a 'beauty contest' and that allocation of organs will not be based on need or capacity to benefit but rather the pulling of heart strings (Neidich et al. 2012). Those advertising will share personal information with strangers, not by personal choice but through necessity. Of course, even if a potential donor is found, they may not be a match, resulting in disappointment if the emotional desire to help another in need is thwarted. There is a greater risk of coercion if the recipient appears to be initiating the process and the BTS states that nondirected altruistic donation is the preferred option where there is no pre-existing relationship between donor and recipient because this maximises equity of access to living donor transplantation.

Key Points
• Directed altruistic donation is lawful.
• Donation can only be directed to an identified recipient; it is not permitted to direct to a particular group of potential recipients on the national waiting list, e.g., by age, ethnicity or gender.
• There must be no reward for or coercion of the donor.

ETHICS AND LAW IN CLINICAL PRACTICE: END OF LIFE

CASE 69: THE DISTINCTION BETWEEN ACTS AND OMISSIONS AT THE END OF LIFE

Tony, a 79-year-old man with a history of hypertension and type 2 diabetes, collapses while playing golf and is taken to the local Accident and Emergency department, still unconscious. A computed tomography (CT) scan reveals a large haemorrhagic stroke and he is transferred to the neurosurgical unit. He fails to regain consciousness, although he does not require ventilatory support. He receives fluids and parenteral nutrition for 11 days and is regularly visited by his wife and two children.

Eventually, senior medical staff discuss with Tony's family the extensive nature of damage to his brain and the likelihood that he will never regain consciousness. The family is asked to consider the possibility of withdrawing nutritional and fluid support and allowing Tony to die 'naturally'. They are warned that this may take some time, as much as a couple of weeks, but that Tony will not be in any pain.

His son approaches you, the FY1 doctor on the ward, during visiting hours and tells you that it is becoming increasingly distressing for his mother to watch her husband die and that, if this is to be the inevitable result, why is it not possible to offer a quicker end to the family's suffering, such as an injection which would stop Tony's heart.

Questions
- What does an 'act' and an 'omission' mean in relation to end-of-life decisions?
- What are the ethical arguments for and against the distinction between the two?
- What is the legal position regarding acts and omissions?

ANSWER 69

Acts and omissions

Is there any moral difference between acting to achieve a goal and omitting to act, knowing it will produce the same result? The distinction between acts and omissions underpins treatment options which are lawful and those which are unlawful at the end of life. Passive euthanasia describes the withholding or withdrawal of life-prolonging treatment (i.e., involves an *omission*), while active euthanasia involves an *act* that will inevitably result in someone's death. The clinical team has proposed the former for the patient in this scenario, and the latter has been requested by his son.

The ethical case for a distinction between acts and omissions

For many, passive euthanasia is deemed the more morally acceptable of the two, supporting the idea that there is an ethical distinction between acts and omissions.

> In certain contexts, failure to perform an act, with certain foreseen bad consequences of that failure, is morally less bad than to perform a different act which has the identical foreseen bad circumstances.
>
> Glover J, *Causing Death and Saving Lives*. Harmondsworth: Penguin (1977)

Many explanations have been offered for this distinction. Some argue that to act is less morally acceptable because it 'interferes' with the natural course of events, i.e., Tony will eventually die, but to give him a lethal injection is to disrupt this natural process. Others argue that in medicine, an omission provides a safeguard against wrong diagnosis whereas an action does not. That is to say, in the unlikely event that a patient can recover, to allow them to die gives the opportunity for this to become apparent. If a lethal injection is given, any chance of recovery (albeit minute) is obliterated.

The ethical case against a distinction between acts and omissions

Tony's son clearly has a different view of acts and omissions, as he thinks an act to end his father's life would be preferable. Many would find it hard to disagree with him on compassionate grounds – they may argue that it is preferable for both Tony and his family that he has a quick resolution to his current situation rather than a long-drawn-out death.

Yet there is the problematic idea of what constitutes an 'act' or an 'omission'. The argument that acts interfere with natural events is flawed as it can be extrapolated to all interventionist medicine – the patient would have died anyway if it were not for doctors intervening with intravenous fluids and nutrition. Healthcare professionals are in the business of disrupting nature if its course happens to be disease or death.

A thought experiment can be used to illustrate that often those who act and omit to act can be seen as equally morally reprehensible if their intention and the result is the same. James Rachels, a philosopher, famously gives the example of Smith and Jones. Both stand to inherit a lot of money if their 6-year-old cousin dies. If Smith were to sneak up on the cousin's bathtime, with the intention of holding his head underwater until he drowned, and succeeded in this, thus inheriting the money, would it be any more morally reprehensible than if Jones went with the same intention, witnessed the boy accidentally trip, knock himself unconscious and drown and did nothing to prevent the death, with the same financially desirable result?

As doctors support the distinction, it could reflect that they are conditioned throughout their training to act – to prescribe the right medicine, to recognise conditions at an early, treatable stage. It could also be a result of the difference in the daily work of bioethicists and doctors – while ethicists use hypothetical thought experiments and moral philosophy, doctors are faced with difficult and very real decisions which need some resolution. As is often the case, it is left to the legal system to try to bridge this divide between complex ethical arguments and practical, real dilemmas.

The legal position

Active euthanasia is not legal in the UK under any circumstances. However, passive euthanasia is, in certain circumstances, permitted. It is obvious therefore that the law *does* draw a distinction between acts and omissions.

Two historical cases occurring within a year of each other in the 1990s illustrate this legal distinction. In *R v Cox* (1992), Dr Cox was convicted of attempted murder for administering a lethal injection of potassium chloride to Mrs Boyes, a 70-year-old woman suffering from intractable pain secondary to rheumatoid arthritis who had repeatedly asked medical staff to end her life. Here Dr Cox's *act* was unmistakable – the potassium chloride had no possible therapeutic benefit and his intention in administering it, however compassionate, was to end Mrs Boyes's life. A year later the case of *Airedale NHS Trust v Bland* (1993) concerned a young man left in a permanent vegetative state following the Hillsborough Football Stadium disaster. The House of Lords established that an *omission* to treat (i.e., withdrawing life sustaining treatment), with the same intention of ending life, *was* acceptable in law. Not all the Lords in the case supported the distinction; in fact one stated that to make such a distinction made the law 'morally and intellectually misshapen'. However, in the *Bland* case, the key issue was how to act in the best interests of a patient who cannot express his wishes. This gives us some insight into why the law maintains a distinction between acts and omissions in the face of many arguments to the contrary – it highly values the individual's right to choose (autonomy) and, where this cannot be expressed, the need to act in the patient's best interests. To allow active euthanasia, e.g., to find Dr Cox not guilty of murder, sanctions action which is, it is feared, open to misuse by those who intend to act dispassionately and without the patient's consent. Although it can be argued that omitting to act by withholding treatment could be exploited in the same way, the idea that people who would have died will die is apparently more palatable in our society than the idea of an act to end the life of a person who otherwise would have lived.

More recently, in *Aintree University Hospitals NHS Foundation Trust v James* (2013), the Supreme Court added further detail by finding that if it is not in the best interests of a patient lacking capacity to continue to receive life-prolonging treatment it would be unlawful *not* to withdraw it. This adds weight to the idea that acting (by introducing life-prolonging treatment) is not always in the best interests of the patient who lacks capacity to choose.

The doctrine of double effect

Traditionally this doctrine states that an action which has a good objective may be performed even though this can only be achieved at the expense of a corresponding harmful effect. In the past the doctrine has been invoked to permit the administration of a high dosage of medication (opioids) for pain relief where the doctor is aware that the dose required to adequately control symptoms may inadvertently contribute to death, but where there is no intention to kill.

However, the doctrine of double effect remains controversial and many feel that with advances in palliative care and careful prescribing the doctrine of double effect has no role in the ethics of end-of-life care. Recently it has been stated that 'there are no circumstances in which the prescription of a lethal dose of opioid is necessary to control suffering, and therefore there is no need to invoke the doctrine of double effect' (Regnard et al. 2011).

An act ending life, for example by lethal injection, even if it is at the request of a competent adult, is unlawful. As a result of a catastrophic stroke Mr Nicklinson was completely paralysed, except that he could move his head and his eyes and was able to communicate by blinking to spell out words. He considered his life 'dull, miserable, demeaning, undignified and intolerable' and wished to end it, but because of his paralysed state this could be achieved only through self-starvation or voluntary euthanasia (that is a doctor taking the final act to end his life). Nevertheless in *R. (on the application of Nicklinson) v Ministry of Justice* (2014), the Supreme Court reiterated that deliberately ending life is murder however benevolent the motive. The law continues to draw a distinction between taking active steps to end a patient's life and withholding or withdrawing life-sustaining treatment.

 Key Points

- The law distinguishes between acts and omissions to act.
- This distinction can seem ethically contentious.
- The acts/omission distinction can be seen to allow inroads into the principle of sanctity of life.

CASE 70: QUALITY OF LIFE AND SANCTITY OF LIFE JUDGEMENTS

Nora is 62 years old and has had multiple sclerosis for 25 years. Initially the disease fol-lowed a relapsing and remitting course, and Nora would have long periods of good health in between months of various disabling side effects, such as temporary paralysis and visual problems. For the past 10 years, however, her condition has become more disabling and Nora has had to move into a nursing home. The staff are friendly and she is well cared for. As a result of the insidious effect of her illness, most of her bodily functions have ceased to work and she is doubly incontinent. On the days when she is well enough to be aware of her sur-roundings she finds her condition extremely distressing. She is embarrassed by her lack of bodily control and the fact that she has to have 24-hour nursing care. Her swallowing is unsafe and, following an admission with aspiration pneumonia a year ago, the decision was made to insert a percutaneous endoscopic gastrostomy (PEG) to provide all the nutrition she requires. She now does not even get pleasure from eating or drinking. Some days she is described by staff as being barely conscious, but when she is, they are concerned that she is lonely as she rarely gets visitors.

Questions

- Does respect for the principle of sanctity of life require that life-prolonging treat-ment should always be provided, irrespective of the quality of that life?
- From whose perspective is quality of life to be judged?

ANSWER 70

Legal issues

A competent adult patient may determine that his quality of life is so poor that he would wish not to continue living. A refusal of initiation of or continuation of life-sustaining medical treatment must be respected.

> The principle of self-determination requires that respect must be given to the wishes of the patient, so that if an adult patient of sound mind refuses, however unreasonably, to consent to treatment or care by which his life would or might be prolonged, the doctors responsible for his care must give effect to his wishes, even though they do not consider it to be in his best interests.
>
> *Airedale NHS Trust v Bland* (1993)

However, taking active steps to end a patient's life, even though this is what the patient wants, is unlawful (Case 69).

A decision about the provision of medical treatment to an incompetent patient centres on whether it is in that person's best interests. Although there is a very strong presumption in favour of a course of action that will prolong the patient's life, this is not an absolute principle and it must be balanced against the patient's quality of life, his pain and suffering and the additional or increased pain and suffering which the treatment itself will cause him. 'For children or adults who lack capacity to decide, when reaching a view on whether a particular treatment would be more burdensome than beneficial, assessments of the likely quality of life for the patient with or without that treatment may be one of the appropriate considerations' (GMC, Treatment and care towards the end of life: good practice in decision making, 2010). Making a judgement about another individual's quality of life is difficult, and where there is discord between physicians and relatives, legal advice should be sought. Quality of life should be assessed on an individual basis and cannot be judged on the quality of life that 'every man' would find unacceptable. The GMC states that doctors should be careful not to rely on their personal views about a patient's quality of life and to avoid making judgements based on assumptions about the healthcare needs of particular groups, such as older people and those with disabilities.

There is a heavy burden on those who are advocating a course which would lead inevitably to death to demonstrate that the quality of that individuals' life is so poor and that further treatment would only prolong suffering. The Mental Capacity Act Code of Practice provides that it may be in the best interests of a patient in a limited number of cases not to receive life-sustaining treatment 'where treatment is futile, overly burdensome to the patient or where there is no prospect of recovery', even if non-provision of treatment is likely to result in death.

But what about where the patient has indicated her views or the family voices an opinion about continuation of treatment? A determination of best interests under Section 4, Mental Capacity Act 2005 requires consideration of the patient's welfare in the widest sense, not only the likely clinical outcomes but also social and psychological factors. The person deciding about best interests *must* consider all the relevant circumstances and *must* consult, if it is practicable and appropriate, anyone engaged in caring for the person or interested in her welfare as to what would be in the person's best interests and, in particular, her past and present wishes and feelings, beliefs and values and other factors that she would be likely to consider if she were able to do so.

Recent court decisions have highlighted the need to consider the quality of life which the patient will experience, from the patient's perspective. This is not to say that the patient's views are determinative. Those involved with Nora's care should try if possible to make contact with those who know her, ascertain her views in more lucid phases and try to put themselves in her place and ask what her attitude to the treatment is or is likely to be.

Ethical issues

The doctrine of sanctity of life states that human life has intrinsic value, and therefore it is wrong to intentionally deprive a person of their life, even to avoid extreme suffering. A religious version of the doctrine states that as life is God given, only God has power to take life away. A secular version of the doctrine provides that all humans are equal and therefore no one has the authority to determine that another's life is not worth living. But even if human life has infinite value, this does not mean that other values such as beneficence, non-maleficence and justice are irrelevant. Where the continuance of medical treatment to preserve life comes at such cost in terms of suffering of the patient, is there an ethical obligation to continue to provide such treatment? Quality of life judgements are relevant to health-care decision making, but the threshold at which sanctity of life yields to quality of life can be notoriously difficult to assess – how can a 'minimum' quality of life, such as to justify withholding/withdrawing treatment, be defined and measured? The assessment of quality of life goes beyond purely medical factors and includes reference to social, emotional and physical well-being. The ability to carry out tasks and intellectual capacity should also be taken into consideration. Therefore, an acceptable quality of life depends from whose perspective it is viewed – the decision maker or the patient.

 Key Points

- Sanctity of life is not absolute; human dignity must also be considered.
- Quality of life assessments are highly fact sensitive.
- A person's quality of life may be suboptimal but still be worth living from the patient's perspective.
- It is lawful to withhold or withdraw treatment when it is not in the best interests of the patient to continue with life-prolonging treatments.

CASE 71: BASIC CARE AND MEDICAL TREATMENT AT THE END OF LIFE

Bertie is an elderly man receiving inpatient care following deterioration at home. He has advanced dementia and prostate cancer that has spread to his bones. He has been lovingly cared for by his wife and children throughout his illness, but they are all aware that he is now dying. It has been many months since Bertie has been able to speak or leave his bed, and he no longer appears to recognise his family. While Bertie would previously chew and swallow food placed in his mouth, over the last few days he no longer does this and has coughed and choked on several occasions when given water to drink. The clinical team has explained that Bertie is dying and that he is likely to die within days. His family has understood the explanation from the speech and language therapist that Bertie is unable to swallow safely, and even though the clinical team would support the family with risk feeding, the family does not wish to cause any coughing or choking. Risk feeding acknowledges that there is a risk of choking and food or drink going into the lungs of a patient unable to swallow safely. This risk may be seen as acceptable if withholding food or drink is felt to be inappropriate, for instance if the patient is in the last days of life. Instead, Bertie's family has asked the clinical team to place a feeding tube, so that their father 'doesn't starve to death'. They accept that he is likely to die in the next few days from his underlying medical issues.

Questions

- What is the difference between medical treatment and basic medical care?
- Can clinically assisted nutrition and hydration legally be withdrawn?

ANSWER 71

The provision of food seems such a 'quintessential example of kindness and humanity that it is hard to imagine a case in which it would be morally right to withhold it' (*Airedale NHS Trust v Bland* 1993). Nevertheless the law draws a distinction between basic care and nutrition and hydration provided by tube or drip. 'Basic' care includes the offer of food and water by mouth, such as a cup or spoon, and should always be offered to patients.

Clinically assisted nutrition and hydration (CANH) is an invasive means of providing nutrition and fluids, for example, PEG feeding, nasogastric feeding and intravenous fluids. Patients who have capacity to make decisions about their treatment may refuse CANH. However, the decision to provide CANH is a clinical one, and patients cannot demand that a doctor administers a treatment which the doctor considers is adverse to the patient's clinical needs.

In respect of a patient who lacks capacity to make such decisions, the decision maker must consider whether the provision of CANH is in the patient's best interests. There is a presumption in favour of prolonging life and this will normally mean that all reasonable steps are taken to prolong a patient's life. Although CANH may prolong life it may be burdensome for the patient. Current evidence about the benefits, burdens and risks of these techniques as patients approach the end of life is not clear-cut. If CANH simply prolongs the process of dying it may not be in the best interests of the patient to provide it. The principle of sanctity of life is not infringed by ceasing to give invasive treatment that confers no benefit on the patient.

There is no obligation to provide treatment which is futile. Futility is an ethically controversial concept because treatment is considered futile relative to its goal. If the goal is to prolong life, then provision of CANH achieves this and it would not be considered futile. It may not, however, return the patient to a quality of life he considers worthwhile. Article 2 ECHR imposes a positive obligation to give life-sustaining treatment in circumstances where it is in the best interests of the patient but does not impose an absolute obligation to treat if such treatment would be futile. In this scenario Bertie's son has requested CANH as although it will not prevent his death, it will prevent him from dying of starvation and therefore would not be considered futile to them.

 Key Points

- Basic care, including oral provision of nutrition and hydration, should always be offered.
- Nutrition and hydration provided by artificial means, i.e., by nasogastric tube, is considered a medical treatment.
- Medical treatments can be withdrawn where it is not in the patient's best interests to continue to receive them.

CASE 72: PROVISION OF FUTILE TREATMENT

Mrs Hauser is a 48-year-old woman with metastatic breast cancer that has spread to her brain, despite numerous treatments over years. She is currently an inpatient at a private hospital, having rapidly deteriorated over the last few weeks. She is now bedbound, requires a feeding tube as she can no longer swallow safely and is finding it difficult to communicate, although she can understand information given to her and clearly indicate her wishes. Mrs Hauser is receiving high-energy nutritional supplements down her feeding tube at her request, even though her body is no longer able to gain energy or nutrition from them due to her advanced disease. She is likely to die within the next few weeks. Mrs Hauser is supported by her husband and three teenage children. The entire family has actively and aggressively pursued all treatment options, switching oncologists to gain access to experimental treatments, some of which are not routinely available in Britain.

Mrs Hauser has repeatedly requested all possible interventions and treatments. Driven not just by a desire to keep living, she has expressed a strong need to prove to her children that she will never give up fighting the cancer, equating giving up with abandoning her family. Mrs Hauser has regularly declined offers of psychological support. She has previously given fully informed consent to risky treatments which did not have a strong body of evidence that they would provide a benefit and accepted significant side effects throughout her treatments. Mrs Hauser had been scheduled for her next chemotherapy in one week's time and both she and her husband are insistent it goes ahead, despite the most recent deterioration. The oncologist thinks it unlikely that the chemotherapy will provide any benefit, although he cannot categorically say it will not keep Mrs Hauser alive for extra hours or days. He is aware she had severe nausea the last time she had this chemotherapy and there is a risk it could actually make her more unwell and hasten her death, as it can be damaging to the liver.

Questions

- Is this 'futile' treatment?
- Is it legal or ethical to provide or even offer treatment, purely for psychological benefit, rather than physical benefit?
- Is there a difference between giving the high-energy supplements and the chemotherapy if both are purely for psychological benefit?

ANSWER 72

Treatment has been considered futile if it cannot cure or palliate the disease or illness from which the patient is suffering. In a decision of the Supreme Court, Lady Hale felt this was setting the bar too high and considered that a treatment is not futile if it provides benefit to the patient 'even though it has no effect on the underlying disease or disability' (*Aintree University Hospitals NHS Foundation Trust v James* 2013). She suggests that if a treatment allows a patient to continue living what *they* regard as a worthwhile life then the treatment has some benefit and could not be said to be futile. Mrs Hauser believes insisting on all and any treatment demonstrates her desire to continue living and therefore is worth pursuing, regardless of anyone else's perception of benefit. It seems, then, that whether treatment is considered futile is for the patient to decide on and not the doctor.

Nevertheless the courts have determined that it is doctors who have the responsibility to decide whether a treatment is clinically indicated or not and that they are under no legal obligation to provide it even if a patient demands it. It may be for a patient to decide if a treatment is futile, but it remains with the doctor to decide if it is clinically indicated and therefore if it is to be provided to the patient.

A doctor has an ethical duty to provide good care for his or her patients, and this encompasses both physical and psychological care. While allowing hope of benefit from taking nutritional supplements carries little risk of harm, the chemotherapy could make the patient nauseated for the remaining few weeks of her life or even hasten her death if it causes liver failure. However, the chemotherapy could provide great psychological comfort to the patient and her family that everything that can be done is being done and allow the family an easier bereavement because they supported Mrs Hauser to fight to the very end. Mrs Hauser has experienced significant side effects from previous treatments and is willing to accept them if it means she can have further treatment. While appropriate counselling and support can assist many people to reach an acceptance of the terminal nature of their illnesses, some people remain resolute in their determination to be cured and never want to acknowledge their impending death. To not give further chemotherapy may leave Mrs Hauser and her family feeling abandoned by her doctors and greatly distressed at the very end of her life. While in most situations, timely and sympathetic discussions with the patient and their family about the goals, benefits and burdens of treatment can result in an agreed withdrawal of burdensome interventions that have no significant benefit, there will be some patients for whom a 'good death' is fighting to the very end.

 Key Points

- Treatment that does not cure or palliate, but that can still provide some benefit to the patient, may not be considered futile by the patient or their family.
- It is a medical decision to decide if a treatment is clinically indicated or not.
- A doctor is not legally obliged to provide treatment that is not clinically indicated.

CASE 73: ASSISTED SUICIDE

A palliative care consultant Zayn has been asked by a clinical colleague to speak to a woman in her 60s. Sally has a progressive neurological condition and she now has limited verbal communication, worsening mobility and some elements of dementia. Her life expectancy is around 4 years. Sally is frustrated by her condition and the prospect of her future deteriorating health and reliance on her husband. She says to Zayn that she has been in contact with Dignitas in Switzerland and intends to go there for assisted suicide. Her husband and two adult children oppose this but are prepared to go with her if there is no way of changing her mind.

Sally has rejected all other forms of counselling and Zayn feels that he should not abandon Sally but rather provide a sounding board for her thoughts and offer support for her family.

Questions

- What support can Zayn offer Sally?
- Are Sally's children at risk of prosecution if they take Sally to Dignitas for assisted suicide?
- Should assisted suicide be lawful?

ANSWER 73

Although suicide itself is not a crime, encouraging or assisting suicide is a criminal offence punishable by up to 14 years imprisonment (Suicide Act 1961 amended by the Justice and Coroner's Act 2009). Assistance might be in the form of providing a lethal substance for the person to take. The final gesture (e.g., swallowing the pills) must be made freely by the person committing suicide.

Dignitas is an organisation in Switzerland offering assisted suicide, including to nonresidents. Friends and relatives taking an individual to Dignitas may potentially face prosecution for assisting suicide even though the final act takes place abroad. Although there might be enough evidence to justify a prosecution it may not be considered to be in the public interest to do so.* It may seem unnecessarily harsh and punitive to prosecute family members who unwillingly support their family member through such a traumatic experience. On the other hand, failure to prosecute may indicate that the law is unworkable and not fit for purpose.

Following the landmark case of *R (Purdy) v Director of Public Prosecutions* (2009), guidance was issued which sets out factors tending toward a prosecution being brought and factors against.† A number of factors tending against prosecution are relevant in this situation. Sally seems to have reached a voluntary, clear, settled and informed decision to commit suicide, her family has sought to dissuade her, they are wholly motivated by compassion and their actions are only of minor assistance.

A person acting in his capacity as doctor, nurse or other healthcare professional is more likely to be prosecuted if there is an existing relationship of care and the healthcare professional exerted some influence. The British Medical Association has issued guidance about responding to patient requests relating to assisted suicide. It advises doctors to avoid all actions that might be interpreted as assisting, facilitating or encouraging a suicide attempt. This means that doctors should not

- Advise patients on what constitutes a fatal dose
- Advise patients on anti-emetics in relation to a planned overdose
- Suggest the option of assisted suicide abroad
- Write medical reports specifically to facilitate assisted suicide abroad
- Facilitate any other aspects of planning a suicide

How then can a doctor act with compassion to his patient who has broached the issue whilst not moving into territory of encouraging or assisting? Zayn is offering emotional support for Sally and her family, taking a neutral and non-judgemental stance on her decision to go to Dignitas. He is not encouraging her nor assisting her to find out information about Dignitas.

If Zayn is asked to provide a medical report for Sally so she can receive assisted suicide at Dignitas, his legal liability is unclear. The BMA states that although no doctor has been prosecuted for providing a report, they should be aware of the possible legal implications as this might be seen as encouraging or facilitating that process. A test case, if brought, will clarify the position.

In some countries, physician-assisted suicide is lawful, and there have been calls for the law here to be changed. 'The debate can no longer be about whether or not we allow for assisted

---

* Crown Prosecution Service, Decision on prosecution – the death by suicide of Daniel James, 9 December 2008.
† Policy for prosecutors in respect of cases of encouraging or assisting suicide, 2010, updated 2014.

dying but how we regulate what is increasingly common practice, balancing respect for autonomy with the need to protect the vulnerable' (Cartwright 2009).

Arguments in favour of change focus on the respect accorded to patient autonomy in allowing patients themselves to decide what quality of life is acceptable to them and enabling them to end their suffering. Good-quality palliative care may ameliorate suffering but may not fully address fears of loss of dignity and choice. Arguments against legalising assisted suicide are that it will undermine the trust between doctors and patients, the value accorded to life would be diminished and that the vulnerable in society may feel pressured to ask for assistance to die.

The Assisted Dying Bill provides for competent adults who are terminally ill to be provided at their request with assistance to end their own life. It includes provision for conscientious objection. Such a change in the law would not be of help to Sally as she is not terminally ill – Section 2 (1) provides that a person is terminally ill if she has been diagnosed with an inevitably progressive condition which cannot be reversed by treatment and the person is reasonably expected to die within 6 months.

 Key Points

- Suicide and attempted suicide are not unlawful.
- It is an offence for a person to encourage or assist a suicide or attempted suicide.
- The fact that a person is a healthcare professional is a fact tending in favour of prosecution.
- A healthcare professional should always act with compassion to a person who raises the issue of suicide and assistance.

CASE 74: ADVANCE DECISIONS

Marjorie is a 70-year-old widow. She was diagnosed with multi-infarct dementia 7 years ago. She was once an intellectual and successful woman, but over the past 7 years her memory has declined to the extent that she no longer recognises her family. Six months ago Marjorie had a much larger stroke due to infarction of the middle cerebral artery. Consequently she is now bed bound, doubly incontinent and has difficulty swallowing. Over the past 3 months there has been minimal improvement in her condition and she has had to remain in hospital.

As an FY1 doctor, you are just starting your third rotation. On your first ward round you find that Marjorie's condition has deteriorated overnight. She is tachycardic and tachypnoeic with a temperature of 38°C. You suspect she has developed bronchopneumonia. This is confirmed by a chest X-ray, and you decide that it would be best to start intravenous antibiotics and fluids. You discuss this with Marjorie's family, but they are adamant that she would not wish to continue living in her current state as she would not consider her quality of life acceptable. Her daughter says that her mother had felt so strongly about this that she had made an advance decision. She gives you a two-sided piece of paper which states 'If, as a result of my illness, I become unable to perform any basic tasks myself, then I would not wish to receive any form of life-sustaining treatment'. It is signed 'Marjorie Jenkins' and dated 5 years ago. You tell the family that antibiotic treatment is likely to cure Marjorie's pneumonia but that she is likely to die without it. However, they say that you should respect their mother's wishes and that all treatment should be withheld except for pain relief.

Questions
- What is an advance decision?
- Is this advance decision valid and applicable to the circumstances?
- If it is, do you have to follow it even if you do not think it is in the patient's best interests?

ANSWER 74

Legal issues

The Mental Capacity Act 2005 (MCA) provides for two forms of advance decision making – advance decisions refusing treatment (ADRT) and Lasting Powers of Attorney (LPA). A Health and Welfare LPA enables the attorney(s) to make healthcare decisions in the event of loss of capacity of the donor, and these can include decisions to consent to or refuse life-sustaining treatment if the attorney has specifically been given this authority. It must be registered with the Office of the Public Guardian.

An ADRT can be made by an adult with capacity stating the treatments they would wish to refuse in the event of loss of capacity and the circumstances of the refusal. A poll commissioned by the charity Compassion in Dying (2011) found that 60% of adults would want only comfort care at the end of life but only 3% had made their treatment wishes known in an advance decision.

An ADRT must state what treatment is to be refused; this can be expressed in layman's terms and should set out the circumstances in which the refusal should apply. Basic care, including oral food and water, warmth and hygiene measures may not be refused by an ADRT. There is no required format for ADRT and examples can be downloaded from relevant websites. However, if the ADRT is refusing life-sustaining treatment then it must be written, witnessed and signed by the person making it, acknowledging that it is to apply to that treatment even if life is at risk.

Healthcare professionals must follow an ADRT if they are satisfied that it is valid and is applicable to the circumstances. They cannot refuse to follow it merely because they consider it is not in the patient's best interests to do so. Prior expression of autonomy trumps current best interests. To treat in the face of a valid and applicable ADRT would render the doctor liable to a claim of battery.

Is Marjorie's ADRT valid and applicable? She made it 5 years ago, 2 years after onset of dementia. There is a presumption of capacity so healthcare professionals should assume the person had capacity to make it unless they are aware of reasonable grounds to doubt it. There is no legal requirement that an ADRT must be recently made or reviewed, although the more recently it was made the more likely it is to be a valid representation of the patient's views.

An ADRT to refuse treatment must state precisely what treatment is to be refused. A statement giving a general desire not to be treated is not enough so Marjorie's ADRT is not specific enough about the treatments which she wants to refuse to be valid. However, it does guide the clinician about what she would have wanted in these circumstances, and this is supported by the views of her family. If there is reasonable doubt about the validity or applicability of the ADRT, then an application should be made to the Court of Protection for a decision, and in the meantime it would be lawful to continue to provide treatment to save the patient's life or prevent serious deterioration in health.

Ethical issues

It may be easy to second-guess the authority of an ADRT and thus fail to give effect to the values that the person has stated would be relevant to them in future circumstances. Some philosophers consider that personal identity, and therefore values, may change with the onset of dementia and therefore a person may not be the best judge of her interests for future unforeseen events. Can an ADRT, written 5 years ago by a healthy person, still reflect the interests of Marjorie now? Conversely, it could be presumed that those who make ADRT demonstrate a high degree of commitment to choices they express.

Advance Care Planning

This is a process of discussion between an individual, and often those close to them, and their care providers about what treatment and care they may want in the future. The General Medical Council states that doctors *should* encourage this for patients who have a condition that will affect the length or quality of their life or where loss of capacity may be anticipated. This supportive discussion may then lead to making an ADRT, an advance statement of wishes (which would inform a best interests' determination) and/or the appointment of a health and welfare LPA. Advance care planning should be initiated before the individual becomes acutely unwell, ideally in a primary care or outpatient setting.

 Key Points

- If an ADRT is valid and applicable, it must be respected even if healthcare professionals do not think that it represents the patient's best interests.
- ADRT may be made by those with views about treatments they may wish to refuse at any stage of life; for example, Jehovah's Witnesses may make ADRT refusing all or specified blood products in line with their beliefs.
- They reflect the autonomy of a person expressed at an earlier point in time.

CASE 75: ADVANCE DECISIONS AND ATTEMPTED SUICIDE

Petra has multiple sclerosis and has struggled with her condition for 20 years. Two years ago, in her early 50s, she wrote an advance decision. In it she states that she does not want to be resuscitated or receive any invasive treatments in the event that there is a deterioration of her physical health. The advance decision was dated and signed by two of her neighbours. Petra had many discussions with her family, her husband and three adult children about her advance decision and why she was making it, and had clearly articulated her view that she never wanted to be admitted to intensive care or to receive life-sustaining treatment.

Petra has now attempted suicide by taking an overdose of co-codamol. She was found unconscious by a carer, who called an ambulance, and she has been admitted to the High Dependency Unit. Petra's husband tells the treating team that his wife had really struggled with her limited physical mobility and that she had told him she had had enough of her life. He says he was not surprised by her suicide attempt and does not think it would be right to treat her and return her to a life she found intolerable. He produces Petra's advance decision which he says was given to the family lawyer and her general practitioner.

Question

- Should an advance decision be respected following a suicide attempt?

ANSWER 75

Ethical issues

It could be argued that suicide is the ultimate exercise of autonomy. But many who attempt suicide are not acting autonomously, perhaps because of a mental disorder or severe personal distress. Intervention after attempted suicide may be justified paternalistically to protect patients against harmful consequences of their own choices. From a consequentialist perspective it could be argued that failure to intervene sends out a message of lack of societal concern for those who have expressed such deep distress. Suicide may be considered morally unacceptable because it goes against the principle of sanctity of life. Many religions believe that life should only be taken by God.

If Petra had not made an advance decision refusing treatment (ADRT) then she would have been provided with life-saving treatment, in accordance with her immediate best interests, as she currently lacks capacity to make decisions about treatment. Should her prior autonomous wish not to receive invasive treatments, expressed through her advance decision, be respected? This seems to be at odds with the duty of non-maleficence. The duty of beneficence, however, could be interpreted either as a duty to keep her alive or, conversely, to respect her view that her life was intolerable.

Legal issues

Particular concerns arise when an ADRT is to be considered following a suicide attempt. A person should be assumed to have capacity at the time of making an advance decision. However, some argue that suicidal ideation is evidence of a mental disorder and demonstrates impairment of rational decision making, giving rise to concerns about the person's capacity at that time. The judge in the case of *A Local Authority v E* (2012) said that where there is an 'alerting background' of previous mental illness, rather than relying on the presumption of capacity, the person making an ADRT should demonstrate that they had capacity at the time of making it. The MCA Code of Practice states that if the person making an ADRT is clearly suicidal, this may raise questions about their capacity to make it at that time. Petra told her family that she wanted to make an advance decision so that she would not be admitted to hospital for invasive treatments, presumably linked to her deteriorating health; there was no indication that she was suffering from depression at the time of making it.

ADRTs must specify the treatments to be refused and should state the circumstances in which the decision will apply. It appears that Petra made the advance refusal of treatment in the context of the progression of her multiple sclerosis. As she made it 2 years ago, her condition is likely to have worsened. Nevertheless it could be argued that the current circumstances of a suicide attempt are very different and thus the ADRT should not be binding on the healthcare team.

If the advance decision is not considered to be binding, it should be taken into account in determining what course of treatment is in Petra's best interests. Section 4(6) MCA requires consideration of the person's past and present wishes and feelings, and in particular, any relevant written statement made by her when she had capacity. The written document, when combined with the views of Petra's family about what they consider to be in her best interests and her prior expression about her quality of life, may result in a decision that intubation, ventilation and other intensive care treatments are not in her best interests.

🔑	Key Points

- An advance decision refusing life-sustaining treatment must be written, signed and witnessed (the witness acknowledging the identity of the person making it) and must acknowledge that life is at risk.
- An advance refusal of treatment made in the circumstances of a progressive medical condition may not apply to the different circumstances of a suicide attempt.

CASE 76: DO NOT ATTEMPT CARDIOPULMONARY RESUSCITATION ORDERS

You are a GP with care of a nursing home. Since your last visit Tim has arrived. He is 87 and very frail. He has a history of ischaemic heart disease but this is well controlled following cardiac stenting. He also has early signs of vascular dementia but can still interact with his environment. Following local clinical commissioning group (CCG) guidance the nursing home has a policy that end-of-life decisions are discussed with patients and their relatives once they have been given a chance to settle in. Part of this involves asking the resident about his wishes regarding cardiopulmonary resuscitation.

Given the medical situation, you believe Tim should not be for resuscitation because the harms of cardiopulmonary resuscitation (CPR) are significant for a person in his physical condition (it is likely that his ribs may break with compressions) and, even if successful at restarting his heart, it is likely that this will only prolong his life by a few months given his past history. The nursing home manager informs you that Tim has an extensive family and at least one member visits him daily.

During one of your weekly visits you decide to chat with Tim about his end-of-life wishes. His grandson is also present. Tim does not recognise you from your previous visits, but Dave, Tim's grandson, tells you that he seems very settled in the nursing home. His grandfather loves to have visits from his family, 'even though he doesn't really know who we are' and he takes great pleasure from the small things in his life, like sitting in the sun in a comfy armchair with a cup of tea.

Questions

- Who makes a decision whether to make a Do Not Attempt Cardiopulmonary Resuscitation (DNACPR) order?
- Does this need to be discussed with the patient/the patient's family/carers?
- What if the family objects to the DNACPR?

ANSWER 76

In 2001 the British Medical Association, the Royal College of Nursing and the UK Resuscitation Council brought out national guidelines on DNACPR orders. They were updated in 2007, and following the Court of Appeal ruling in *R (Tracey) v Cambridge University Hospitals NHS Foundation Trust & Others* (2014), guidance was produced in respect of recording and communicating decisions about CPR. In 2009 the UK Resuscitation Council also published standardised DNACPR forms which are widely implemented throughout the country.

A DNACPR decision should be requested by the patient or be made by the most senior member of the medical team or GP after discussion with the patient where appropriate and potentially also with their relatives. All decisions should be clearly documented.

In the *Tracey* case, a woman with lung cancer was admitted to hospital with life-threatening injuries following a road traffic accident. A DNACPR order was implemented in view of her comorbidities. When the family discovered this they challenged the order and it was removed. It was implemented again a few days later after discussion with Mrs Tracey and her family, and a few days after that she died. Posthumously the family challenged the lawfulness of the first DNACPR. The Court of Appeal ruled that the hospital trust had breached Article 8 ECHR (the right to respect for private and family life) as, despite having capacity, Mrs Tracey had not been consulted about the DNACPR order.

The Resuscitation Council (Recommended standards for recording decisions about cardiopulmonary resuscitation 2015) states that there must be

    a. Effective recording of decisions about CPR in a form that is recognised and accepted by all those involved in the care of the patient

    b. Effective communication with and explanation of decisions about CPR to the patient, or clear documentation of reasons why that was impossible or inappropriate

    c. Effective communication with and explanation of decisions about CPR to the patient's family, friends, other carers or other representatives, or clear documentation of reasons why that was impossible or inappropriate

    d. Effective communication of decisions about CPR among all healthcare workers and organisations involved with the care of the patient.

It is, however, important to emphasise that even a patient with capacity cannot insist on cardiopulmonary resuscitation if the medical professional feels that this would not be in the patient's best interests. The issue in the Court of Appeal ruling was not that Mrs Tracey had a DNACPR but that it had not been discussed or explained to her. The decision to make a DNACPR imposes an obligation on clinicians to discuss such decisions with patients (there is a presumption in favour of patient involvement) unless to do so would cause the patient physical or psychological harm.

Where a DNACPR decision is made on the grounds that CPR will not work, and a patient or their relatives do not accept that decision, a second opinion should be offered. In reality if a patient and their relatives were adamant that the patient wanted to be resuscitated, it is likely that the medical professional would agree to this, as enforcing a DNACPR against someone's wishes would inevitably lead to a breakdown in the doctor–patient relationship.

The reasons behind making a DNACPR order are usually multifactorial. Each case should be considered by itself, and blanket decisions about DNACPR's should not be made, e.g., making all patients over the age of 80 'not for resuscitation'. Some examples of when a decision is appropriate are when CPR is unlikely to restart the patient's heart, when the patient is in the terminal stages of an illness or where it is believed that the patient's quality of life is such that the benefit of CPR would not improve their quality of life. In some critical but not necessarily terminal cases, resuscitation decisions may change. Because of this a review date should also be added in case the patient's circumstances improve and the DNACPR order is then re-evaluated.

Discussing end-of-life plans with patients can be very challenging, and healthcare professionals need to learn how to do this in a sensitive and supportive manner. Many patients may never have been asked how and where they would like to die, so where possible, time should be given to allow the patient a chance to reflect on these decisions and discuss them with their loved ones before they are put in place. Explaining what is meant by cardiopulmonary resuscitation is also useful. There is still a general perception that a DNACPR equates to discontinuation of medical treatment. Although in some circumstances the two can go hand in hand, it is important to discuss in detail what treatment a patient would or would not want at the end of their life and to counter this from a professional point of view of what would and would not be clinically effective or appropriate. In the above scenario the GP quickly establishes that Tim does not really comprehend some of the information you are discussing. However, his grandson is able to explain that because Tim is happy in the nursing home and becoming increasingly confused whenever change occurs, the family would not want him to be admitted to a hospital in the event of illness and would definitely not want him to be resuscitated.

These conversations can be emotionally challenging and cause distress to a patient, and there was a real fear that doctors would simply avoid the subject altogether and that end-of-life care planning would be avoided. In the *Tracey* ruling the judge went as far to say that if a professional failed to address end-of-life issues for someone with a terminal illness and they ended up being inappropriately resuscitated, then this too could breach their human rights.

Key Points
• All DNACPR forms should be discussed with the patient if they have capacity. If the patient lacks capacity, discussions should be held with relatives, where possible.   • The patient, the consultant and other members of the healthcare team should be involved in making DNACPR decisions.   • A patient cannot insist on resuscitation where a clinician feels that this would be a futile treatment.

CASE 77: BRAINSTEM DEATH

Holly Poulter is 35 years old. She had been trying to conceive over the past 5 years and was successful after three cycles of IVF. At 23 weeks gestation, she was discovered unconscious at home by her husband. She was rushed to hospital but deteriorated further in the A&E department. She required intubating and was transferred to ITU. Over the next few days multiple tests are performed to try and determine the cause of collapse. She is found to have suffered a catastrophic intracranial haemorrhage. Despite multiple attempts to wean ventilation and see if she could breathe alone, there was no return of spontaneous respiration. Review by two independent consultants confirms that she has suffered brainstem death and that there is no chance of recovery. The review and scan by the obstetricians show that she has a healthy 23 week live foetus.

Her husband pleads that the life support machine is not switched off in order to nurture the baby to a viable gestation. He feels that this is what Holly would have wanted.

Questions

- What tests are performed to diagnose brainstem death?
- Does a person who is declared dead have any interests?
- Is it lawful and ethical for somatic support to be continued until viability of the foetus?

ANSWER 77

Brainstem death

Historically, death was confirmed when there had been cardiac and respiratory arrest. With advances in medical technology, the way in which death is confirmed has had to change. The ability to mechanically ventilate someone has meant that a different method of confirming death has been introduced. Brainstem death is confirmed by establishing that the cerebral cortex is no longer active and that without ventilation the patient would not be able to breathe spontaneously. It is the 'irreversible loss of the capacity for consciousness combined with the irreversible loss of the capacity to breathe' (Kumar and Clark 2012).

Before attempting to diagnose brainstem death, it is essential to exclude other causes of coma such as drug overdose, a change in metabolic state, hypothermia, hypoxia, infection and structural lesions.

! Confirmation of brainstem death
The examination must be performed by two senior doctors: • Absence of oculocephalic reflexes (doll's eye movements) • Absence of corneal reflexes • Pupils fixed bilaterally and unresponsive to light • Absent vestibulo-ocular reflexes (normally, ice-cold water inserted into the ear canal will cause nystagmus. This is absent in brainstem death.) • Absence of any motor response to painful stimuli • Absent gag and cough reflex • Absence of spontaneous respiration (a trial off the ventilator will be needed to establish this)

Although it would be legally permissible to switch off the ventilator since continued ventilation is futile, in practice, agreement should be sought from the next of kin. Holly's husband does not think ventilation is futile because he believes it is keeping her alive and she would have wanted this so that their baby has a chance to continue to mature and be delivered at a safe gestation. The medical ability to physically do this is uncertain. There has been a reported case where a woman has been kept on a ventilator and provided with inotropic support, artificial nutrition and hormones in order to allow a foetus to mature. Even with very intensive support the foetus itself showed signs of physical deterioration after less than 3 weeks. Decisions to continue somatic support need to take this clinical uncertainly into account.

The foetus has no legal status and has no interests which outweigh the interests of the mother in pregnancy (Case 15). What interests does Holly have? As Holly and her husband wanted a child, some may argue that it is in her best interests to receive medical intervention because she would be benefitted by the birth of a much-longed-for child in accordance with her wishes up to and immediately prior to brainstem death. An assessment of a patient's best interests takes into account non-medical considerations, and the beliefs and values which would be likely to influence Holly's decision, if she had capacity to make it, are a relevant factor. Case law provides that altruistic wishes of the patient can be relevant in determining best interests, even if the patient has no awareness of, and no reaction to, the fact that such wishes are being respected (*In the Matter of G (TJ)* 2010).

The interventions would not be of therapeutic benefit to Holly as she is dead. However, as she is not aware of what is happening to her body the interventions could not be considered burdensome. How could Holly benefit if she is dead and would not be aware of the birth of her child or the joy of its life? The birth would attest to her legacy, but it would not benefit her life in any way as she is not alive. The balancing of benefits and burdens of an intervention is relevant in determining whether it is in the person's best interests, but in the case of *Airedale NHS Trust v Bland* (1993) it was said that a person in permanent vegetative state 'has no best interests of any kind'. Of key concern is the dignity accorded in death.

Ethical issues

Some may argue that Holly is being kept alive as an incubator to promote the interests of the unborn child, her husband and the wider family. It seems that she is being used simply as a means to others' ends.

From a utilitarian point of view, the morally right thing to do is to promote the greatest happiness for the greatest number. Enabling the life of this much-sought-after baby is likely to bring joy to her husband and the wider family. However, ITU facilities are expensive and scarce and as there is no hope for Holly to make a recovery, it could be argued that her life support should be switched off in order to provide resources for other patients with the prospect of survival.

 Key Points

- Brainstem death is a clinical assessment.
- Before turning off a ventilator relatives should be informed of the differences between brainstem death and the ability of a machine to keep someone artificially alive.

CASE 78: AFTER DEATH – CORONERS AND CREMATION FORMS

Scenario 1

Maureen, a 90-year-old spinster, has been found dead at home. Neighbours raised concerns as she had not taken her milk in for a few days. There is no sign of foul play and she appears to have died peacefully in her sleep.

Scenario 2

Derek is a 54-year-old driving instructor who presents to the surgery with central crushing chest pain. An ECG demonstrates that he is having a heart attack. Whilst waiting for the ambulance he continues to deteriorate and goes into ventricular tachycardia. Staff begin CPR and shock him back into a normal rhythm, but he does not regain consciousness. He is intubated at the scene and taken to the nearest intensive care unit. Unfortunately, less than 24 hours later he suffers another cardiac arrest and doctors are unable to resuscitate him.

Scenario 3

Evangeline is a 22-year-old ballet dancer who has been involved in a road traffic accident. She is confirmed dead at the scene by the paramedics.

Scenario 4

Mabel has end-stage lung fibrosis. She is seen by her GP due to an exacerbation in her condition. He feels she needs hospital admission but Mabel declines. She fully understands that refusing admission is likely to result in her death but she has made a conscious decision to die at home surrounded by her extensive family. They are all in support of her decision. Some days later her daughter rings to inform the GP that Mabel has died.

Questions

- What is the role of the coroner?
- When should deaths be referred to the coroner?
- How do you refer to the coroner?

ANSWER 78

The office of the coroner is one of the oldest in English history and possibly dates back to the Saxon times. The primary function of the medieval coroner was to keep records of all events leading up to a court case. However, these days the coroner has the much simpler job of investigating death. Most coroners are lawyers although in London some are doctors and a few are dual qualified.

❗ When to report a death to the coroner

- Infant death
- Traffic accidents
- Alcoholism
- Industrial disease
- Drugs and poisons
- Suicide
- Sudden death
- Murder
- Deaths in custody
- Domestic accidents
- Perioperative deaths
- Cause of death unknown
- If a patient has not been seen by a medical professional during the last 2 weeks of life

---

In practice, if a doctor is in any doubt about whether a death needs to be reported to the coroner, it is advisable to first discuss the case with senior members of the team that has been looking after the patient prior to his death. If a decision cannot be made about the exact cause of death, it should be discussed with one of the coroner's officers, who can decide whether a post-mortem should be performed. Sixty per cent of cases reported to the coroner result in a post-mortem being carried out to determine the exact cause of death. When a post-mortem has not fully confirmed the cause of death or where the death was violent and unnatural, then the coroner must hold an inquest into the death. There is also still a common law duty for any member of the public to report a suspicious death to a coroner. However, there is no statutory duty for doctors to report a death.

In the above scenarios Maureen, Derek and Evangeline ought to be discussed with the coroner or a coroner's officer. It may be that Maureen's GP would be happy to put the cause of death as Old Age and a post-mortem would not need to be performed. Although Derek has only been in hospital for less than 24 hours, because the cause of death is known, again a post-mortem would not necessarily be required. Evangeline would undoubtedly need a post-mortem to discover the cause of death. Mabel would not need to be discussed as her death was expected and she had been seen the week before by her GP.

The Coroners and Justice Act (2009) set out improvements to the way coronial investigations are carried out. Some of these changes include providing a coroner with better access to medical advice and allowing bereaved relatives to make a larger contribution to any investigations surrounding the death of their loved ones.

Cremation forms

The Shipman inquiry was held as a result of a GP, Dr Shipman, being found guilty of murdering 15 of his patients. Its aims were to investigate how this could have happened and what measures could be implemented to prevent something similar from happening in the future. It considered several areas of medical practice but focused particularly on death and cremation certification. As a result, proposals to the practice of cremation were suggested. Now two doctors must complete the cremation forms. Form B must be completed by a doctor who was involved in the patient's care prior to their death. Form C must be completed by an independent doctor who is at least 5 years post full registration with the GMC. This doctor should speak with a relative or carer of the deceased to ascertain whether they had any concerns surrounding the death of the patient or the cause of death. Both doctors must also view the body after death.

Doctors are paid for filling in cremation forms and the fee is colloquially known as 'ash cash'. It is worth considering whether this is ethical. Doctors can often charge patients fees for services that go beyond those of caring for a sick patient, for example, signing passport photographs or providing letters for insurance companies. Is assessing a patient posthumously for any evidence of an unnatural death or any cardiac implants a continuation of their duty of care or an extra duty for which doctors should be reimbursed?

 Key Points

- Suspicious, unexpected or violent deaths *must* be discussed with a coroner.
- The Shipman Inquiry resulted in much tighter regulations for doctors completing cremations paperwork.

DUTIES OF A DOCTOR

CASE 79: COMPASSION AND RESILIENCE

Dr Ruth Clarke has been working as a GP partner for the past 3 years. During this time the practice has had a change in staff; they have had to replace the practice manager, one GP retired and another emigrated to Canada. Despite advertising to fill their positions, there has not been any interest. Workload has increased due to the building of a new nursing home and housing estate within the practice boundaries. Financial income is beginning to suffer as there is not enough time to meet additional government targets. Although she has previously enjoyed her job, Ruth is becoming emotionally exhausted by the constant stream of patients – both the chronically ill and the worried well. Last week she overheard one of the secretaries telling the receptionist that there was concern that patients were beginning to notice that she was less interested in their problems and some had even mentioned that they found her manner quite curt.

Questions

- In an increasingly stretched NHS, how important is compassion?
- Is compassion something that can be faked?
- How does burnout affect compassion?

ANSWER 79

Compassion is considered an emotive response to the suffering of others which motivates a desire to provide support and help. The nature of healthcare means that most clinicians are naturally empathetic and compassionate people who thrive themselves by being able to help others. But in modern-day medicine could compassion be considered more of a hindrance to clinical care than an essential attribute? Is demonstrating compassion something that can be taught whilst simultaneously ensuring that clinicians learn to keep themselves emotionally detached from their patients? Analogies have been made between frontline medicine – general practice and A&E departments – and battlefields. Constant exposure to sustained levels of human suffering, complex conditions and a loss of autonomy over working conditions is leading to higher rates of clinician burnout. One critical symptom of burnout is a loss of emotional integrity and compassion. The clinician becomes so overwhelmed by absorbing the emotions of others that subconscious barriers go up as a self-protective mechanism. This in turn can be significantly detrimental to the patient, who will not feel listened to or cared about.

Ironically, it is often the most compassionate clinicians who burn out quickest, and in the current work environment there is increasing emphasis on how to become more resilient to both the emotional intensity of the job and the increasing demands from patients. In this context resilience has been defined as 'the ability to maintain professional and personal well-being in the face of ongoing work stress and adversity' (McCann et al. 2013). Several studies have explored ways of increasing resilience, and all of these suggest that factors such as a supportive work environment, socialising, humour and high levels of job satisfaction are all protective factors against burnout. One particular study suggested that resilience can actually be taught and that the concept of resilience should be 'introduced in all training programmes (including education on ways to strengthen one's own resilience, such as building a positive identity and increasing social support, coping skills and spiritual connection)' (McAllister and McKinnon 2009). Following the Francis Report in 2013, which demonstrated systemic failings in care at Mid Staffordshire NHS Trust, it appeared that this could all be blamed on a lack of compassion from staff at all levels. This prompted public debate about how to increase compassion in the healthcare setting. Should it be tested for when interviewing job applicants? Should compassion be incentivised, with nurses who demonstrate higher levels of compassion being paid more? Conversely, one could argue that a surgeon does not need to care about the patient in order to do their job well and the Health Care Assistant does not need to care about their patient in order to empty a bed pan or provide food to a patient. Incentivising compassion in the current climate would be disastrous – persistent understaffing and lack of resources have put many healthcare workers at breaking point, and being made to 'act out' compassion would be more stressful and likely to result in more work-related stress than trying to rectify the underlying problems. Yet compassion does improve patient experience of healthcare and has been shown to help improve recovery. Finding ways to support healthcare workers remaining compassionate is the key to preventing another crisis like the one in Mid-Staffs. Better staffing, more job autonomy and the feeling that someone will listen if things are going wrong will all support a better work environment and will help promote natural compassion.

 Key Points

- Compassion is undoubtedly beneficial for a positive experience of patient care but does not necessarily equate to being able to provide good-quality and safe clinical care.
- Compassion without resilience can cause clinician burnout.

CASE 80: GOOD SAMARITAN ACTS

James is an FY1 doctor, 3 months into his job. He has just finished a 12-hour on-call night shift when he decides to go to his local supermarket to pick up some groceries on his way home. Whilst there, he hears someone shout for help. He rushes over to find a body lying on the floor. It appears that the person has fainted and hit their head on the floor, causing a significant head wound. James introduces himself as a doctor and applies pressure to the site of bleeding to stem blood flow, having checked that the patient was breathing. He asks for an ambulance to be called. James continues to monitor the patient's breathing whilst applying pressure to the head wound. After a short while, an ambulance arrives and the paramedics take over. The supermarket manager takes down James' details and asks for a description of what happened.

The next day, James arrives at work and recounts the story to a colleague. His colleague expressed his concern at James' actions, saying that he could get sued. Several days later, two letters arrive for James in the post. He becomes slightly anxious after hearing what his colleague had said about legal action. He opens the letters; one is from the supermarket manager and the other is from the patient. They both expressed their gratitude for his actions.

Questions
- What is a Good Samaritan act?
- Is there a legal duty to perform a Good Samaritan act?
- What standard of care would the doctor be held to in a court of law?
- Is there an ethical and professional duty to act as a Good Samaritan?

ANSWER 80

A Good Samaritan act can be defined as one where emergency medical assistance is provided, free of charge and in an environment where the doctor is present in a personal rather than a professional capacity. Good Samaritan acts appear to be quite common. In a Medical Defence Union survey of GPs, GP trainees and hospital doctors, approximately 40% of respondents had acted as a Good Samaritan two to three times, whilst 13% had assisted more than five times (*Pulse*, June 2014). Most incidents were not serious, with assistance most commonly required for fainting, sprains and broken bones.

It is very rare for a Good Samaritan act to result in legal action. Neither the Medical Defence Union nor the Medical Protection Society has come across a case of this happening in the UK at the time of writing. Therefore, James' colleague's opinion regarding legal action is misplaced.

In the UK, there is no legal duty to give medical assistance provided that the incident occurs away from your place of work. There is a contractual duty under the General Medical Services contract of a GP to provide treatment in an emergency within their practice during 'core hours'. Further, some GPs will have a duty of care not only within their premises but also in their practice area, when specified in their contract. The position of the law in the UK differs from many other countries which have Good Samaritan laws. In the United States and most Canadian provinces, there are laws in place to protect the 'Samaritan' from legal claims. In Quebec, Japan and many European countries, such as France and Germany, there is a requirement for a doctor to assist in an emergency unless doing so would endanger the doctor.

The Social Action, Responsibility and Heroism Act 2015 protects people who carry out good deeds from being sued, resulting in the provision of extra protection for doctors acting as Good Samaritans.

Once any kind of medical assistance has been provided, a duty of care is established. This raises the issue as to what standard the doctor would be held to. In this situation the standard of care that James can deliver at the supermarket aisle is going to differ greatly from that in an intensive care unit, for example. The standard of care is that which could 'reasonably' be expected in the circumstances.

It is also important to consider that the doctor may not be in the best position to provide care, for example, he may have consumed alcohol. In the case scenario, James has just finished a long night shift and must have been very tired. The doctor may feel he does not have a choice but to treat the person, but the GMC requires doctors to work within the limits of their competence. In such a situation, the MDU advises that you should explain this to the person beforehand if possible.

There is an ethical and professional duty to provide care in an emergency. It would be difficult to justify non-intervention, unless there was a significant risk of harm to the individual offering help. The GMC guidance is unequivocal; it says 'you must offer help if emergencies arise in clinical settings or in the community, taking account of your own safety, your competence and the availability of other options for care' (GMC, Good Medical Practice 2013).

The GMC guidance goes on to state that doctors have an ethical requirement to ensure that they have adequate insurance or indemnity. Medical defence organisations provide worldwide protection to their members against the unlikely event of legal action. It is important to note that 'good neighbour acts', such as volunteering medical support at an event, is not the same as a Good Samaritan act, as the doctor is attending the event in a professional capacity.

 Key Points

- In the UK, a doctor does not owe a passer-by a duty of care.
- If a doctor provides medical assistance outside of work, a duty of care is established. The standard is one that can 'reasonably' be expected in the circumstances.
- An off-duty doctor is under an ethical and professional duty to provide medical care in an emergency.
- Medical defence organisations provide worldwide protection for their members if litigation occurs.

CASE 81: DELEGATION AND HANDOVER

It is Friday night and you have almost finished admitting your patient. You are just waiting for his blood test results. The locum doctor taking over your shift is running late, and you are getting a bit stressed as you have a train to catch back to London so that you can make it home in time for your cousin's birthday party. Just as you are about to leave your bleep goes off. A nurse informs you that one of your patients, Eric, is having some chest pain. He was admitted 2 days ago with pneumonia and you suspect that the pain is related to the infection. You ask the nurse to do a set of observations and an electrocardiogram (ECG) and say you will ask the doctor taking over to assess him. You then receive an incoming call. It is your cousin, who is very drunk and urging you to hurry up as you are missing out on all the fun. You tell her you are on your way. The locum arrives 20 minutes later and you rush off straight away. Later that night you remember that you completely forgot to hand over the patient who was having chest pain. You decide to ring the hospital and find that he is now a patient on the coronary care unit, having had a massive heart attack.

Questions

- Who has a duty of care to this patient?
- Did you, as the FY1 who received the call, have a duty of care to a patient you have not seen since the onset of new symptoms?
- Should hospitals have systems in place to ensure that ill patients are handed over to night staff?

ANSWER 81

The question, 'When does a doctor owe a duty of care to a patient?' has often been discussed in the courts. Duty of care can be established if it was reasonably foreseeable that the doctor's actions (or lack of) could harm the patient, that the doctor and patient were in a sufficiently proximate relationship and if it would be fair, just and reasonable to owe a duty of care. The hospital also has a duty of care to its patients. There are two types of liability:

> **! Types of liability**
>
> - Direct liability: this includes a duty to provide competent and qualified employees, necessary equipment and safe communication systems in the hospital.
> - Vicarious liability: an employer would be vicariously liable for negligent acts performed by an employee during the course of employment.

A duty of care exists when there has been doctor–patient interaction in a professional capacity. This particular case is fairly straightforward. The on-call hospital doctor had a duty of care to the patient having chest pain. The hospital is also deemed to have a duty of care to that patient. Consequently, if a claim were to arise it could be brought against the hospital under NHS indemnity. The doctor involved in the case would probably be subject to investigation, either internally or via the GMC. Medical defence organisations provide support and advice for any investigations or disciplinary actions held against individual doctors.

In its guidance Good Medical Practice, Delegation and Referral (2013) the GMC states that you must 'share all relevant information with colleagues involved in your patients' care within and outside the team, including when you hand over care as you go off duty, when you delegate care or refer patients to other health or social care'. Handing over sick patients is an important part of a doctor's job. All hospitals should have a system in place to enable the on-call doctors to be aware of which patients are acutely unwell and may need medical attention or review following a changeover of staff. Doctors should check with the hospital they are working in to find out how to hand over patients and how to find out which patients need reviewing on-call. In the scenario the FY1 doctor failed in his duty of care because he did not hand over information regarding an ill patient.

Written communication is just as important as verbal communication. Patient notes and job lists should always be legible and accurate to avoid mistakes being made through misinterpretation.

> ** Key Points**
>
> - A duty of care is established when there has been interaction between a doctor and a patient in need of medical attention.
> - Doctors have a duty to ensure that patients are handed over to the out-of-hours team.

CASE 82: PROFESSIONAL RESPONSIBILITY TOWARD AN ABUSIVE PATIENT

Ben is a 48-year-old man with terminal metastatic melanoma. Originally diagnosed 3 years ago, the cancer has spread despite all treatments, including surgical resection, chemotherapy and radiotherapy. He is angry at having terminal cancer and has been verbally abusive to numerous staff members, face to face, on the telephone and via email, and including senior consultants, junior doctors, specialist cancer nurses and ward nurses. Ben has made several formal complaints against the hospital, in addition to his local District Nursing service and community palliative care team. He has, however, maintained strong and friendly relationships with a few oncology team members and his own GP. Ben has had his care transferred from another hospital and between oncologists at his current hospital due to recurrent breakdowns in relationships with his doctors and nurses due to his behaviour.

Ben attends the emergency department at 2 a.m. with uncontrolled pain. The emergency department doctors have referred him to oncology as he is a cancer patient and have refused to see him. You are the junior oncology doctor working overnight in the hospital. After politely introducing yourself and appropriately commenting on the difficulties you are aware he is facing from his disease, Ben tells you aggressively to stop being condescending, swears at you and makes a derogatory comment about your physical appearance. He demands to see a senior oncology team member who he says knows his case and he has a good relationship with. You are the only oncology doctor available to see the patient for the next 7 hours when the shift changes.

Questions

- Does a doctor's duty extend to treating patients who are aggressive and verbally abusive?
- Does it make a difference if the behaviour is as a result of the patient reacting badly to their condition or illness?
- What if there is no one else able to take over care?

ANSWER 82

Professional integrity

The General Medical Council guidance Good Medical Practice (2013) states that good doctors 'do their best to make sure all patients receive good care and treatment'. All patients include those that are upset or distressed. It is not uncommon for doctors to be required to care for a patient who is angry or upset about their condition or treatment they have received, and dealing with them sensitively is a skill that develops with experience. Patients have the right to complain about care they are unhappy with. However, behaviour that becomes aggressive or verbally abusive can damage the trust required for a doctor–patient relationship. The GMC guidance, Ending Your Professional Relationship with a Patient (2013) is clear that this relationship should only be ended if the trust has broken down such that good clinical care can no longer be provided. It includes violent, threatening or abusive behaviour to the doctor or a colleague or the patient persistently acting inconsiderately or unreasonably as reasons for this trust to break down. The doctor must warn the patient that the relationship may end, should try to do what they can to restore the professional relationship, explore alternatives to ending the relationship and discuss the situation with a more senior colleague. If no resolution can be reached, after ending the professional relationship, the doctor must, amongst other things, ensure prompt on-going care of the patient. Not to follow this guidance could put a doctor's registration at risk.

It may be that warning a patient about the consequences of further abusive behaviour is enough for it to cease. Compassion for an individual patient's situation should be common to all doctors; however, each doctor will have their own limits on this compassion in the face of verbal abuse and aggression. The GMC guidance recognises this, but clarifies that it must be balanced by the need to provide care for the patient. In a situation in which there is no one else promptly available to provide necessary care to a patient who needs it, for example, who is acutely unwell or in extreme pain, it may be difficult to justify ending the professional relationship because of verbal abuse.

Moral responsibility

Patients come from diverse backgrounds. It is not realistic for doctors to only treat patients whom they like or would have as friends. Doctors have a professional responsibility to treat all patients regardless of their own personal views or the patient's beliefs or life choices. This includes people who may be rude or offensive. The limit to which any one doctor will endure abuse, verbal or physical, will depend on the individual circumstances of that situation. A doctor slapped by an elderly patient with advanced dementia may find it difficult to justify ending their professional relationship, while a doctor repeatedly racially abused may be justified in doing so. The latter may be harder to justify if the patient was very unwell and needed immediate life-saving treatment, but a lack of repercussion could be seen as condoning what is an illegal behaviour that encourages repetition by the patient in the future. The cause of the behaviour may have some bearing. A patient shocked by bad news, for instance being told they have terminal cancer, may react aggressively to the doctor, yet be apologetic and upset at their own reaction if responded to appropriately. An experienced oncology doctor, aware of this possible reaction and of the need for an on-going professional relationship, may be more forgiving of aggressive behaviour.

🔑 Key Points

- There are limitations to a doctor's duty of care in the face of violent, threatening or abusive behaviour from a patient.
- A doctor can only end a professional doctor–patient relationship if the breakdown of trust means good clinical care can no longer be provided.
- After the relationship has ended, the doctor must ensure continuing care has been arranged and medical records passed on without delay.

CASE 83: DISCHARGE AGAINST MEDICAL ADVICE

Nora, a frail 82 year old lady with advanced lung cancer, is brought to A&E late at night by ambulance. Her husband, her main carer, was admitted yesterday with pneumonia. He mentioned to staff that his wife was at home alone and was concerned she might not be managing without him.

After she failed to answer the staff's phone calls, an ambulance was dispatched, and she was found in her chair, dehydrated and unable to mobilise. Since her husband's admission she had been too weak and breathless to get up, and had been unable to get herself anything to eat or drink.

Fortunately her test results are normal and the A&E doctor suggests she stays overnight so a carer can be arranged the following morning. The doctor explains to Nora they are concerned that if she goes home she may become dehydrated or have a fall. Nora is adamant she wants to go home, stating that she is fine, would rather sleep in her own bed, and will take a sandwich from A&E for supper. She starts getting up and making her way towards the door. She has no history of mental health problems.

Questions
- How should doctors approach patients who make decisions they consider unwise?
- What issues arise from the complex interplay between health and social care, particularly during out of hours?

ANSWER 83

The fact that Nora's decision to go home is one the doctor might think is unwise is not grounds for overriding her decision, as all adults should be assumed to have capacity unless it is demonstrated otherwise. The Mental Capacity Act Code of Practice states that 'anybody who claims that an individual lacks capacity should be able to provide proof. They need to be able to show, *on the balance of probabilities*, that the individual lacks capacity to make a particular decision, at the time it needs to be made' (paragraph 4.10). The doctor should formally assess Nora's capacity (particularly given that she is making a decision which could potentially result in harm), and explore the reasons behind Nora's decision. It may be that Nora attributes different weight to the risks and benefits compared with the doctor, and that she is willing to accept the risk of a fall or becoming unwell in exchange for the benefit she perceives of being in her own home.

If Nora is deemed to have capacity, her decision must be respected and she must be allowed to go home. In this scenario, the doctor will probably feel uneasy. Doctors have a duty of care towards their patients, and it may be difficult for the doctor to reconcile this duty to look after Nora and avoid harm, with the requirement to respect her autonomous decision. This uneasiness could be partly addressed by considering what measures they could take to try to support Nora and respect her wishes whilst reducing potential risks. As it is out of hours and she is in A&E it may be practically difficult to arrange additional care, although some areas have emergency social care services and district nurses. The doctor may consider contacting out of hours support networks, informing Nora's GP of the situation, or calling her in the morning to check her progress.

If there was anything to suggest that Nora lacks capacity, a different set of challenges arise. If a patient lacks capacity they should be treated according to their best interests, but these can be difficult to determine as they extend beyond only medical issues. One may argue that keeping Nora in hospital is in her best interests as it will prevent potential harm, preserving her future autonomy. However, keeping her in hospital against her will, particularly where there is no medical treatment indicated and where doing so is purely a preventative measure to reduce risk of potential (not definite) harm, is a significant infringement of her autonomy. This could amount to a deprivation of her liberty (Case 33), contravening Article 5 (right to liberty) and Article 8 (right to respect for private and family life) of the ECHR. Furthermore, keeping Nora in hospital against her will could result in further harm, as she may be less willing to engage with health and social services in the future, something that is likely to become increasingly important given her current health status and her husband's role as her sole carer.

This case demonstrates that assessing capacity, and subsequent decision-making, can be complex, particularly in environments such as A&E where things are busy, time-pressured, and the doctor may lack any prior knowledge of the patient. It may be further complicated where a patient makes a decision the doctor considers unwise, because although this does not necessarily indicate a lack of capacity, it will cause unease for the doctor. However, when a patient has capacity their autonomous wishes should be respected, and doctors should seek to explore potential practical methods and utilise other healthcare and social professionals to enable their wishes to be met.

 Key Points

- Assessing capacity may be difficult in certain circumstances, particularly where there are time-pressures in busy departments and a lack of prior knowledge of the patient.
- Senior support should be sought if there are doubts about a patient's capacity, particularly where they are making a decision that may put them at risk.

CASE 84: CHILD SAFEGUARDING

An 18-month-old girl, Lilly, presents to A&E with vomiting. She is well known to the paediatric department for vomiting and poor feeding. She was born at 29 weeks' gestation and was very ill as a neonate. She spent the next 4 months in hospital with various infections and difficulty tolerating feeds. Since coming home, her mother struggled to feed Lilly and ensure she put on weight. Her mother coped as well as she could but had to give up her job as an office manager, as she felt no one else could spend the time Lilly needed to feed. Lilly's mother also has to look after her 3-year-old son, who is healthy.

Lilly has no defined diagnosis and this makes managing her condition difficult. Her mother has consulted a number of different hospitals in a desperate attempt to help her daughter. Each hospital performed the same tests and came to the same conclusion – that Lilly was malnourished but no firm diagnosis could be made.

At presentation, Lilly looks thin and small. Her mother says Lilly has not been able to keep anything down for days because she has been coughing. You think she looks a little dehydrated but otherwise not too bad. Her chest is clear. You ask for a chest X-ray to rule out a chest infection. The radiologist later alerts you to the multiple rib fractures of differing ages. He also tells you the bones look osteopenic, consistent with chronic metabolic bone disease. You discuss the case with your consultant, who is not convinced of any child abuse. He asks you to focus on making the child better and ready for discharge.

Questions

- What are your legal obligations in this case?
- How would you proceed?
- Do you have any ethical obligations to Lilly's mother?

ANSWER 84

The welfare of the child is paramount (Children Act 1989). Lilly's welfare may be compromised if she is suffering as a result of directly inflicted damage (abuse) or as a result of failure to protect her from harm (neglect). The latter includes failing to provide adequate nutrition or appropriate medical care.

Has Lilly's mother failed in these respects? If no, then no further action needs to be taken. If yes, any concerns should be discussed with a consultant. In this case, where the consultant has disregarded the possibility of child abuse if you have ongoing concerns, the GMC (Good Medical Practice, 2013) states that 'you should follow up your concerns and take them to the next level of authority if you believe that the person or agency you told about your concerns has not acted on them appropriately and a child or young person is still at risk of, or is suffering, abuse or neglect'. A doctor may find it useful to discuss the situation with peers, other senior colleagues or even other agencies while preserving patient anonymity. If, after all this, a doctor still suspects child abuse, they have a positive obligation to disclose information promptly (GMC, Confidentiality, 2009). After contacting social services on the phone, a doctor should send a written referral within 48 hours. If they have not had a reply within 3 working days the doctor should contact social services again.

There are three outcomes of referral:

- No further action
- The child may need to be assessed
- Urgent action to safeguard the child if there are concerns about the child's immediate safety (e.g., admitting the child into hospital)

It is important that anyone involved in the care of the child accurately documents events and concerns in the patient's notes, including discussion with senior colleagues. It is the duty of the doctor to recognise and follow up child protection concerns. This applies not only to those who have suffered significant harm but also to those at risk of suffering in the future.

When speaking to the child, it is important not to ask any leading questions or attempt to investigate alleged abuse as this may be detrimental to any criminal prosecution. All hospitals will have a protocol which should be observed by every doctor, e.g., some trusts have a policy of referring all unexplained fractures directly to social services.

The diagnosis and misdiagnosis of non-accidental injury carry obvious ramifications for the parents (or guardians) and of course the child. Perhaps a less apparent consequence may be the subsequent reluctance of the parents to present to medical services in the future. An honest approach by keeping parents informed and discussing concerns and the processes involved with them is good medical practice and may help prevent these outcomes. This should be attempted as far as is compatible with the welfare of the child.

 Key Points

- The welfare of the child is the paramount consideration.
- Suspected child abuse cases are complex and should be handled sensitively with advice from senior colleagues and social services.
- NHS trusts should have local protocols, which should be adhered to. They will also have a designated lead specialist for child safeguarding who can be contacted for advice in an emergency.

CASE 85: TREATING FRIENDS AND RELATIVES

Since you graduated from medical school you have been bombarded with people asking you about their possible medical problems. When you went home for a weekend to escape from the hospital, your brother-in-law asks you to give him some advice on his hayfever. You felt able to do this so you made some suggestions. Your aunt then asked you about her arthritis and whether you could prescribe her some extra pain relief. Later that day your grandparents come to visit. Your grandma confides in you that she is worried about the number of times your grandpa is getting up to go to the toilet in the night. She wants some reassurance that this is normal.

Questions

- What should a doctor do when a friend or relative asks for medical advice?
- Can a doctor write a prescription for a friend?

ANSWER 85

Medical training means that a doctor should have extensive knowledge of different medical illnesses. A newly qualified doctor may discover that friends and relatives suddenly view them as a professional with a vast amount of medical knowledge. They may assume that you will be able to accurately diagnose any condition they present with and will feel more comfortable asking advice rather than going to see a doctor they don't know. A lot of medical knowledge, however, comes with experience.

General Medical Council: Good Medical Practice, Treating Friends and Family (2013) states that 'wherever possible, you should avoid providing medical care to anyone with whom you have a close personal relationship'. Although the recommendation is not to treat, consultation discussion explored some contrary views to this. It went as far to say that imposing restrictions on whether a doctor can treat a loved one could be considered a breach of their human rights under Article 8 ECHR – a right to private and family life. The consultation process also considered that being treated by a relative can be beneficial to a patient as the doctor will have a much better understanding of their ideas, concerns and expectations.

The main reason against treating loved ones is the inability to be impartial, which could be detrimental to patient care. The patient may feel unable to say no to treatment they do not want, and both parties may feel uncomfortable if the need for intimate questions or examinations is required. A doctor treating friends or relatives also risks being accused of nepotism if the patient is seen quicker or referred for urgent investigations. Conversely, a doctor could be accused of negligence or neglect if they stand to benefit from a relative's death. There may also be massive psychological consequences if reassurance is given to a friend or relative when actually they may have a more sinister illness, which then goes undiagnosed.

In more rural locations or small villages, relatives may be official patients. This should be avoided if there is another surgery a patient can register at, or measures should be taken to ensure that the patient is seen by another doctor within that practice. In smaller hospitals it can raise issues of confidentiality and it may make either the doctor or the patient feel uncomfortable.

Fully registered doctors are allowed to write private prescriptions. Again, it is advised that this does not happen too frequently. A course of antibiotics would be considered an acceptable use of this privilege. However, long courses of medication should be monitored by doctors and consequently prescribed by a general practitioner.

 Key Points

- Treating friends and relatives is not advisable because it raises important issues regarding confidentiality and the nature of the doctor–patient relationship.
- Doctors could be accused of giving preferential treatment to their relatives.

CASE 86: PROFESSIONALISM AND SOCIAL MEDIA

A colleague from the hospital has invited you to join a special Facebook group for doctors as they have found it a useful source of information. The group provides a forum in which individuals can ask the other members questions about difficult cases or can write about their experiences with interesting patients. Although you think that you would find the group very beneficial you raise some concerns with your colleague about the safety of discussing cases with strangers over the Internet. You decide to see if there is any ethical guidance about using Internet forums as a doctor.

Questions

- Can you think of any benefits of using social media to discuss cases?
- Can you think of any dangers that using social media sites may present – either on a professional or personal level?
- What guidance has the GMC and BMA issued about this subject?

ANSWER 86

Over the past decade access to public information has been dramatically changed by the evolution of numerous social media websites. These range from educational based forums such as doctors.net to more personal forums such as Twitter and Facebook. Although there are advanced privacy settings on these sites, it is important to realise that essentially any information on them is potentially accessible to the general public.

Professional guidance from both the BMA and GMC acknowledges that these forums can be beneficial by enhancing professional sharing of knowledge and case studies in an easy-to-access manner. They can also be used as a way to learn about different protocols in other areas of the country and can be used to network with other healthcare professionals in different parts of the world.

There are two very obvious ethical issues surrounding the use of online media by medical professionals.

The first is the duty of confidentiality that a doctor owes a patient. Discussing cases and posting pictures of unusual rashes on a forum can be educationally beneficial *but* it is imperative that the person doing this is aware that they are potentially breaching confidentiality if enough detail is provided to enable the patient to be identified. GMC guidance states that 'although individual pieces of information may not breach confidentiality on their own, the sum of published information online could be enough to identify a patient or someone close to them' (GMC, Doctors' Use of Social Media, 2013). Patient consent to publish information about them should be obtained and documented in the correct way.

Perhaps a less obvious risk of using social media websites as a professional is the blurring of doctor–patient boundaries. This is particularly important to be aware of when working in small communities where being friends with your patients is sometimes inevitable. Professionals need to be aware that anything they post on personal sites is potentially accessible to their patients and may make them vulnerable to abuse or manipulation. The BMA gives clear guidance that doctors should not accept Facebook friend requests from patients (BMA Guidance: Using Social Media: practical and ethical guidance for doctors and medical students).

It is also recommended that doctors regularly review privacy settings on any social media websites they use to ensure they are set at the most conservative levels in order to prevent risks to themselves. It is also important to remember that informal comments about patients or colleagues should not be made on social media sites – particularly if the comments are derogatory in nature.

 Key Points

- Doctors should consider any information they post on a social media website as being in the public domain and must retain high levels of professionalism at all times.
- The Internet can provide supportive and educational forums to doctors at all stages of training.

CASE 87: DOCTORS AND DVLA REGULATIONS

Fabian is a 38-year-old taxi driver who is admitted to A&E following a collapse. He was at home with his wife and son when he 'fell to the floor and just started shaking'. He has no memory of the event and does not recall feeling strange beforehand. A collateral history is taken from his wife who describes the collapse as sudden with all of his body jerking. She says it lasted about a minute 'but felt like a lifetime'. There is no history of tongue biting or incontinence and he recovered spontaneously, although he felt a little drowsy afterwards. Nothing like this has happened before and there is no history of epilepsy in the family. He did, however, start taking a new drug called Pellidron for his headaches 3 days ago. Fabian has a history of headaches, oesophagitis and mild depression. He does not smoke and drinks about 20 units a week. He is taking omeprazole 20 mg daily and citalopram 20 mg daily, and he says he takes a baby aspirin as his brother, aged 47, recently had a myocardial infarction. He does not have any known allergies.

Questions

- Can Fabian continue to drive because he has only had one unexplained seizure?
- Is there a legal requirement to inform the Driver and Vehicle Licensing Agency (DVLA) of Fabian's seizure?
- Is there a legal requirement to tell his employer?

ANSWER 87

The DVLA publishes guidelines on medical conditions that disqualify an individual from holding a driving licence. These restrictions vary, depending on the vehicle being driven. It is the responsibility of the patient to inform the DVLA of any 'notifiable' medical condition or disability which may affect their ability to drive and these include:

- Epilepsy
- Cardiovascular disorders
- Diabetes mellitus
- Psychiatric conditions
- Drug and alcohol misuse
- Visual disorders
- Renal disorders
- Respiratory and sleep disorders

The DVLA will assess the medical condition or disability and decide if the person should stop driving. DVLA guidance also states that the person should stop driving if his doctor tells him to because of his medical condition. Taxi licence applicants should pass a medical examination prior to a licence being granted and licence holders should not drive for 5 years following an unprovoked seizure as long as all neurological investigations are otherwise normal. In this case it will be prudent to advise Fabian both to abstain from driving due to the risk of having a seizure and losing control of his vehicle, and to tell Fabian that he ought to inform his employer and the DVLA that he has had a seizure of unknown aetiology and is currently under continued medical investigation. Information like this can have a severe effect on an individual's livelihood. It is important when breaking the bad news that doctors emphasise why the regulations are so strict.

If a doctor discovers that a patient is continuing to drive against medical advice the GMC advises that it is acceptable to break patient confidentiality and inform the DVLA (GMC, Confidentiality: reporting concerns about patients to the DVLA or the DVA, 2009). The GMC provides guidance on the steps that should be taken. The patient's legal duty to inform the DVLA and the risks of continuing to drive should be discussed with the patient again and they should be asked to inform the DVLA. Alternatively, it would be appropriate to gain consent to inform the DVLA on the patient's behalf. If the patient refuses, a doctor has a professional obligation to inform the DVLA and the patient should be informed that this will be done. It is important to inform the patient once a disclosure has been made.

There is no absolute legal obligation to inform either the DVLA or the patient's employer.

Confidentiality is an important factor in the doctor–patient relationship and as such should only be broken in specific circumstances. Breaking patient confidentiality can be ethically justified using a consequentialist argument; it is done to protect the health of the patient and protect the general public from harm. In this case informing the DVLA that the patient has had a seizure may prevent harm to the patient and the general public by preventing a road traffic accident caused by having a seizure while driving.

 Key Points

- When a patient has a medical condition that may prevent them from driving they should inform the DVLA.
- If a patient refuses to inform the DVLA, a doctor has a professional and moral obligation to do so but must inform the patient that this will be done.

CASE 88: THE ROLE OF CLINICAL AND RESEARCH ETHICS COMMITTEES

Scenario 1

You are an FY1 doctor on your general practice rotation. At medical school you were interested in the law on advance decisions and you now wish to do a research study to look at the prevalence of advance decisions in general practice. You have drafted up a questionnaire which you want to send out to all general practices in the Clinical Commissioning Group.

Scenario 2

You are an FY2 doctor on an intensive care rotation. A patient with multiple sclerosis is admitted to the unit and treated for pneumonia. The patient was adamant that she did not want to receive intravenous antibiotics but no specific reasons were given. The patient's condition deteriorated rapidly and she became unconscious. It was considered clinically necessary to give intravenous antibiotics since they were more likely to be effective against her sepsis, and she was no longer able to swallow oral medication. You think that the patient's prior refusal of intravenous antibiotics should be taken into account, and you would like an opportunity to discuss the ethical issues.

Questions

- In what circumstances is research ethics approval required?
- What does a clinical ethics committee do?

ANSWER 88

Clinical ethics committees and research ethics committees have distinct functions.

Research ethics

The NHS Health Research Authority (HRA) was established in 2011 'to protect and promote the interests of patients and the public in health research, and to streamline the regulation of research' (www.hra.nhs.uk). It ensures that any research involving humans is ethical, safe and of high quality. Prior approval from a research ethics committee (REC) is required for any research involving patients or NHS resources (including NHS staff). Members of RECs are volunteers, and at least one-third of REC members must be lay people, i.e., not in a clinical role.

All applications must be through the Integrated Research Application System (IRAS). This is an online system where applications can be made to a number of different organisations involved in research including research ethics committees. Additional details on the processes involved in getting ethical approval for a research project are all found on the HRA website. An audit or service evaluation does not require ethical review by an NHS research ethics committee. Where it may be unclear, advice should be taken.

Clinical ethics

A clinical ethics committee (CEC) considers the ethical implications of the treatment and care of patients. These are multidisciplinary committees and members include clinicians, other healthcare professionals, and religious, legal and lay members. Although the role of CECs varies, many will provide ethics input in trust policy (e.g., limitation of treatment plans), ethics education (e.g., open days for trust staff) and consider the ethical implications in individual cases referred by health professionals (e.g., conflict within the treating team about the best interests of a patient). The role of the CEC is advisory only – it does not direct healthcare professionals. CECs can provide a supportive forum for discussion of difficult ethical issues.

There is no requirement that an NHS trust must have a clinical ethics committee. Currently there are more than 85 CECs in the UK. The UK Clinical Ethics Network provides information and support to developing and existing clinical ethics committees and the website contains ethics education materials (www.ukcen.net).

In scenario 1, approval by a research ethics committee is not required, as this is an audit. However, there may be different views about what defines an audit. Advice from the HRA may be required. In scenario 2 there is a conflict of views between the priority accorded to the best interests of the patient and respecting her autonomy. These issues can be usefully discussed in a clinical ethics committee and can provide a good basis for ethics education. However, this does not replace the need for legal advice where necessary, in this case whether there is a valid advance decision that applies in the circumstances.

 Key Points

- Healthcare research *must* be approved by a research ethics committee.
- Clinical ethics committees are not compulsory and have no legal status but can be a useful resource for individual patient ethical dilemmas, ethics education and guidance on hospital and community policies.

FAITH, VALUES AND CULTURE

CASE 89: MEDICALISATION OF HUMAN EXPERIENCE

Toby is 6 and has been referred by his GP to the child development centre as his school has expressed concerns over his lack of social interaction and mild speech problems. The referral letter describes him as being 'a happy, friendly child most of the time but who can have periods of agitation in some situations. He has a few close friends at school but struggles with larger group activities. He also likes to know the times of breaks and lunch and struggles if these are delayed. He is progressing well in most areas of learning but we have noticed that he does not engage in conversation with others and rarely initiates questions. He has a special interest in sports cars and can talk about this happily for long periods of time.'

Toby has been brought to the clinic by his parents. They too have noticed that Toby's behaviour is different from his peers. They say that they first noticed this around 2 years of age as he would prefer to play alone than with others at nursery and would also have repetitive speech and movements. They say that he has mainly grown out of these but that if he faces significant changes to his routine he will get agitated and start flapping his hands. His parents are not concerned about his behaviour and feel that he is doing well at school. Although they are aware he is different they do not see how assigning him a 'label' will benefit him.

Questions
- When does a spectrum of normality become an illness?
- Who should make decisions about a child's health if the parents do not have any concerns?

ANSWER 89

The last half century has seen a marked change in societal perception of illness. The medicalisation of human experience – from childbirth to bereavement and alcoholism to obesity – has presented anthropologists, physicians and bioethicists with a pandemic of new medical problems with perhaps the only real beneficiaries being pharmaceutical companies. Interestingly, only two 'conditions' – homosexuality and masturbation – have been de-medicalised.

Medicalisation of normal human experiences such as childbirth and bereavement can also have detrimental effects on individuals who perceive that their 'experience' should fit societal expectations. Feelings of abnormality and failure if a birth does not go according to a birth plan, or if feelings of grief do not resolve within a pre-existing expectation of when life should get back to normal, can all have significant psychological consequences. The same thought process can be applied to simple maladies such as premenstrual tension and menopause. Although not abnormal experiences, the ability to 'treat' the condition with pharmaceutical or psychological interventions has medicalised unavoidable physiological changes.

There are many examples in clinical medicine where diagnoses are assigned to individuals who are perceived to lie outside of a normal spectrum of development or behaviour. Autism spectrum disorder is one of the most common 'modern' diagnoses. First identified in the 1970s it now has a prevalence of roughly 5/1000 children (Taylor et al. 2013). There was a dramatic increase in prevalence in both the UK and the United States in the 1990s, but this has now plateaued and there has been little annual variation over the past decade. One theory is that prior to the increase in diagnosis in the 1990s the condition was not medically recognised and individuals with the classic triad of difficulties with social communication, social interaction and social imagination were merely considered slightly reclusive or socially awkward. Similarities can be drawn with other newer medical disorders such as attention-deficit hyperactivity disorder and emotionally unstable personality disorder, both of which could be considered part of the spectrum of human behaviour.

The ethical debate revolves around the benefit of assigning diagnoses and the impact that medicalisation of human behaviour has on the individual, their family and society as a whole. The latest research suggests that the earlier autism is diagnosed the better the outcome for the child, as the brain is more malleable and can be taught how to improve social interaction. But is medicine tampering with something more innate than just trying to prevent disease? Is there a risk that these changes fundamentally alter personality at a young stage? Retrospective analysis of historical figures suggests that many of the most celebrated geniuses showed typical autistic traits and by 'curing' individuals of autism we may be denying society the very people who have the intense, single-minded focus to produce brilliance.

It is widely accepted among clinicians that the behavioural and developmental features of autism lie on a spectrum, ranging from people with exceptional skills and flexibility of thought, to individuals with really marked difficulties. The difficulty in making a diagnosis thus throws into sharp relief a dilemma which is present across multiple conditions but is seldom discussed: the difficulty of placing a dichotomy on the continuum of human development. There are individuals who undoubtedly will benefit from the additional educational and psychological support that a diagnosis brings. It can also bring some comfort to family to have a reason to explain behaviour or habits that may be perceived as socially unacceptable. However, there are others who may feel 'labelled' with a disease by professionals who feel that treatment is needed in order for them to conform to social expectations of behaviour.

In the case scenario Toby may well be exhibiting autistic traits which could be ticked off on a medical checklist as meeting arbitrary criteria for a diagnosis of autism. This would no doubt enable him (and his school) to have access to additional funding for educational support. What may be more important to consider, however, is Toby's 'lived experience'. Does he perceive himself as having problems which need medical and social input? His parents' views and beliefs should also be taken into consideration. In a supportive environment differences may be celebrated and individuals able to flourish without medicalisation of behaviour. This could be in contrast to a more rigid environment where another child with fewer autistic traits may actually benefit more from support in order to conform to societal expectations of behaviour. Given the problems outlined, a flexible and collaborative approach to diagnosis and prognosis is not only empowering for families, but also intellectually honest.

 Key Points

- Careful consideration should be given to whether someone is experiencing normal emotions that can be helped with emotional support rather than medication.
- Diversity in abilities and interests should be encouraged unless there is evidence that further intervention is needed for the support of that individual.

CASE 90: JEHOVAH'S WITNESSES AND BLOOD TRANSFUSIONS

Zoe has given birth to her first child. She subsequently develops a postpartum hemorrhage and informs the doctors of her refusal to receive blood products, if they are needed in treatment, because she is a Jehovah's Witness.

Joshua, age 15, sustained multiple injuries in a car accident. He refuses blood products because he is a devout Jehovah's Witness.

A newborn baby has been diagnosed with a serious heart condition requiring surgery. His parents consent to him undergoing the cardiac surgery, but because of their religious beliefs they cannot consent to him receiving blood during the course of that surgery or subsequently, if it is needed.

A 27-year-old devout Jehovah's Witness, Gemma, is attacked whilst walking home from work. A passer-by calls an ambulance and she is rushed to A&E, where she is found to have a ruptured spleen. She is unconscious but she is carrying a document that informs doctors that she does not wish to receive a blood transfusion even if the outcome would be death. When Gemma's husband arrives, he informs the doctors that her wishes have not changed since signing the document.

Questions

- What is the religious constraint on Jehovah's Witnesses refusing blood products?
- Is a refusal respected in all situations?

ANSWER 90

Jehovah's Witnesses obey the Biblical injunction to abstain from blood (Acts 15:29). As a result of their beliefs they may refuse the administration of whole blood and primary blood components (red blood cells, white cells, plasma and platelets). However, individual beliefs vary and some may accept blood salvage techniques and the use of minor blood fractions. The Jehovah's Witness Hospital Liaison Committee can be contacted to provide information about practises and beliefs.

As a competent adult, Zoe's refusal to accept a blood transfusion must be respected.

A refusal by a teenager of life-sustaining treatment, even if competent to make that decision, may be overruled to preserve his life and thus his future autonomy. This *may* be so even if the refusal is for religious reasons.

Although his parents may have understandable objections on religious grounds, surgery is clearly in the baby's best interests and as it is inevitable that he must receive blood transfusions during the course of or subsequent to the surgery it would be lawful for the baby to be given blood products. The welfare of the child is paramount. However, in a situation which is not imminently life-threatening, doctors should consult with parents and consider if it is appropriate to use alternative forms of management.

Gemma was unconscious on arrival at hospital. As a practising Jehovah's Witness she is carrying an Advance Decision Document prohibiting blood transfusion. The Mental Capacity Act Code of Practice provides that an advance decision (AD) refusing all treatment in any situation, for example with an explanation of her personal or religious beliefs, may be valid and applicable (paragraph 9.13).

The lack of advance dialogue with Gemma about whether she really understands the nature and effect of her AD is a concern. It would be easy to err on the side of caution and treat in her medical best interests irrespective of her AD. This is legally and ethically problematic; treating in the face of a valid and applicable advance refusal may be subject to a claim of battery.

There is protection from liability if a healthcare professional provides treatment when they were unaware of an advance decision. If somebody tells a healthcare professional that the patient has made an AD, reasonable efforts should be made to find out what it says. Healthcare professionals should not delay emergency treatment to look for an AD if there is no clear indication that one exists. If no such document is found on an unconscious person, they should be treated in their best interests.

 Key Points

- A refusal of blood products by a competent adult is respected.
- It is in the best interests of babies and young children to receive blood products which are necessary as part of the treatment, irrespective of their parents' religious views.
- Blood products may be refused in an advance decision and it is the responsibility of the person who is in charge of the care of the patient when treatment is required to determine whether a valid and applicable advance decision exists.

CASE 91: RAMADAN AND PROFESSIONAL RESPONSIBILITY

Ahmed is a newly qualified doctor and is due to be on-call for 4 days in a row. This involves consecutive 14-hour days and can be very busy and tiring. His on-call week has coincided with the last week of Ramadan and since it is May the hours of darkness where he is allowed to eat and drink are more limited. He is adamant that he does not want to break his fast during the on-call as he is a devout Muslim. During the second of his on-call days, the ST2 trainee calls in sick and the consultant asks Ahmed to assist with surgery. Things are going well and Ahmed is really enjoying the extra surgical experience and responsibility he is gaining. During a lunch break the consultant praises Ahmed's skills but notices that he has nothing to eat or drink at all, not even a glass of water. During the next operation an emergency arrives in A&E. A 70-year-old man has been diagnosed with a leaking abdominal aortic aneurysm. He is rushed to theatre and Ahmed is told to scrub. The additional concentration needed to learn new skills all morning combined with not having eaten is beginning to affect Ahmed's focus, and on several occasions he has to be retold what he needs to do.

Questions

- What does the Qur'an say about Ramadan and illness?
- What advice should you give Ahmed?
- Who else can you ask for help in this situation?

ANSWER 91

Ramadan is the month during which Allah revealed the contents of the Qur'an to Muhammad. To commemorate this, Allah instructed all devout Muslims to fast from sunrise to sunset during the month of Ramadan. Fasting during Ramadan is one of the five pillars of Islam. It involves abstaining from food and all medication to demonstrate obedience and learn sympathy for the poor and hungry. People who are healthy and intentionally do not fast commit a sin in the eyes of Allah. However, there are exceptions to fasting. Those with chronic illnesses, the acutely unwell, children and people with learning disabilities who would not understand the reason behind fasting are not expected to fast. It could also be argued that certain professionals should be able to abstain from fully fasting as reduction in their concentration and physical skills may have a negative impact on other people. In this instance fasting could cause significant health repercussions for his patients.

Although there does not appear to be any definitive research on the impact on patient safety by fasting, it is recommended that clinicians should avoid it if they feel they are putting patients at risk. In a letter in the British Medical Journal this point is raised and the clinician writing the letter had discussed the dilemma with The Fiqh Council of Birmingham (an Islamic committee of clerics that address modern religious problems) (Iqbal 2012). It may be that Ahmed could speak to his Imam to see whether it would be considered acceptable to consider semi-fasting so that he would be at least able to take water and basic nutrition to prevent patients from being put at risk, or delaying Ramadan until he was on a section of his rota which was not so intensive. There are also many blog-style forums which discuss this with a large amount of debate about whether fasting does cause significant reduction in concentration. There does not appear to have been any cases where mistakes have been made and blamed solely on fasting for Ramadan.

Doctors and other healthcare professionals also have a duty of responsibility to ensure that Muslims with chronic diseases such as diabetes are given extra support during Ramadan. This may be by encouraging them to consider that Allah allows exceptions to fasting or by ensuring that they have appropriate dietary advice on what to eat in order to optimise glycaemic control whilst fasting.

 Key Points

- Ramadan is a religious festival during which Muslims fast from sunrise to sunset.
- This can affect the health of people with chronic disease, including diabetes.
- Healthcare professionals should advise patients on how to fast safely.
- An Imam can offer help and guidance to Muslims who feel their professional role is being affected by following their religious beliefs.

CASE 92: FEMALE GENITAL MUTILATION

Sayida, 21 years old, has recently arrived in the UK with her husband and 2-year-old daughter from their home country, Sierra Leone. The family left Sierra Leone because of war and continuing political unrest and are seeking asylum in the UK. Sayida is 10 weeks pregnant when she attends the antenatal clinic for her first booking appointment, accompanied by her husband and a middle-aged female relative of her husband. The latter explains that she has come along to act as chaperone and interpreter because Sayida speaks no English and her husband very little. During initial assessment it transpires that a friend already living in London has told Sayida about the African Well Woman Clinic (AWWC) and Sayida's husband has telephoned for an appointment. Through the interpreter Sayida explains that she had problems with her first pregnancy and during the birth, and her friend has told her that the AWWC would be able to help her with this and 'difficulties' she has had since the birth of her daughter.

Clinical examination by a female genital mutilation (FGM) public health specialist reveals that Sayida has FGM III and is presenting with symptoms consistent with problems associated with urinary tract infection and the menstrual cycle.

Questions

- What is FGM?
- What are the laws in the UK regarding the practice of FGM?
- Should a competent adult be able to consent to the procedure?
- What is cultural relativism?

ANSWER 92

Across the globe the controversy of FGM has ignited arguments by human rights activists, healthcare professionals and feminists for nearly half a century. In 2000 the World Health Organisation (WHO) defined FGM as 'all procedures which involve partial or total removal of the external female genitalia or other injury to the female genital organs whether for cultural or any other non-therapeutic reasons'.

> **! WHO classification of FGM**
>
> - Type I: excision of the prepuce, with or without excision of part or all of the clitoris
> - Type II: excision of the clitoris with partial or total excision of the labia minora
> - Type III: excision of part or all of the external genitalia and stitching/narrowing of the vaginal opening, also known as infibulation
> - Type IV: unclassified. This includes pricking, piercing or incising of the clitoris and/or labia, stretching of the clitoris and/or labia, cauterisation by burning of the clitoris and surrounding tissue.

In many countries, FGM is accepted as the norm – an expected part of the customary practice of many local communities. For many women FGM is a fact of life, a pain that must be borne because they must conform to social expectation. People with little or no knowledge, skill or training in female anatomy and surgical techniques perform FGM. It is usually performed on girls between the ages of 4 and 13 years, but sometimes it is done in newborns or on young women before marriage or pregnancy. It is often performed in unhygienic conditions and without anaesthesia. Despite worldwide attempts to end the ancient tradition, every year millions of women and girls are being 'circumcised'. There are three main arguments against the practice of FGM:

- It is a dangerous tradition with horrific medical consequences.
- It is primarily performed on girls who cannot consent to the procedure.
- It is a misogynistic practice carried out in patriarchal societies to repress female sexuality.

Ethical issues

In a multicultural environment, it is important to respect others' religious and cultural beliefs and value systems. Many of the arguments centred on FGM are tied up in an intricate web of ethical issues with the main conflict arising between cultural and individual rights. Opponents of FGM argue against the practice on the ethical basis that some human rights are fundamental and supersede differences in cultural morality. The counterargument to this is that different moral codes are applied by different cultures and that these should not be criticised by people who do not have an intimate understanding of that culture. In bioethics this argument is described as cultural relativism.

Relativism is a strain of ethical theory that holds that there are no absolute truths or morals. Mackie, a contemporary philosopher, cites that the proof of this is the existence of diverse moral values, which have changed greatly over time and culture. Cultural relativism argues that morals are merely socially approved habits, and the moral code that one culture follows does not have to be the same as that of another culture. It holds that the morals of other cultures should not be subjected to criticism from the subjective view of an outsider. It encourages diverse cultural expression and harmonious living in pluralistic societies because it fosters an attitude of acceptance of other cultures.

A strong example of the ethical hypocrisy of criticism of FGM and of moral double standards is reflected in the law concerning it. The UK and other countries have legislation making it a crime to 'excise, infibulate or otherwise mutilate the whole or any part of the labia majora or labia minora or clitoris of another person' (Female Genital Mutilation Act 2003, Section 1). Yet in these same countries, genital cosmetic surgery in terms of piercings or labioplasty is rarely criticised and has not resulted in prosecution.

Legal issues

In 1985 the Prohibition of Female Circumcision Act was introduced due to pressure from global conventions to criminalise the practice amid fears that FGM was occurring in Britain by African immigrants who had fled their own countries to escape from war and poverty. This Act made it a criminal offence to circumcise any girl or woman living in the UK no matter what her nationality, religion or culture. In 2003 this Act was repealed by the Female Genital Mutilation Act 2003, which was introduced to close a loophole in the law. It prevented British inhabitants from taking their children away on 'holidays' to be circumcised. This is an unusual step to take since crimes usually committed abroad are not liable to prosecution under the British penal system.

Section 6 of the 2003 Act clarifies that no distinction is made between FGM being performed on minors or competent adults and prosecution can occur no matter in which country FGM is performed. Note that the 2003 Act specifically forbids mutilation 'required as a matter of custom or ritual', even if not performing it may have adverse mental health consequences. The Act also extended the prison sentence from 5 years to 14 years, demonstrating once again how serious a crime this is considered to be in the UK.

There are several defences to FGM:

> No offence is committed by a registered medical practitioner who performs a surgical operation necessary for a girl's physical or mental health. Nor is an offence committed by a registered midwife or a person undergoing a course of training with a view to becoming a registered medical practitioner or registered midwife, but only if the operation is on a girl who is in any stage of labour, or has just given birth, and is for purposes connected with the labour or birth.
>
> Crown Prosecution Service, Female Genital Mutilation Guidance

Despite FGM being illegal since 1985, there have been no successful prosecutions. In a recent landmark case, the Crown Prosecution Service charged a trainee obstetrician with the crime of re-infibulation following the need for an episiotomy in a woman who had undergone circumcision in Somalia at the age of 6. The jury cleared the doctor very quickly and there was a public outcry that this attempted prosecution was detracting from the real crime of circumcision and making midwives and obstetricians vulnerable. In comparison, France has had over 100 successful prosecutions and has a zero tolerance policy on FGM, to the extent that girls who are taken abroad during school term time and are at risk of being mutilated are examined first, the parents are warned about the law and grave consequences and then they are re-examined on their return to ensure they remain intact. The Serious Crime Act 2015 (by making changes to the 2003 Act) now imposes a duty on healthcare professionals, teachers and social care workers, to notify the police when, in the course of their work, they discover that an act of female genital mutilation appears to have been carried out on a girl who is under 18. Such a notification would not breach any duty of confidence or other restriction on the disclosure of information. A court can make a protection order to protect a girl against the commission of FGM.

Child protection issues

Healthcare professionals have an obligation to safeguard girls who are at risk of FGM and must report cases to the child protection team. Refugees, asylum seekers and migrants to the UK need to be given information about their health and the UK legal and child protection issues regarding FGM. Sensitivity is an essential component of any interaction with patients and their families. Wherever possible the aim must be to work in partnership with parents and families to protect children through parents' awareness of the harm caused to the child.

A girl may be considered to be at risk if it is known that older girls in the family have been subjected to the procedure. Pre-pubescent girls aged 7–10 years are the main subjects, although the practice has been reported among babies. If any agency is informed that a girl has been or may be subjected to these practices, a referral must be made to social services in accordance with child protection procedures. In planning any intervention it is important to consider cultural factors because culture and cultural identity are frequently given as the reason that FGM is performed, and any intervention is more likely to be successful if it involves workers from, or with a detailed knowledge of, the community concerned.

Female genital mutilation is different from other child protection issues since it is a one-off event of physical abuse (albeit one that may have grave permanent sexual, physical and emotional consequences). A girl who has already been genitally mutilated should not usually be registered on the child protection register, unless additional protection concerns exist, although she should be offered counselling and medical help. Consideration must be given to any other female siblings at risk.

	Key Points
	• In the UK, FGM is illegal. But despite this it continues to be practised due to the growing number of refugees and asylum seekers from countries where FGM is widespread.
	• People who *might* perform FGM on their children should be educated sensitively about the dangers of the practice and its illegality.
	• In a multicultural environment it is important to respect others' religious and cultural beliefs and value systems, but some human rights are considered universal.

CASE 93: CHILDHOOD MALE CIRCUMCISION

A 3-year-old boy has been referred to the urology clinic for consideration for circumcision under general anaesthetic. Both parents are practising Muslims and want him to be circumcised for religious reasons. He was not circumcised at birth in accordance with custom because he had been in special care due to complications from congenital heart disease. Although the boy is now thriving, due to his underlying condition a general anaesthetic would present a heightened risk. As there are no clinical indications for circumcision, the urologist is uncertain about whether to proceed, despite the parents' insistence that circumcision is performed.

Questions

- Is neonatal circumcision for religious or social reasons ethically and legally appropriate?
- Do the increased risks of circumcision being performed in the community justify NHS provision of the procedure even if it is not clinically indicated?

ANSWER 93

Circumcision for religious, cultural and social reasons has become increasingly controversial. Fox and Thomson suggest that 'infant male circumcision is characterised by an acceptance of levels of risk unimaginable in other health care contexts' (Fox and Thomson 2005). Non-therapeutic circumcision continues to be performed in stark contrast to female genital mutilation which is prohibited (Female Genital Mutation Act 2003), even for competent women who would choose to be circumcised (Case 92).

The BMA states that male circumcision is generally assumed to be lawful, and both parents must give valid consent (The Law and Ethics of Male Circumcision 2006). But is neonatal circumcision a legitimate choice for parents to make? There are limits to parental decision-making authority. BMA guidance states that the child's parents have to demonstrate that non-therapeutic circumcision is in their child's best interests and this requires consideration of the harms and benefits for the child.

There is no convincing evidence of medical benefits and indeed the World Health Organisation does not recommend routine circumcision in developed nations to prevent urinary tract, HIV and other sexually transmitted infections.

The parental view is that neonatal circumcision benefits their child by connection to a religion and adherence to those norms. This may be engendered through involvement with worship and therefore development of a sense of belonging to a religious faith or cultural group. If parents are non-practising and the child would be brought up in a secular community then this benefit of circumcision would not be made out.

The procedure is not pain-free, and there are potential risks, both physical and psychological. The NHS identifies bleeding and infection as the most common problems associated with circumcision but lists other complications including damage to the urethra and septicemia. The evidence of the psychological impact and altered sensation with neonatal circumcision is conflicting and indeterminate. Inadequate pain relief results in at least transient suffering, but there are risks if general anaesthetic is used. Although complication rates from routine circumcision are low, they can be severe in nature.

Performing the circumcision in a hospital would be safer than allowing it to be performed by a lay person. There is no indication that if the urologist refused, these parents would proceed with circumcision by a lay person. Even if the only two options were NHS or lay circumcision, the surgeon can anticipate a real likelihood of harm, which means that surgery cannot be justified.

The philosopher Joel Feinberg defends the notion of enabling children to have maximally open options (Feinberg 1992). Children possess 'anticipatory autonomy rights' which are violated when children's future options are prematurely closed. An irreversible non-therapeutic procedure performed to respect the parent's religious beliefs limits the child's future options to make a decision on the matter.

 Key Points

- Non-therapeutic neonatal circumcision is lawful if the child will be brought up in adherence with the religious views that promulgate it.
- Unless both parents agree, the court decides whether the procedure is in the child's best interests.
- This parental decision limits the child's right to make an autonomous choice at a later date.

CASE 94: DISCLOSURE OF DIAGNOSIS AND CULTURAL RELATIVISM

An 85-year-old Japanese man, Aiko, who came to the UK 10 years ago to live with his children, is admitted with haematuria. He has known bladder cancer but has been under surveillance with regular cystoscopy for many years and during this time has had multiple admissions with frank haematuria. These have usually been secondary to urinary tract infections. Unfortunately, on this occasion it is discovered that his bladder cancer has turned aggressive and spread rapidly. He is found to have multiple metastases and it is likely that he is in the terminal stage of his disease.

His son and daughter arrange a meeting with the oncologist and are insistent that their father should not be informed of his prognosis, since they feel that he will 'give up'. Rather, they ask that 'we should respect him and not directly tell him of his prognosis so that he might enjoy the last part of his life'. The oncologist agrees to discuss their request with the other members of the clinical team.

The palliative care nurse insists that the patient has a right to know so that any palliative treatment that is given can be obtained with informed consent. The senior ward nurse takes the view that the team should balance the risks and benefits of telling the truth to this patient. The registrar believes that Aiko himself should be asked how much he wants to know.

Questions
- Is there a moral obligation to tell Aiko his prognosis?
- To what extent should cultural beliefs and practices influence your decision making?

ANSWER 94

When informing patients of their prognosis, it is appropriate to consider the cultural slant on patient-centred decision making, since it may not be universally endorsed. In contemporary bioethics it is considered that respect for autonomy is best served when individuals make decisions for themselves without influence from others, even on the part of their own families. The dominant view of those involved in Aiko's care is that autonomy should be promoted through openness and truth telling.

Legally, it is imperative that informed consent be gained for any treatment course. In the case of palliative nursing, healthcare professionals must ensure that as a team they do not create any medico-legal implications for the nurse or her department. The request of Aiko's family that he should not be informed of his prognosis may lead to future problems of obtaining consent. For instance, if, to offer a good standard of care, later a long-term catheter is thought to be appropriate, Aiko would require the information surrounding this treatment option in the light of his prognosis for him to give informed consent. However, while it may be taken for granted that telling patients the truth about terminal illness is always the right thing to do, many cultures assume the opposite. The nurse suggests that the doctor should inform Aiko regardless of his family's views but wider issues should be considered.

From an ethical point of view, respect for patient autonomy must take patient values into consideration. If members of the patient's family have informed the doctor that nondisclosure of prognosis to elderly relatives is culturally acceptable, this should be taken into account. Disclosing prognosis against the family's advice may inadvertently cause distress to the patient and set up tensions within the family. If, as the ward nurse suggests, the doctors balance the risks and benefits of fully informing the patient, then the additional knowledge given by the family about Japanese culture is important to take into consideration. In the sphere of Japanese health culture even the interpretation of 'risk' and 'benefit' may be different. Considering the concept of respect for the elderly, it may seem a benefit to fully inform Aiko, yet this is perceived by his family as a potential harm to his dignity. Hence we cannot use the traditional utilitarian way of measuring harm and good in order to dictate the information the doctor gives. The suggestion of the registrar to ask Aiko whether he wants his family to make healthcare decisions for him may seem to be the most sensible in this situation.

From a legal point of view, patients being treated in the UK are of course subject to UK healthcare laws, and in particular informed consent must be gained for any treatment. However, it is important to be culturally sensitive in conveying the truth, and not disrupt family communication patterns.

 Key Points

- Faith, cultural and individual values should be taken into account when determining the exercise of healthcare choices.
- The legal requirements for disclosure should be interpreted with consideration of different cultural practices.

CASE 95: CULTURAL CONSIDERATIONS IN POST MORTEM EXAMINATION

Latisha is a 24-year-old woman who has been admitted to hospital after being found drowsy and uncommunicative at home by her younger sister. Her family has requested that she is only seen by female staff and that she is treated in a side room since the patient and her family are all strict Muslims. The hospital has managed to accommodate these requests. Initial investigations do not reveal why Latisha is critically unwell and her Glasgow Coma Scale score continues to drop. Her younger sister comes to speak to you to tell you that she is worried that Latisha may have attempted to commit suicide since she had a massive argument with their father, who had found out that Latisha has a non-Muslim boyfriend. You decide to test her blood for drug levels. Before being able to take more blood for toxicology screening Latisha has a cardiac arrest. Despite three cycles of cardiopulmonary resuscitation (CPR) she never regains a heartbeat. She is pronounced dead at 20.17 hours, 3 hours after her admission to hospital. You know that a postmortem is legally required and go to discuss this with her family.

Questions

- Which religions do not allow postmortem examinations?
- Can a postmortem not be performed if there is religious or cultural opposition to it?
- What should you say to Latisha's family in this situation?

ANSWER 95

Postmortem examinations are a legal requirement in specific circumstances (Case 78). Some religions, such as Judaism and Islam, do not allow postmortems. Many other individuals also find the concept of a postmortem distressing, regardless of their religious beliefs. In this scenario Latisha's death must be referred to the coroner for consideration of a postmortem for several reasons; the cause of death is unknown, she was in hospital for less than 24 hours and it is possible that she may have committed suicide.

When discussing the legal requirement for a postmortem with the family it is important to be sensitive to their beliefs. Postmortems are most often required when a person has died unexpectedly, so the relatives will be in shock or denial about what has happened. It is useful for a doctor to be accompanied by another healthcare professional to offer additional support to the family. The family should also be asked if they would like anyone else to be present during the discussion, for example, a religious leader. The first thing that should be explained is that the postmortem is a legal requirement. The family cannot refuse a postmortem and their consent is not being requested. It can help if the doctor can acknowledge an understanding of their religious beliefs regarding postmortem examinations as part of the discussion surrounding the need for one to be performed.

Discussing sensitive issues with recently bereaved people is one of the hardest things a doctor has to do, and good communication skills are essential. During the discussion the doctor should be as honest and open as possible about the reasons a postmortem is required. Euphemisms should not be used to protect the family as they can be misconstrued. Before the discussion the doctor should find out when the postmortem will be done and how this will affect the funeral arrangements, as these are questions that the family will have. The doctor could also ask them if there are any religious or cultural traditions that can be followed to see if these can still occur despite the necessity for the postmortem.

In some areas of the country coroners are allowing initial postmortem examinations to be carried out simply by MRI scanning. This has to be self-funded and done on the understanding that it may not reveal the cause of death, and if it doesn't, traditional postmortem examination will still be required.

In general, doctors should be aware that people from different religions and cultures will want to follow certain procedures during the dying process and after death. Being aware of what these are can make the experience less traumatic for the patient and their relatives.

 Key Points

- Some religions do not allow postmortem examination of the body.
- If there is a legal requirement to have a postmortem, this takes precedence over religious and cultural beliefs.
- Always be sensitive to religious needs during the dying process. If in doubt, ask if there is anything you can or should not do.

CASE 96: REQUESTS TO SEE A 'BRITISH' DOCTOR

You are an Asian FY2 doctor working in A&E. During an unusually busy night shift, a patient starts shouting about how the department is too slow and is staffed by lazy foreigners. Various members of staff have tried to diffuse the situation but this encourages him even more. At first, other patients join in his banter. Every time you walk through the waiting area, the patient makes increasingly insulting comments about you and other nonwhite staff members and patients. Other patients are beginning to feel uncomfortable and the atmosphere in the waiting room is changing. He is next to be seen by you. You call him into the treatment area but he refuses, stating he wants to be seen by a 'British' doctor only.

Questions
- How will you deal with this situation?
- What is your legal duty of care to this patient and the other patients?
- What are your ethical obligations?

ANSWER 96

Legal issues

The doctor and indeed the hospital owe this patient a duty of care, which encompasses the provision of adequate and timely treatment irrespective of the patient's choices and beliefs. There is no duty to provide a particular doctor to treat a patient. If a patient refuses to be seen by a doctor this raises the practical problem of fulfilling the ongoing duty of care to the patient. The patient may choose not to be treated if his request is not met. If the patient needs urgent treatment and the only doctor available is the Asian FY2, then there may be some difficulty 'in drawing a line between the unreasonable demand of a racist patient and a sensitive response from a caring profession to a difficult situation'.[*] Acceding to this request would divert resources, by way of an 'acceptable' doctor to this patient, based on demand rather than clinical need, and it impacts on other patients and staff. It also condones such behaviour.

The Macpherson report defined the term 'institutional racism' as the collective failure of an organisation to provide an appropriate and professional service to people because of their colour, culture, or ethnic origin. The NHS is under a legal duty, by virtue of race relations legislation, to promote race equality, and the Equality Act 2010 requires the NHS to work toward eliminating discrimination and reducing inequalities in care. However, the number of racist verbal and physical attacks in the NHS rose 65% in a 5-year period – from 420 in 2008–2009 to 694 in 2012–2013.[†]

Patients might have a request for a particular doctor for different reasons. The Royal College of Obstetricians and Gynaecologists provides that 'any O&G department will do their best to provide a woman doctor for you if you state a preference …. If it's not possible, and the situation isn't urgent, it may be possible to arrange a further appointment at a time when a female doctor is available for you'.[‡] In respect of provision of abortion 'special arrangements should be made for some women and this includes access to a female doctor if requested'.[§] If female patients are accommodated in their request for a female doctor, then why not a request to see a 'British' doctor? The first is based on promoting the therapeutic relationship, whilst the latter is founded in discrimination.

Ethical issues

To what extent do we respect the autonomy of patients? Although respect for patient autonomy is given high priority, it cannot trump all other interests. The patient's demand for respect for his 'autonomous' choice of the type of doctor he sees is justifiably limited because of the harm to the respect and dignity of the Asian doctor and to healthcare professionals of different ethnicity in general.

 Key Points

- The hospital owes the patient a duty of care. However, there is no requirement that a patient must be seen by a particular doctor.
- Racism in the workplace will not be tolerated in the NHS.

---

[*] Rapid response to Moghal, N, Allowing patients to choose the ethnicity of attending doctors is institutional racism, *BMJ* 2014;348:g265.

[†] http://www.bbc.co.uk/news/health-25368332

[‡] https://www.rcog.org.uk/en/patients/faqs/your-appointment/#q3

[§] https://www.rcog.org.uk/en/news/campaigns-and-opinions/human-fertilisation-and-embryology-bill/qa-abortion-and-mental-health/

CASE 97: CHAPERONES

An attractive 25-year-old woman presents to A&E with a 3-day history of abdominal pain. She has not had her bowels open for 2 days but says she has not been eating either. As part of her investigations you need to perform a digital rectal examination. You explain this to her and she consents but is obviously unhappy about it. She asks you if it can be done by a female doctor. Unfortunately the only female doctor on duty is busy with a trauma call. You decide to go ahead and perform the examination. The patient is diagnosed with constipation and discharged home with Movicol. A few weeks later your consultant calls you into his office. He has received an angry letter from the patient saying she has been extremely distressed by the experience and felt violated by the rectal examination. She has requested a written apology.

Questions

- In what circumstances should a chaperone be present?
- Who is an appropriate chaperone?

ANSWER 97

Practising medicine often requires a doctor to ask personal questions and perform intimate procedures on strangers. This can often occur in a very short space of time, and a doctor needs to have the skills to establish rapport and make a patient feel comfortable very quickly. If a patient feels at ease because the procedure has been fully explained, they are less likely to feel intimidated, and therefore the risk of complaints against the doctor is reduced.

Guidance in most trusts states that patients having an intimate examination should be offered a chaperone. A chaperone is an impartial observer.

The GMC has produced specific guidance on intimate examination and chaperones:

> When you carry out an intimate examination, you should offer the patient the option of having an impartial observer (a chaperone) present wherever possible. This applies whether or not you are the same gender as the patient. A chaperone should usually be a health professional.
>
> General Medical Council, Intimate Examinations and Chaperones, 2013

The GMC and the Medical Protection Society recommend that chaperones should always be offered when performing examinations of the breast, genitalia or rectum. Patients do have a right to decline a chaperone, but if they do, it should be documented in the medical notes. Occasionally it may not be possible for a chaperone to be present. If no chaperone is available, the examination should be delayed until one is available, unless it is a medical emergency.

An awareness of the fact that some individuals may feel uncomfortable with any type of physical examination is important and cultural and religious sensitivity should always be taken into consideration. If the doctor is in doubt about what a patient would find acceptable, he/she should ask first. Intimate examinations should be performed in a well-lit room or cubicle. If there is a lockable door the doctor should explain that the door is being locked to prevent someone walking in on the patient.

When asking personal questions, it can help to explain why the questions are relevant, and that the questions being asked are routine and used to exclude different medical problems. Time should be spent building a rapport with the patient before proceeding to external or internal examinations. The doctor should explain what they are doing, why they are doing it and how long it will take.

In the above scenario the doctor should contact his medical indemnity insurer to ask for advice and to let them know a complaint has been made. The doctor should write a letter of apology, as requested by the patient, saying that he did not mean to make the patient feel uncomfortable and that next time he will ensure that he has a chaperone present.

 Key Points

- A chaperone should always be offered to a patient when a doctor is going to perform intimate examinations or procedures.
- All procedures should be fully explained to ensure the patient knows what to expect.

CASE 98: PROFESSIONAL BOUNDARIES

John is admitted to hospital following a car accident. He has multiple injuries and requires full nursing care. During his stay in hospital he becomes very attached to one of the junior doctors. He sees her every day on the ward round and she often stays to talk to him after taking his blood or changing his dressings. As John recovers he starts flirting with the doctor. She is flattered and is finding more and more reason to stay and talk to him. While she is removing the sutures from a scar on his face, he tells her that she is beautiful and tries to kiss her. Uncertain about what to do and her own feelings, the doctor leaves and avoids seeing John for a few days. However, when he is discharged a week later she gives him her number and says they should go out for a drink now that he is no longer an inpatient.

Questions

- Is it appropriate for a doctor to have a relationship with a patient?
- What should a doctor do if she is serious about having a relationship with a patient?
- Are their situations where relationships would be inappropriate even if the therapeutic relationship had ended?

ANSWER 98

The GMC guidance on relationships between doctors and patients is quite straightforward – it does not condone it. As a healthcare professional it undermines the trust that a patient places in them and potentially takes advantage of vulnerable individuals.

> You must not use your professional position to establish or pursue a sexual or improper emotional relationship with a patient or someone close to them.
>
> General Medical Council, Good Medical Practice, 2013

The same reasoning applies to medical students who are expected to establish their own professional relationships with patients and must learn the importance of professionalism (General Medical Council, Medical Students: professional values and fitness to practise, 2009).

In some small villages it can be very difficult to meet people who are not patients. If it looks like a relationship may be establishing itself then the doctor–patient relationship should be stopped so that the two roles do not overlap. In its guidance 'Maintaining a Professional Boundary between You and Your Patient' (2013), the GMC gives further recommendations about what to do if a relationship is being considered with a former patient. It suggests looking at how long ago the patient had been treated by the doctor and what the nature of the therapeutic relationship was. For example, it is unlikely that a relationship between a psychiatrist and their former patient would ever be condoned due to the vulnerability of the patient. The guidance also states that where possible the therapeutic relationship should not end merely so that an intimate relationship can begin. Special consideration also needs to be given to the nature of relationships through social media networks (Case 86).

When caring for patients, doctors should keep their distance professionally by not engaging in conversations about their own personal life. They should also dress appropriately and not wear provocative clothing. When performing intimate procedures they should have a chaperone with them so that the purpose of the procedure cannot be misconstrued (Case 97).

There are several ethical arguments in favour of zero tolerance for sexual patient–doctor relationships. These include the premise that sexual relationships will nearly always be harmful to the patient due to the imbalance in power between doctors and their patients. It is, however, worth considering whether this is still relevant since medical practice is much more patient oriented and less paternalistic. Virtue ethics argues that a good doctor is one who extols virtues and that a doctor who commences a sexual relationship with a patient would not be adhering to these virtues. Consequentialists could argue that any sexual relationship between patients and doctors would inevitably lead to a breakdown in trust and respect of the medical profession as a whole and as such should not be allowed as it would reflect poorly on the profession.

 Key Points

- Doctors and medical students must not enter into intimate or sexual relationships with patients.
- It is unethical to have a relationship with a patient since it jeopardises the trust that the public has in healthcare professionals.

CASE 99: ETHICAL ISSUES ON ELECTIVE

As a final-year medical student you have just arrived in Western Samoa to undertake an 8-week elective at the local hospital. You have spent the last week getting to know the area and some of the other medical students who are also on attachment with you. Although you were feeling relaxed you are now quite nervous about your first day in the hospital. On arrival the first thing you notice is how busy it is everywhere. Whole families are queuing outside a door, waiting to see the doctor. Everyone is very subdued. Despite seeming exceptionally busy the doctor in charge of paediatrics is extremely pleased to see you. After a brief introductory talk he gives you a list of names and shows you to a big room. On one side a large group of mothers and their children are sitting on benches. On the other side are a desk and an examination couch. He gives you a prescription pad and then waves goodbye. Nervously you call your first patient, a 5-year-old boy. His mother tells you in very stilted English that he has a sore throat and painful knees. Could this be rheumatic fever? You feel out of your depth but do not know what to do about it.

Questions

- Should students follow the ethical guidelines that they would follow in their own country or do they not apply in the host country?
- Do medical schools provide guidelines for their students?
- What would you do in this situation?

ANSWER 99

The ethical framework within which an individual practises medicine should not change simply because they are practising in a different country. The Hippocratic Oath and the more contemporary Declaration of Geneva set out ethical principles and the General Medical Council echoes these principles in its guidance for medical students and doctors (Good Medical Practice, 2013).

Electives offer students the chance to experience medicine in a different country. It enables them to become more self-sufficient and can give them increased confidence. About 40% of electives are spent in developing countries. Working in developing countries with severe resource issues and fewer doctors provides an opportunity to gain more experience as there are often more patients to learn on and more procedures which are done by junior members of the team. However, it is essential that students are aware of their own limitations and should not feel pressurised to perform procedures until they have been taught how to do them correctly and safely. Above all a medical student must 'do no harm'. This applies both in the UK and when working abroad. When students are unsure of what to do and do not feel they have the necessary knowledge or experience they should seek help or supervision. Attempting to perform a procedure or treat a patient when a student is not sure of what they are doing is both potentially harmful for the patient and not educational for the student. The BMA states that 'where students believe they are being asked to act beyond their clinical competence they should politely but firmly decline' (BMA Ethics and Medical Electives in Resource Poor Countries: A Toolkit 2009).

Medical treatment is often seen as a privilege in developing countries, and while patients may seem grateful for attention, they are still owed the same respect that a patient would receive in the UK. They should be told that you are a medical student and not a qualified doctor and their informed consent should be sought for any procedure they undergo. Medical students abroad are representatives of their country and medical school and it is important that they should behave in a mature and responsible way. Professional values should be the same as those used at home. Students should be dressed respectably, even in hot weather. They should be polite and courteous to patients, their relatives and everyone else working in the hospital.

Electives can be an amazing and memorable experience. Students should not let preventable bad experiences impact on the rest of their medical career.

 Key Points

- Electives abroad are a useful learning experience and an opportunity to experience a different culture.
- Medical students should follow the same ethical principles that they do when working in the UK.
- Students should never perform procedures they are not able to do without appropriate supervision.

CASE 100: PROFESSIONAL EXPERIENCE OF ILLNESS

I was a final-year medical student when I was diagnosed with Hodgkin's lymphoma. In the space of 3 weeks I went from initial presentation at the general practitioner to disease diagnosis, including grading and staging. Pretty impressive, considering this involved going for two consultations (one with a hospital specialist), a blood test, chest X-ray, computed tomography (CT) scan, fine needle aspiration and biopsy under general anaesthetic. My world had been turned upside down.

Looking back, the majority of those 3 weeks are a hazy memory. However, my first consultation with the hospital specialist remains in my head, but for all the wrong reasons. Initially there were no introductions, which meant I had no idea who anyone was. I remember there being another person in the room besides the doctor, my mother and myself. I assumed at the time that she was a student nurse, but this is pure supposition based on my own experiences as a student in outpatient clinics. I certainly was not asked whether I minded her being present and she did not say or do anything to indicate that her being there was necessary. The consultant appeared in a hurry and spent most of the consultation speaking to my mother about everything that had happened, despite the fact that at 23, I was not only the patient, but also a competent adult (and nearly qualified medical professional!).

The worst thing about the consultation was the provisional diagnosis. It was not broken to me in the way I would have expected. The consultant asked me what I thought was wrong with me. By that point, most differentials had been ruled out; the only one left was Hodgkin's, yet still I thought I was just being a hypochondriac. I made my suggestion and the consultant responded, but not with the answer I'd been expecting: 'Yes, I think it is Hodgkin's too'. From that point on, the rest of that consultation is a blur. I can't remember any of the other information I was given; my mind had gone into overdrive and the only thing I could think was that I had cancer and might die. A week later, after the diagnosis had been confirmed histologically, I went for CT staging. Again, I found this a terrifying experience. I was scared it might show the cancer had already metastasised, but also of having the scan itself. Nobody had explained the procedure to me – that I would need to be cannulated and have intravenous contrast injected. By the time I got into the CT scanner, I was hysterically upset. A form was thrust at me, which I was asked to sign. To this day I have no idea what I signed for, whether it was to consent to the scan, confirm I didn't have any allergies to iodine/shellfish or to confirm I wasn't pregnant.

Despite having spent 2 years on hospital ward as a student, being an inpatient while I received chemotherapy was a completely different experience. It made me really think about what my own patients must have been going through. There are things that you don't appreciate as a student (and perhaps even as a junior doctor). Privacy was a big problem. I was paranoid about sleeping since everyone would see me and possibly hear me snore. I was constantly tired as the nurses are always coming to do observations or give drugs. Machines bleeping constantly were also a huge annoyance! I was also always asked about how I was feeling and about my intimate bodily functions in front of an entire ward of patients and relatives. It was also very lonely being a patient; I would see doctors on their rounds for less than 10 minutes and then speak to no one till visiting hours in the afternoon.

I spent 6 months as a patient, and thankfully now I'm a doctor. But my experience was more valuable than any lectures or clinics, since it made me think a lot about the way we treat our patients.

Questions

- Should I have been treated quicker just because I am a medical professional?
- Should the consultant have assumed I knew what all the investigations and treatments involved?
- Is informed consent ever possible when a patient is scared? Or in pain? Or in emergency situations?

10 years later ... An update

Ten years on and I still reflect on my own personal experience as a patient. I have no doubt that it strongly influenced my career choice, as I now specialie in palliative medicine. I recognise and accept that unfortunately, despite our best efforts as medical professionals, sometimes patients die. In a strange way, I think being forced to confront my own mortality has enabled me to reconcile the fact that patients die too. Being able to ease patients' suffering and support them and their families at such a difficult time is both rewarding and extremely humbling.

What I learnt through personal experience is echoed time after time by the patients I care for. Patients value honesty and clear and timely communication from the medical team. Lack of information leads to a sense of loss of control and a negative patient experience. In any medical condition, the patient has already lost a degree of control, so anything a doctor can do to improve that perception is welcomed by patients.

Sometimes 'being alongside' the patient is enough. You may not have all the answers and you may not be able to solve their problem or cure their illness, but being there for the patient and listening to them goes a very long way, and often doesn't take up as much of your time as you think it will.

Kindness is one of the most valuable clinical skills you have. Patients appreciate empathy; if you treat every patient as you would wish a close relative to be treated, then it's difficult to go far wrong.

One of the biggest lessons I've learnt is that the human spirit is amazing. Even in the face of adversity, people can show great strength and resilience. Patients can teach us a lot, not just about medicine, but also about life itself. As health professionals, we are very privileged indeed to be able to do the job we do

ANSWER 100

Using your knowledge of medical ethics, write your answers to the questions for this scenario.

RESOURCES

Foreword
Warnock G. (1971) The Object of Morality (London, Methuen).

Ethical Principles
Beauchamp T. and Childress J. *Principles Biomedical Ethics*, 7th edition, OUP, USA, 2013.

British Medical Association, Ethics tool kit for students.

British Medical Association. *Medical Ethics Today*, 3rd edition, Wiley Blackwell, 2012.

Charon R. Narrative medicine: A model for empathy, reflection profession and trust, *JAMA* 2001; 286(15): 1897–1902.

Fenwick A., Johnston C., Knight R., Testa G. and Tillyard A. *Medical Ethics and Law: A Practical Guide to the Assessment of the Core Content of Learning*, A report from the Education Steering Group of the Institute of Medical Ethics, 2013.

Gardiner P. A virtue ethics approach to moral dilemmas in medicine, *J Med Ethics* 2003; 29: 297–302.

Gillon R. Medical ethics: Four principles plus attention to scope, *BMJ* 1994; 309: 184.

Stirrat G., Johnston C., Gillon R. and Boyd K. Medical ethics and law for doctors of tomorrow: The 1998 Consensus Statement updated, *J Med Ethics* 2010; 36: 55–60.

UK Clinical Ethics Network.

Beginning of Life
An NHS Trust v MB [2006] EWHC 507 (Fam).

An NHS Trust v SR [2012] EWHC 3842 (Fam).

BBC Radio 4, Inside the Ethics Committee Series 5, Programme 3, Screening.

British Medical Association, Expression of Doctors' Beliefs.

CP (A Child) v First-tier Tribunal (Criminal Injuries Compensation) [2014] EWCA Civ 1554.

Doogan v Greater Glasgow and Clyde Health Board [2014] UKSC 68.

General Medical Council, Personal Beliefs and Medical Practice 2013.

Glass v UK (App no 61827/00) 2004.

Glover J. Should the child live? Doctors, families and conflict, *Clinical Ethics* 2006; 1(1): 52–59.

Harris J. The concept of the person and the value of life, *Kennedy Institute of Ethics Journal* 1999; 9(4): 293–308.

Kings College Hospital NHS Foundation Trust v Y [2015] EWHC 1966 (Fam).

Larcher V. et al. Making decisions to limit treatment in life-limiting and life-threatening conditions in children: A framework for practice, *Arch Dis Child* 2015;100 (Suppl 2):s1–s26.

Larcher V. and Brierley J. Fetal alcohol syndrome (FAS) and fetal alcohol spectrum disorder (FASD) diagnosis and moral policing: An ethical dilemma for paediatricians, *Arch Dis Child* 2014; 99: 969–970.

Nuffield Council on Bioethics. Critical care decisions in neonatal and fetal medicine: Ethical issues, 2006.

Parker M. The best possible child, *J Med Ethics* 2007; 33: 279–283.

Paton v British Pregnancy Advisory Service Trustees [1979] QB 276.

Re Ashya King (A Child) [2014] EWHC 2964 (Fam).

Re G (A Child) [2013] EWHC 134 (Fam).

Re P-M [2013] EWHC 2328 (Fam).

Savulescu J. Conscientious objection in medicine, *BMJ* 2006; 332(7536): 294–297.

Scott R. Reconsidering "Wrongful Life" in England after thirty years: Legislative mistakes and unjustifiable anomalies, *Cambridge Law Journal* 2013; 72(1): 115–154.

Slowther A. Selection of embryos, *Clinical Ethics* 2008; 3: 60–62.

Children and Adolescents

An NHS Trust v SR [2012] EWHC 3842 (Fam).

British Medical Association, Children and young people toolkit.

Doig C. and Burgess E. Withholding life-sustaining treatment: Are adolescents competent to make these decisions? *CMAJ* 2000; 162(11): 1585–1588.

General Medical Council, 0–18 years: guidance for all doctors, 2007.

Gillick v West Norfolk & Wisbech Area Health Authority [1985] UKHL 7.

Johnston C. Overriding competent medical treatment refusal by adolescents: When 'no' means 'no', *Arch Dis Child* 2009; 94: 487–491.

P (a Child) v NHS Foundation Hospital [2014] EWHC 1650 (Fam).

Re W (A Minor) (Medical Treatment: Court's Jurisdiction) [1993] Fam 64.

Slowther A. Clinical ethics committee case 3: Should parents be able to request non-therapeutic treatment for their severely disabled child? *Clinical Ethics* 2008; 3: 109–112.

United Nations Convention on the Rights of the Child, 1989.

Consent, Refusal and Capacity

British Medical Association, Consent tool kit.

British Medical Association, Ethics tool kit for students.

British Medical Association, Mental Capacity Act toolkit.

Department of Health, Reference guide to consent for examination or treatment, 2nd edition, 2009.

DH NHS Foundation Trust v PS [2010] EWHC 1217 (Fam).

General Medical Council, Consent: Patients and doctors making decisions together, 2008.

Health Protection Agency, Eye of the Needle: United Kingdom surveillance of significant occupational exposures to bloodborne viruses in healthcare workers, London, 2012.

Johnston C., Baty M. and Adewole C. King's College London Student Clinical Ethics Committee case discussion: A patient changes her mind about surgery – Should her later refusal be respected? *Clinical Ethics* 2015; 10: 34–36.

Law Commission Report 231, Mental Incapacity, HMSO, London, 1995.

Ms B v An NHS Hospital Trust [2002] EWHC 429 (Fam).

Newson A. Clinical ethics committee case 9: Should we inform our patient about animal products in his medicine? *Clinical Ethics* 2010; 5: 7–12.

P v Cheshire West and P & Q v Surrey County Council (2014) UKSC 19.

Re T (Adult: refusal of treatment) [1992] EWCA Civ 18.

Schloendorff v Society of New York Hospital 211 NY 125 105 N.E. 92, 1914.

Confidentiality

BBC Radio 4, Inside the Ethics Committee Series 9 Programme 3, Genetic Testing in Children.

British HIV Association UK National Guidelines for HIV Testing, 2008.

British Medical Association, Confidentiality and disclosure of health information toolkit.

British Society for Human Genetics, Report on the genetic testing of children, 2010.

Chalmers J. Criminalization of HIV transmission: Can doctors be liable for the onward transmission of HIV? *Int J STD and AIDS* 2004; 15: 782–787.

Danish Council of Ethics, Ethics and mapping of the human genome, Copenhagen, 1993.

Fraser J. Ethics of HIV testing in general practice without informed consent: A case series, *J Med Ethics* 2005; 31: 698–702.

General Medical Council, Confidentiality, 2009.

Joint Committee on Medical Genetics, Consent and confidentiality in clinical genetic practice: Guidance on genetic testing and sharing genetic information, 2011.

Good medical ethics, *Journal of Medical Ethics* 2015; 41(1): 1–140.

Liao S. Is there a duty to share genetic information? *J Med Ethics* 2009; 35: 306–309.

Myers H. Huntington's disease genetics, *NeuroRx* 2004; 1(2): 255–262.

Rayment M. et al. HIV testing in non-traditional settings – The HINTS study: A multi-centre observational study of feasibility and acceptability, *PLoS ONE* 2012; 7(6): e39530.

Royal College of Physicians, Testing for HIV, 2009.

R v Dica [2004] EWCA Crim 1103.

Sheehan M. The right to know and genetic testing, *J Med Ethics* 2015; 41(4): 287–288.

Slowther A. Sharing information in health care: The nature and limits of confidentiality, *Clinical Ethics* 2006; 1: 82.

The Caldicott Committee, Report on the review of patient-identifiable information, Department of Health, London 1997.

Negligence

British Medical Association, NHS complaints procedure.

British Medical Association, Whistleblowing.

Freedom to Speak Up – A review of whistleblowing in the NHS, Sir Robert Francis QC, 2015.

General Medical Council, The State of Medical Education and Practice in the UK, 2014.

Montgomery v Lanarkshire Health Board [2015] UKSC 11.

NHS Litigation Authority Report and accounts 2012/13, London: The Stationery Office, 2013.

Reporting of Injuries, Diseases and Dangerous Occurrences Regulations, 2013.

Selected summaries of investigations by the Parliamentary and Health Service Ombudsman, April to June 2014. HMSO, 2014.

Slowther A. Truth telling in health care, *Clinical Ethics* 2009; 4: 173–175.

Wilsher v Essex Area Health Authority [1988] AC 1074.

Mental Health

General Medical Council, Supporting medical students with mental health conditions, 2013.

MD v Nottinghamshire Health Care NHS Trust [2010] UKUT 59 (AAC).

Mental Health Act 1983, Code of Practice, Department of Health, 2015.

Morriss R., Kapur N. and Byng R. Assessing risk of suicide or self-harm in adults, *BMJ* 2013; 347: f4572.

Re C (Adult: refusal of treatment) [1994] 1 WLR 290.

Rethink Factsheet, Detention under the Mental Health Act, 2014.

Rethink Mental Illness, Mental capacity and mental illness: Treatment and consent, https://www.rethink.org/living-with-mental-illness/mental-health-laws/mental-capacity/treatment-and-consent.

Sulek J. The Mind guide to the Mental Health Act 1983, Mind, 2012.

Truth hurts: The report of the national enquiry into self harm amongst young people, 2006.

Wong J., Poon Y. and Hui E., I can put the medicine in his soup, Doctor! *J Med Ethics* 2005; 31: 262–265.

Public Health

Alex Matthews-King. *Pulse* magazine, 1 April 2015. http://www.pulsetoday.co.uk/about-pulse/.

Al Hamwi v Johnston [2005] EWHC 206.

Barratt A. Overdiagnosis in mammography screening: A 45 year journey from shadowy idea to acknowledged reality, *BMJ* 2015; 350: h867.

Behrman A. W. and Offley W. Should influenza vaccination be mandatory for healthcare workers? *BMJ* 2013; 347: f6705.

Biller-Andorno N. and Jüni P. Abolishing mammography screening programs? A view from the Swiss medical board, *N Engl J Med* 2014; 370: 1965–1967.

Burns T. and Shaw J. Is it acceptable for people to be paid to adhere to medication? *BMJ* 2007; 335: 232–233.

Cole P. Human rights and the national interest: Migrants, healthcare and social justice, *J Med Ethics* 2007; 33(5): 269–272.

Dare T. Mass immunisation programmes: Some philosophical issues, *Bioethics* 1998; 12: 125–149, 146.

Diekema D. Parental refusals of medical treatment: The harm principle as threshold for state intervention, *Theor Med Bioeth* 2004; 25(4): 243–264.

F v F [2013] EWHC 2683 (Fam).

Flanigan J. A defense of compulsory vaccination, *HEC Forum* 2014; 26: 5–25.

Forbes K. A. and Ramirez A. Communicating the benefits and harms of cancer screening, *Curr Oncol Rep.* 2014; 16(5): 382.

General Medical Council, Leadership and management for all doctors, 2012.

Glasziou P. et al. When financial incentives do more good than harm: A checklist, *BMJ* 2012; 345: e5047.

Godlee F. Wakefield's article linking MMR vaccine and autism was fraudulent, *BMJ* 2011; 342: c7452.

Kalager M., Adami H. O., Bretthauer M. and Tamimi R. M. Overdiagnosis of invasive breast cancer due to mammography screening: Results from the Norwegian screening program, *Ann Intern Med.* 2012:3; 156(7): 491–499.

Kendall T. Paying patients with psychosis to improve adherence, *BMJ* 2013; 347: f5782.

National Institute for Health and Care Excellence. Guidance on the identification, assessment and management of overweight and obesity in children, young people and adults, 2014.

National Institute for Health and Care Excellence. Immunizations: Childhood, 2014.

Offit P. Should childhood vaccination be mandatory? Yes, *BMJ* 2012; 344: e2434.

Priebe S. et al. Effectiveness of financial incentives to improve adherence to antipsychotic maintenance treatment with antipsychotics: Cluster randomised controlled trial, *BMJ* 2013; 347: f5847.

Public Health England, Guidance; Criteria for appraising the viability, effectiveness and appropriateness of a screening programme, 2013.

Royal College of Physicians, Guidelines on the practice of ethics committees in medical research with human participants, 4th edition, 2007.

Salisbury D. Should childhood vaccination be mandatory? No, *BMJ* 2012; 344: e2435

UK National Screening Committee, Review of the UK National Screening Committee (UKNSC), Recommendations, 2015.

Organ Donation

British Transplantation Society Guidelines for Directed Altruistic Organ Donation, 2013.

Cohen C. Selling bits and pieces of humans to make babies: The gift of the magi revisited, *Med Philos* 1999; 24: 288–306.

Costello K. Ethical implications of searching for a kidney donor online, *Proc Am Soc Info Sci Tech* 2013; 50: 1–5.

Emson H. It is immoral to require consent for cadaver organ donation, *J Med Ethics* 2003; 29: 125–127.

Erin C. and Harris J. An ethical market in human organs, *J Med Ethics* 2003; 29: 137–138.

MacKellar C. Human organ markets and inherent human dignity, *The New Bioethics* 2014; 20(1): 53–71.

Neidich E., Neidich A., Cooper J. and Bramstedt K. The ethical complexities of online organ solicitation via donor-patient websites: Avoiding the 'beauty contest', *Am J Transplant.* 2012; 12(1): 43–47.

NHS Blood and Transplant, Taking Organ Transplantation to 2020.

Wright L. and Campbell M. Soliciting kidneys on web sites: Is it fair? *Seminars in Dialysis* 2006; 19(1): 5–7.

End of Life

Aintree University Hospitals NHS Foundation Trust v James [2013] UKSC 67.

Airedale NHS Trust v Bland [1993] AC 789.

A Local Authority v E [2012] EWHC 1639 (COP).

Baines P. Death and best interests: A response to the legal challenge, *Clinical Ethics* 2010; 5: 195–200.

British Medical Association. Ethics, medicine and morals: A changing landscape, Webcast, http://bma.org.uk/practical-support-at-work/ethics/withdraw-withhold-artificial-nutrition-and-hydration.

British Medical Association. Responding to patient requests relating to assisted suicide: Guidance for doctors in England, Wales and Northern Ireland, 2015.

Cartwright N. 48 years on, is the suicide act fit for purpose? *Med Law Rev* 2009; 17(3): 467–476, 475.

Compassion in Dying, Knowledge of end-of-life rights and choices – YouGov poll 2011.

Dresser R. Pre-commitment: A misguided strategy for securing death with dignity, *Tex L Rev* 2002–2003; 81: 1823.

English V. *Withholding and Withdrawing Life-Prolonging Medical Treatment*, 3rd edition, Blackwell Publishing, 2007.

General Medical Council. Treatment and care towards the end of life: Good practice in decision making, 2010.

Glover J. *Causing Death and Saving Lives*. Harmondsworth: Penguin 1977.

In the Matter of G (TJ) [2010] EWHC 3005 (COP).

Kumar P. and Clark M. *Clinical Medicine*, 8th edn. Edinburgh: Elsevier Saunders, 2012.

Johnston C. Advance decision making: Rhetoric or reality? *Legal Studies* 2014; 34: 497–514.

Johnston C., Baty M. and Dollman G. King's College London Student Clinical Ethics Committee case discussion: Is it appropriate to insert a Percutaneous Endoscopic Gastrostomy for an elderly man who has already pulled out a naso-gastric tube? *Clinical Ethics* 2015; 10: 37–40.

Nicklinson and Lamb v. UK (application nos. 2478/15 and 1787/15).

NHS Improving Quality, Planning for your future care: A guide, 2014.

R v Cox (1992) 12 BMLR 38.

R. (Nicklinson) v Ministry of Justice [2014] UKSC 38.

R (Purdy) v Director of Public Prosecutions [2009] UKHL 45.

R (Tracey) v Cambridge University Hospitals NHS Foundation Trust & Others [2014] EWCA Civ 822.

Regnard C. et al. So, farewell then, doctrine of double effect, *BMJ* 2011; 343: d4512.

Saunders J. Guiding practical care in feeding at the end of life, *Clinical Ethics* 2010; 5: 172–174.

Schneiderman L. Defining medical futility and improving medical care, *Journal of Bioethical Inquiry* 2011; 8(2): 123–131.

The gold standards framework: Advance Care Planning, http://www.goldstandardsframework.org.uk/advance-care-planning.

Duties of a Doctor

British Medical Association, Using social media: Practical and ethical guidance for doctors and medical students.

De Zulueta P. Compassion in twenty-first century medicine: Is it sustainable? *Clinical Ethics* 2013; 8(4): 119–128.

Driver and Vehicle Licensing Agency, Current medical guidelines: DVLA guidance for professionals, 2015.

General Medical Council, Delegation and Referral, 2013.

General Medical Council, Doctors' Use of Social Media, 2013.

General Medical Council, Ending your professional relationship with a patient, 2013.

General Medical Council, Good Medical Practice, 2013.

General Medical Council, Medical students: Professional values and fitness to practise, 2009.

General Medical Council, Protecting children and young people: The responsibilities of all doctors, 2012.

HM Government, Working together to safeguard children, A guide to inter-agency working to safeguard and promote the welfare of children, 2015.

Larcher V. The development and function of clinical ethics committees in the United Kingdom, *Diametros* 2009; 22: 47–63.

McAllister M. and McKinnon J. The importance of teaching and learning resilience in the health disciplines: A critical review of the literature, *Nurse Education Today* 2009; 29: 371–379.

McCann C., Beddoe E., McCormick K., Huggard P., Kedge S., Adamson C. and Huggard J. Resilience in the health professions: A review of recent literature, *International Journal of Wellbeing* 2013; 3(1): 60–81.

Medical Protection Society, Removing patients from the practice list, 2013.

Office of the Public Guardian Safeguarding Policy, 2013.

Faith, Value and Culture

An NHS Trust v Child B, Mr & Mrs B [2014] EWHC 3486 (Fam).

BMJ Blogs, Autonomy and circumcision wars, Guest post Akim McMath, 27 February 2015, http://blogs.bmj.com/medical-ethics/2015/02/27/autonomy-and-the-circumcision-wars/.

British Medical Association, The law and ethics of male circumcision: Guidance for doctors, 2006.

British Medical Association, Ethics and medical electives in resource poor countries: A toolkit, 2009.

Darby R. The child's right to an open future: Is the principle applicable to non-therapeutic circumcision? *J Med Ethics* 2013; 39: 463–468.

Dowell J. and Merrylee N. Electives: Isn't it time for a change? *Medical Education* 2009; 43: 121–126.

Feinberg J. The child's right to an open future. In: *Freedom and Fulfilment: Philosophical Essays*, Princeton University Press, Princeton, NJ, 1992, 76–97.

Female Genital Mutilation Act 2003.

Fox M. and Thomson M. A covenant with the status quo? Male circumcision and the new BMA guidance to doctors, *J Med Ethics* 2005; 31: 463–469.

General Medical Council, Intimate examinations and chaperones, 2013.

General Medical Council, Maintaining a professional boundary between you and your patient, 2013.

General Medical Council and Medical Schools Council, Medical students: Professional values and fitness to practise, 2009.

House of Commons Home Affairs Committee, Female genital mutilation: The case for a national action plan, Second Report of Session 2014–15.

Iqbal F. What should doctors do about fasting during Ramadan? *BMJ* 2012; 345: e5629.

Medical Protection Society, Chaperones, 2013.

Moghal N. Allowing patients to choose the ethnicity of attending doctors is institutional racism, *BMJ* 2014; 348: g265, doi: 10.1136/bmj.g265.

NHS Clinical Governance Support Team, Guidance on the Role and Effective Use of Chaperones in Primary and Community Care Settings, Model Chaperone Framework, 2005.

Newcastle upon Tyne Hospitals Foundation Trust v LM [2014] EWCOP 454.

Selby M. Dealing with racist patients, *BMJ* 1999; 318: 1129–1131.

Taylor B., Jick H. and MacLaughlin D. Prevalence and incidence rates of autism in the UK: Time trend from 2004–2010 in children aged 8 years, *BMJ Open* 2013; 16; 3(10): e003219.

Index

Printed and bound by CPI Group (UK) Ltd, Croydon, CR0 4YY

23/10/2024

01777682-0005